Eight Contemporary Poets

Calvin Bedient

Eight
Contemporary Poets

CHARLES TOMLINSON   DONALD DAVIE

R. S. THOMAS   PHILIP LARKIN   TED HUGHES

THOMAS KINSELLA   STEVIE SMITH

W. S. GRAHAM

OXFORD UNIVERSITY PRESS
London   Oxford   New York

OXFORD UNIVERSITY PRESS

London   Oxford   New York
Glasgow   Toronto   Melbourne   Wellington
Cape Town   Ibadan   Nairobi   Dar es Salaam   Lusaka   Addis Ababa
Delhi   Bombay   Calcutta   Madras   Karachi   Lahore   Dacca
Kuala Lumpur   Singapore   Hong Kong   Tokyo

To Cadence and Van

First published by Oxford University Press, London, 1974
First issued as an Oxford University Press paperback, 1975
Printed in the United States of America

Contents

Acknowledgements

For permission to reproduce copyright passages grateful acknowledgement is made to publishers and copyright holders as follows:

for Donald Davie: *Brides of Reason, Events and Wisdoms, Essex Poems, A Winter Talent and Other Poems* to Routledge & Kegan Paul; (*Events and Wisdoms*, Copyright © 1965 by Donald Davie, reprinted by permission of Wesleyan University Press, Middletown, Connecticut); *Six Epistles to Eva Hesse* to Alan Ross, London Magazine Editions;

for W. S. Graham: *Second Poems, Cage Without Grievance*, to the author; *The White Threshold, The Nightfishing, Malcolm Mooney's Land* reprinted by permission of Faber and Faber Ltd.;

for Ted Hughes: *Hawk in the Rain, Lupercal, Wodwo, Crow, Poetry in the Making*, reprinted by permission of Faber and Faber Ltd., Harper & Row, Inc., New York, Miss Olwyn Hughes;

for the work of Thomas Kinsella to The Dolmen Press, Dublin;

for Philip Larkin: *The Whitsun Weddings, The North Ship, Jill* and *A Girl in Winter* reprinted by permission of Faber and Faber Ltd., and A. P. Watt & Son; *The Less Deceived* by permission of The Marvell Press, England;

for Stevie Smith: *Selected Poems*, Copyright © Stevie Smith, 1962, *Scorpion and Other Poems*, Copyright © Stevie Smith, 1972, *The Frog Prince and Other Poems*, Copyright © Stevie Smith, 1966 to Penguin Books Ltd.; (*Selected Poems*, Copyright © 1964 by Stevie Smith, reprinted by permission of New Directions Publishing Corporation); *The Best Beast*, Copyright 1950, © 1964, 1965, 1966, 1967, 1968, 1969 by Stevie Smith, reprinted by permission of Alfred A. Knopf, Inc.; *Harold's Leap, Mother, What Is Man?, Not Waving But Drowning* to James McGibbon;

for the work of R. S. Thomas to Rupert Hart-Davis;

for the work of Charles Tomlinson to Oxford University Press.

I should also like to make acknowledgement to the following:

to Carol Buckroyd, my editor at Oxford University Press, for her advice and watchfulness;

to Gerald Goldberg and Stephen Yenser, my colleagues at the University of California, Los Angeles, for their criticism of a considerably different version of the Introduction;

to Philippa Foote, for her kindness in reading the chapter on Stevie Smith;

to the editors of *The Critical Quarterly, The Iowa Review* and *The New York Times Book Review*, in which magazines various chapters or passages of this book were first published;

to Vanessa, my wife, for her patience and encouragement.

Introduction

The English poetic 'Movement' of the Fifties (the very name suggesting an excess of dull plainness) did much to fix the image of contemporary British poetry as deliberately deficient, moderate with a will. This image has gradually frayed and will probably give way altogether, for the truth is that, however *deliberate*— and after a faltering start—postwar poetry in Britain and Ireland has proved increasingly robust, varied, responsive to the times, felicitous, enjoyable. Donald Davie and Philip Larkin, the two best poets temporarily covered by the barracks-blanket characterization of the Movement, transcended from the first the gentility, the triviality, the meagreness embroidered by the critics, with reason enough, on its corners: the first poet through a glowing tonality and a penchant for risk that have increased with the years, the second through an elegiac note that approaches grandeur and a glance that, though certainly gentle, looks straight through life. And in the Sixties it became apparent to those who listened for the rare, fresh, genuine, precious accent of necessity in various voices—some new, some old—that British poetry had lucked upon, dedicated itself to, a remarkable decade, and not least remarkable because the highest talents were so heterogeneous that they could not be found in any School, any Movement, but had to be looked for in this corner and that, writing themselves out in isolation. Even today some are still hardly known, reputed, *found*. W. S. Graham and Stevie Smith and often R. S. Thomas are still so meagrely anthologized that they look hole-in-corner indeed. Charles Tomlinson has been accepted only cautiously, as if he were too strange an amphibian, too Americanized, too peopleless, to be trusted. The English make so little of Austin Clarke and Thomas Kinsella that Ireland might be farther away than America. And there was the English poet C. H. Sisson, working all through the decade, out of earshot of almost everyone but writing brilliantly. (In Larkin's symptomatic selections for

The Oxford Book of Twentieth-Century English Verse only Davie
and, very naturally, Larkin himself received anything like a frame
large enough to show their truest expression, most being reduced
to an incomprehensible mouth, an eyelash, not so much as a
meaningful glance.)

Of course compared to the raging 'black holes' in the American
firmament—Robert Lowell, Sylvia Plath, John Berryman—
postwar British poets, Ted Hughes excepted, have been moderate
enough, permanently stunned as they were by the war, as if
they had suffered from it more, learned more, remembered.
'. . . We shan't, not since Stalin and Hitler', wrote Auden,
'trust ourselves ever again: we know that, subjectively, all is
possible.' And yet the genius of the British poets has lain in
getting around their own knowledge, around in it, creating
original poetry despite their lucidity. Their energy characteristically a *sceptical* energy, they have breathed an atmosphere
that, while not encouraging life, has yet proved bracing, like
upland air. They are alert, not anaemic; lean, not meagre;
austere, not genteel.

Except for Larkin, who has sat down with despair, these other
sceptics, ironists, doubters, these others who will never trust
themselves again, have worked out, toughly, resiliently, certain
arrangements between faith and distrust in life—between risk
and caution, energy and defeated weariness. Stevie Smith,
Donald Davie, and R. S. Thomas migrate unpredictably between
loving or gallant engagement with the world and grim or dour
withdrawal. Still others mix extremes unexpectedly: Charles
Tomlinson's dry-dewy mixture of contemplation and sensory
delight, W. S. Graham's *spry* isolation and self-consciousness,
Ted Hughes's monstrous marriage of nihilism and vitality.
By comparison with Yeats and Lawrence, with Dylan Thomas
and even Robert Graves, with Pound and T. S. Eliot, too—though
not of course with Edward Thomas or Hardy—most inhabit a
world truncated in possibilities, cramped metaphysically and
politically, just too large for despair and too shut down for con-
fident hope or trusting joy. None is so naïve, so ready for a wager,
as to attempt a resolving vision, though R. S. Thomas, an Anglican priest, has adopted one.

Yet one could just as easily stress the divergencies among these
poets, and perhaps more truly. So if R. S. Thomas is a man of the
cloth and faith, Hughes and Larkin, on the other hand, fly a

black flag of nihilism, have an essential view of life as devouring
its own value. Thomas Kinsella, having fought away from this
view, is now in its jaws. C. H. Sisson, too, has been there.
And the darkly laconic Geoffrey Hill is just a held breath, an
exquisite touch, away. Charles Tomlinson, Donald Davie, and
R. S. Thomas are all intent moralists, students of noble self-
restraint, and yet three more various moralists could hardly be
found: the first a man of the woods, the second of the city, the
last of God's shrill chorus of stars. Stevie Smith and the new W. S.
Graham stand aside as formidable, comic sophisticates, greatly
original and determined eccentrics, neither moralists nor nihilists,
outside the usual categories. The English *will* go their own way,
as often noted, but, more significant, the new poets have little
choice, being as Contemporary as they are English (or Welsh or
Scottish or Irish), having been thrown out into a world powerless
to help them—a world made up of everyone else exiled from
village walls.

As a consequence of this scattering of minds and talents, this
explosion as of raindrops on a speeding car, this speaking each
alone—though in one sense poets have never had a choice about
this—poetry in Britain and Ireland is now more modernist than
ever (even if the contrary impression prevails). At its most durable,
earlier twentieth-century English and Irish poetry largely missed
out on 'modernism'. Stomach-dropping gaps between a few of
Yeats's stanzas, Edith Sitwell's manic babble, Lawrence's occasionally rapt repetitions and running balances, a general contrac-
tion upon the image, a new adherence to the little company of
the moment—this was about the extent of its concession to
experimentation. The ferment, as A. Alvarez has argued, was
'largely an American importation and an American need'. The
Americans, after all, had to hunt up a tradition, the English
already had one, there like the fireplace.

Nowadays, however, particularly in Graham, Hughes, and
Kinsella, as earlier (almost as a lark) with Dylan Thomas, this
poetry is becoming more difficult, 'American' in the way it
approaches its subjects cold, indeed in a cold sweat, without help,
alone in an undefined silence. At the same time the tradition (with
its fealty to the consecutive, the clear, and the climactic) still
attracts gifted poets, Larkin being scarcely more modern than
Hardy, who claimed famously that 'All we can do is to write
on the old themes in the old styles, but try to do a little better

than those who went before us'. The new poets in fact form a cautious poetic chain, Davie, Sisson, R. S. Thomas, Stevie Smith, Tomlinson, and Hill extending the tradition out from Larkin towards and, finally, with Hill's *Mercian Hymns*, right down into the gorge of modernism—where the unwritten law is the risk of the greatest chaos that can yet give a poignant hint of a difficult order. And there, as I have said, Graham and Hughes and Kinsella also descend.

The formal English tradition is gently, tentatively being loosened, pulled so that the new spaces between words can reveal significant silences, metaphysical holes, perplexities. As if on tightropes, the new poets shift stress unexpectedly, their poise precarious. And most favour a short line as nervously lean as their trust and times. Often their lines break abruptly, seek a balance outside themselves. And though their structures are usually continuous, sometimes they are seried like stones dotting a mountain river, and you leap across at your own risk. The poets both explore and shrink from their undetermined limits. Only Hughes, and Hughes only lately, has with his desperate and detonative energy razed the old formal lines, substituting instead the wild-wheeling catalogue. All would agree with an acidulous statement made by Keith Douglas in the thick of the war: 'I see no reason to be either musical or sonorous about things at present.' Their lyricism, when it comes, is like the nervous whistling of a man crossing a once-mined field.

The chapters of this book are attempts at once to sight and be inward with the poets who, though by no means the only fine contemporary poets in Britain and Ireland, have perhaps achieved most to date, having made often enough to count, and indeed each instance counts, the all-but-impossible transposition from the arbitrary to the necessary—the crossing that, part happy start and skill, part sweat and endurance, distinguishes the accomplished artist. Mysteriously assured, their best poems are emotional inventions of deep contemplative value. They give the wonderful impression of having been born without consulting their authors —or consulting them only after the fact, for they are subtle and powerful structures, carefully composed structures of language. By all the resonance of execution these poems are what they had to be and thus are triumphs over contingency, indefiniteness, banality—nests in the void of the uncertain significance, the inarticulateness in which we lead our lives.

Charles Tomlinson

CHARLES TOMLINSON is the most considerable British poet to have made his way since the Second World War. There is more to see along that way, more to meditate, more solidity of achievement, more distinction of phrase, more success as, deftly turning, hand and mind execute the difficult knot that makes the poem complete, than in the work of any of his contemporaries. It is true that the way is strait; but Tomlinson would have it so. For his is a holding action: he is out to save the world for the curious and caring mind. And if he is narrow, he is only so narrow as a searching human eye and a mind that feeds and reflects on vision—an eye that to everything textured, spatial, neighbouring, encompassing, humanly customary, and endlessly and beautifully modulated by light, dusk, weather, the slow chemistry of years, comes like a cleansing rain—as also like a preserving amber. The quality everywhere present in Tomlinson's poetry is a peculiarly astringent, almost dry, but deeply meditated love; this is true whether his subject is human beings, houses, lamplight, chestnuts, lakes, or glass. Tomlinson is a poet of exteriority and its human correlatives: the traditional, the universal, the unchangeable, the transparencies of reflection. And he is thus the opposite of a lyric or 'confessional' poet. Yet what a mistake it would be to confuse this outwardness with superficiality. To read Tomlinson is continually to *sound*: to meet with what lies outside the self in a simultaneous grace of vision and love. Tomlinson's chief theme is, in his own phrase, 'the fineness of relationships'. And though his poetry is in great measure restricted to this theme, the theme itself is an opening and a wideness.

Tomlinson's theme, or his strict relation to it, is one with his originality; and this originality is most salient in his poems on the world's appearances. We have been asked to admire so many poets of 'nature' that we can but sigh, or look blank, to hear it announced that still another one has come along; and we will greet with scepticism any claims to originality. But Tomlinson is unmistakably an original poet. There is in him, it is true, a measure of Wordsworth: the at-homeness in *being* as against *doing*, the wise passivity, the love of customariness, and what Pater spoke of as Wordsworth's 'very fine apprehension of the limits within which alone philosophical imaginings have any place in true poetry'. Both poets awaken, moreover, in Shelley's phrase, 'a sort of thought in sense'. But how different in each is the relation of sense to thought. In Wordsworth, sense fails into thought. Nature strikes Wordsworth like a bolt; it is the charred trunk that he reflects upon. His thought looks back to sense and its elation, hungering. In Tomlinson, by contrast, the mind hovers over what the eye observes; the two are coterminous. Together, they surprise a sufficiency in the present; and if passion informs them, it is a passion for objectivity. For the most part, Wordsworth discovers himself in nature—it is this, of course, that makes him a Romantic poet. Tomlinson, on the other hand, discovers the nature of nature: a classical artist, he is all taut, responsive detachment.

The sufficiency (or something very near it) of the spatial world to Tomlinson's eye, mind, and heart, the gratefulness of appearances to a sensibility so unusual as his, at once radically receptive and restrained, separates him from such poets as D. H. Lawrence and Wallace Stevens—though the latter, indeed, exerted a strong early influence. This marked spiritual contentment—which makes up the message and quiet power and healing effluence of Tomlinson's work—may be conveniently illustrated by one of his shorter poems, 'The Gossamers':

> Autumn. A haze is gold
> By definition. This one lit
> The thread of gossamers
> That webbed across it
> Out of shadow and again
> Through rocking spaces which the sun
> Claimed in the leafage. Now
> I saw for what they were
> These glitterings in grass, on air,
> Of certainties that ride and plot

The currents in their tenuous stride
And, as they flow, must touch
Each blade and, touching, know
Its green resistance. Undefined
The haze of autumn in the mind
Is gold, is glaze.

This poem is in part a parable on the propriety of the self-forgetting mind. The mind—it seems to hint—is in itself a wealth, like a gold haze; the mind turned outward, however, is wealth piled upon wealth, a glaze upon particular things—a haze lighting up glittering gossamers. This reflection, which encloses the poem, forms part of its own wealth; and yet it is to the poem only what the enclosing haze is to the gossamers: an abstract richness outdone by and subservient to the vivid interest of the concrete. The poem is as good as its word: proclaiming the supremacy of the particular, it stands and delivers. To the tenuous intellect it presents a living, green resistance. Tomlinson's poem discovers gossamers as a scientist might discover a new chemical; indeed, Tomlinson himself has quoted with covetous interest from Lévi-Strauss's *The Savage Mind* a phrase applicable to his own cast of thought: 'the science of the concrete'. Of course the phrase omits the grateful quality of Tomlinson's attention: a scientist observes, Tomlinson regards, has regard. The gossamers are his host, he their thankful guest. And as a consequence of this humble gratitude, of this self-abnegating attention, Tomlinson brings into the human record—as nothing else has ever done—the look and being of gossamers, an obscure yet precious portion of articulated space. Impossible, now, not to know how gossamers plot currents, ride air, tenuously stride, connect and resist. Modest as it is, the poem is as good as a front row, a microscope, the opening of a long-buried treasure.

With this example before us, we may perhaps approach to a sharper view of Tomlinson's originality as a poet of nature. Among such poets, he is the anchorite of appearances. To poetry about them he brings an unexpected, an unparalleled, selflessness and objectivity. An ascetic of the eye, Tomlinson pushes poetry closer to natural philosophy than it has ever been before—and at the same time proselytizes for fine relationships with space, writes and persuades in earnestness, if not in zeal. Into an area crowded with hedonists, mystics, rapturous aesthetes, he comes equipped with a chaste eye and a mind intent upon exactitude. Nature may indeed be a Book; but not until now, say the chaste eye, the intent mind, has the book been more than scanned. The fine print, the difficult clauses, the subtle transitions, the unfamiliar words—Tomlinson will pore over them all. And his language will be as learned and meticulous, his dedication as passionate, his ego as subdued, as that of the true scholar—though mercifully he will also exercise, what few scholars possess, a deft and graceful feeling for form.

The clue to Tomlinson's originality lies in the apparent incongruity between his chosen subject and his temperament. In part, the subject is all the opulence of the visual world—jewelled glass, golden gossamers, fiery clouds. The temperament, by contrast, is strict and chaste, not far from sternness, flourishing only in an atmosphere of 'fecund chill', of 'temperate sharpness'. It is akin to that grain of wheat which, unless it die, cannot bring forth fruit. Ordinarily, of course, men of such temperament turn to God, to the State, to the poor, to science, to learning. They would no sooner turn to the sensual earth than the pious would turn to the Devil. Or if they did they would bring a scourge, not a strict curiosity indistinguishable from the most discreet and delicate love. A nature of which there is no 'point' to seize, as the first of the 'Four Kantian Lyrics' suggests, exists, after all, only to the senses; and the senses are notorious panders to the self, tributary streams of the torrential Ego. And yet what the chaste temperament desires is, precisely, to be selfless. Men of such mould would fall to the ground and emerge—something else, something richer. An anti-hedonist who cultivates his senses, an ascetic of

> . . . the steady roar of evening,
> Withdrawing in slow ripples of orange,
> Like the retreat of water from sea-caves

—these are patent contradictions in terms. Tomlinson, politely denying the contradiction, steps in among the hullabalooers and coolly and dedicatedly clears serious ground of his own in the region of the senses, in the forests and 'further fields' of non-transcendent space. The result is a nature poetry as unique in its classical temperateness as in its consecration to the Being of Space, to the face and actions of our natural environment.

Tomlinson looks outward, and what he sees becomes, not himself exactly, but his content. Seeing discovers his limits— but they are the limits of a vase or a window, not of a prison. Indeed, to Tomlinson it is a happy circumstance that the world is 'other'; were it identical with the self, there would be no refuge from solitude, nothing to touch as one reaches out.

> Out of the shut cell of that solitude there is
>   One egress, past point of interrogation.
> Sun is, because it is not you; you are
>   Since you are self, and self delimited
> Regarding sun . . .

Observer and observed stand apart, then, as the necessary poles of a substantiated being. The eye is the first of philosophers; seeing turns up the soil of ontology. Beholding thus applies to the spirit a metaphysical balm. The 'central calm' of appearances, their very thereness, gives a floor to the world. So Tomlinson walks and looks, and he finds it enough. Philosophically, he begins in nakedness—in nakedness, not in disinheritance; for the scrutinizing eye detects no twilight of past dreams of trans- cendence, only a present wealth of finite particulars, an ever shifting but sharply focused spectacle. In Tomlinson, the spirit, as if ignorant of what once sustained it—Platonic forms, Jehovah, the Life Force, the whole pantheon of the metaphysical mind— finds bliss in trees and stones that are merely trees and stones. And doubtless this implies an especially fine, not a particularly crude, capacity for wonder. Tomlinson is one of the purest instances in literature of the contemplative, as distinct from the speculative, mind. No poet has ever before regarded the intricate tapestry of Space with such patient and musing pleasure, with so little dread or anxiety to retreat through a human doorway or under the vaulted roof of a church. On the other hand, neither has any poet been less inclined to eat of the apples in his Eden. Tomlinson holds up to the tapestry a magnifying glass: he is all absorption, but, courteously, he keeps his place. And evidently his reward is a sense of answered or multiplied being. Let others— Dylan Thomas, D. H. Lawrence, E. E. Cummings—mount nature in ecstatic egoism. They will not really see her, except distortedly, through the heat waves of their own desire for union; they will not be companioned. Let still others—Thomas Hardy,

Robert Frost, Philip Larkin—suspect the worst of her, dread her, hint at wrinkled flesh beneath the flowered dress. They, too, will be left with only themselves. Tomlinson, putting himself by, will gain the world.

What Tomlinson values in human beings is a similar facing-away from the self, a rock-like, disciplined submergence in *being*. For the most part, the people in his poems are either models of subservience to task or tradition, as in 'Return to Hinton', 'The Farmer's Wife', 'The Hand at Callow Hill Farm', 'Oxen', 'Geneva Restored', 'Maillol', or examples of the discontent of desiring: the ambitious castellan of 'The Castle', the Symbolists of 'Antecedents', the 'Black Nude' who is sullen until she learns the 'truce' of the eye, the restless poet in 'Up at La Serra', and 'Mr. Brodsky', the American 'whose professed and long / pondered-on passion / was to become a Scot'. Like the hills and seas of his poems, Tomlinson is conservative through and through. If he could, one feels, he would bring all the world to a halt: to the 'luminous stasis' of contemplation. The dread he conveys is not of nature, nor even of human nature, but of the 'rational' future and its present busy machines—of what is happening to the earth, our host, and to the distinctively human source of our content-ment, the filaments of custom that hold us lovingly to place. Better a contented poverty, he believes, than a standardized prosperity:

> No hawk at wrist, but blessed by sudden sun
> And with a single, flaring hen that tops the chair
> Blooming beside her where she knits. Before the door
> And in the rainsoaked air, she sits as leisurely
> As spaces are with hillshapes in them. Yet she is small—
> If she arrests the scene, it is her concentration
> That commands it, the three centuries and more
> That live in her, the eyes that frown against the sun
> Yet leave intact the features' kindliness, the anonymous
> Composure of the settled act. Sufficient to her day
> Is her day's good, and her sufficiency's the refutation
> Of that future where there'll be what there already is—
> Prosperity and ennui, and none without the privilege
> To enjoy them both . . .

No doubt this leaves much to be said; but there is wisdom, passion, and sting in it, as well as beauty. In Tomlinson, the present as the latest and brimming moment of the past has both a first-rate poet and an able defender. 'Farm-bred certainties', 'ancestral certitude', or, as here, 'three centuries and more'—these, to him, have the same sanctifying use as a beech tree or a mood of light: all are alike, for human beings, the conditions of an 'anonymous / Composure'. All conduce to, all are food for, a contemplative life.

The Tomlinson of these portrait poems beholds not so much his subjects' individuality as their fine or fumbled relation to time and place: he beholds, in other words, their beholding. He is thus himself once removed—though, in another sense, also himself twice over. In the rest of his poems he beholds natural objects directly and minutely—standing back only so far as will allow him to reflect on the virtue of the eye. In either case, he is the poet of contemplation. It is this that gives him his strong and peculiar identity. The atmosphere of his work is that of a calm and cherishing attention. It is an atmosphere in which the objects of this world suddenly stand forth as part of the beautiful mystery of the founded. Whatever can be apprehended as the locus of a fine relation, dwelt on with intent devotion—whether gossamers slung in a haze, or a woman knitting in the rain-soaked air—becomes, to this poet, an 'Eden image'; at once pristine and per-manent, it radiates being. Tomlinson's sensibility homes to everything well established, and alights, and broods. And though it comes for grace, it comes also like a grace. It consecrates. This rare and valuable quality, never in excess but always temperate and chaste, is the essence of almost every Tomlinson poem.

It is this patient intention to consecrate that saves Tomlinson from the rapids of the senses. Indeed, it is doubtless a fear of the sensual and gluttonous Ego that gives thrust to his intention to consecrate. Accordingly, beholding in his work often seems as much a discipline as a delight. In such recent poems as 'Clouds' and 'In the Fullness of Time' he comes through as impressively equal to what he contemplates—a large, gracious, and answering stability. In many of his early poems, by contrast, he seems a trifle *determined* to see chastely and feel calmly. Indeed, so little excitement, so little spontaneous joy do these poems convey that their seeing sometimes seems *more* a discipline than a delight. The description never blurs, but neither does it glow, with enthusiasm; no sentiment ever spills over the detail into a general, joyful reference. Here contemplation is, in the poet's own word, a shriving. Light, he says in 'Something: A Direction', is split by human need: accept the light, and you heal both the light and your need. At each dawn the sun is recovered

> . . . in a shriven light
> And you, returning, may to a shriven self
> As from the scene, your self withdraws . . .

So it is that Tomlinson would make of beholding an *ascesis*, a chaste, chill atmosphere to cool the hot and clouding Ego.

In consequence, Tomlinson's poems have something of the severity of a religious cell. Whitewashed of the self, chill, close-packed as stone walls, they are rooms for intense and selfless meditation. Austerity marks both their language and their movement. The diction has the dryness of exposure to mental weather—though the dryness of living bark, not of stones. Learned and exact, it joins the concrete with academic abstraction: in 'Gossamers', for example, the sun is said to *claim* the spaces that *rock* in the leafage; and if the gossamers *ride* and *plot*, they are *certainties* that do so. Tomlinson's descriptions, accordingly, both feed and ration the eye. Seeing passes somewhat difficultly into thought and stops just short of an easy clarity. At the same time, the depictions give out only so much emotional warmth as they counter with the chill of a rational diction. Even when almost entirely concrete, this poet's delineations remain anatomy:

> A trailed and lagging grass, a pin-point island
> Drags the clear current's face it leans across
> In ripple-wrinkles. At a touch
> It has ravelled the imaged sky till it could be
> A perplexity of metal, spun
> Round a vortex, the sun flung off it
> Veining the eye like a migraine—it could
> Scarcely be sky . . .

Like a window that allows vision through only one side, this looks out lucidly towards surfaces, is blind and indifferent to the inner life. Concrete with respect to spatial things, it is abstract to feeling. Not that it fails to touch feeling; for there is delight here—the delight of detected resemblance and, deeper still, the pleasure that comes from perceiving that a thing has escaped being simply itself—'it could / Scarcely be sky. . . .' And this is to say that there is considerable imaginative life in the description—an aspect of the poetry that we must return to. All the same, Tomlinson analyses and photographs the current as one who stands over against it, alien though not estranged. He neither attempts to become the water, as any number of poets might have done, nor leaves chinks in his description for sentiment. With Robbe-Grillet, his passage declares that 'to describe things . . . is deliberately to place oneself outside them, facing them', and also that 'there is in existence in the world something that is not man, that takes no notice of him.' So the stream is itself, and the words merely serve its being. While Tomlinson stands over against the water, his language, as it were, stands over against him and on the side of what faces him. Indeed, until recently, it has even turned a deaf ear to itself, avoiding all but the most discreet self-echoing—as here, for instance, the tucked-away rhyme of 'lagging' and 'drag'.

Metre is also, of course, a self-reference of sound, and Tomlinson's verse logically eschews it, is 'free'. It is not, however, free as the verse of D. H. Lawrence or William Carlos Williams is free: it is not free to empathize with its subjects. Empathic rhythm, like metre, awakens feeling: the difference is that metre is emotionally introverted, empathic *vers libre* extroverted. So the metre of Christina Rossetti's

> My heart is like a singing bird
>   Whose nest is in a water'd shoot;
> My heart is like an apple-tree
>   Whose boughs are bent with thick-set fruit . . .

turns feeling around and around, like a dancer in a music box, while the rhythm of Lawrence's 'Fish',

> Aqueous, subaqueous
> Submerged
> And wave-thrilled . . .

or Williams's 'Rain',

> the trees
> are become
> beasts fresh risen
> from
>   the sea—
> water

> trickles
> from the crevices of
> their hides . . .

sends feeling outward into objects. Tomlinson's rhythm, by
contrast, is neither extroverted nor introverted, but emotionally
suspended, stilled and poised in meditation. It springs free of the
hypnotic spin of metre, but holds itself back from the emotional
free-lancing of *vers libre*. It is free, not to dance new steps to
the music of a vital happening, but free, precisely, from the tug
and engulfing tide of feeling. Just as a rational element checks
emotional participation in Tomlinson's descriptions, so an
approximate accentual balance and a kind of sanity of iso-
chronism reins in feeling in Tomlinson's rhythm—a rhythm
that moves narrowly between the mind-lulling security of metre
and the mind-dissolving fluidity of free verse:

> Two stand
> admiring morning.
> A third, unseen as yet
> approaches across upland
> that a hill and a hill's wood
> hide. The two
> halving a mutual good,
> both watch a sun
> entering sideways
> the slope of birches . . .

Here the first two lines have an approximate quantity or length;
they also balance in beat. The next three add a beat and balance
one another. The sixth, though it drops an accent, keeps the length
with its long vowels and caesura. And in the last two lines the
rhythm quickens back to its initial measure. Reading Tomlinson,
one comes instinctively to look for this sort of rough yet reliable
recurrence. Like the next bead in a rosary, the accentual repetition
provides a necessary sense of stability. On the other hand, shifting
and uncertain as it is, it discourages complicities of the pulse. It
leaves the mind strung, alert, and waiting.

This condition is heightened by the frequent breakage of the
lines *against* phrasal expectations and unities. The lines end long
or short, in mid air; and thus left jutting and jagged, they spur
the mind to attention. So of the swan in 'Canal' we read:

> . . . Sinuously
> both the live
> bird and the bird
> the water bends
> into a white and wandering
> reflection of itself,
> go by in grace
> a world of objects . . .

Obviously the lines here work against any sharing of the swans'
sinuous motion. The swans may be all grace, but the lines, as
such, are all stiff angles. Typically fragmenting sentences down
to phrases, then further fragmenting some of the phrases, omitting
expected and interjecting unexpected commas, Tomlinson's
lines retard and brake the mind, suspend and distance its grasp,
so that when full comprehension finally comes, it arrives, as it
were, soundless and clear, unaccompanied by the resonant surge
of an affective rhythm.

Altogether, then, there is in Tomlinson's slow, inorganic
rhythm of stops and starts and precarious, uncertain balances
no wave for imagination to surf on, no independence and autonomy of accent. And yet, for all that, it has character and charm;
one acquires a taste for it. Toughly flexile, it introduces a new
quality into verse, as if after centuries of beating the drum of the
blood, a rhythm had at last been found for the mind. Anything
more fluent and facile—so one feels while reading him—would
be intolerably flaccid. Whether in short lines, as in 'Canal', or
in medium lines like these,

> It happened like this: I heard
> from the farm beyond, a grounded
> churn go down. The sound
> chimed for the wedding of the mind
> with what one could not see,
> the further fields, the seamless
> spread of space . . .

or in the longer lines he has favoured of late,

> Cloudshapes are destinies, and they
>   Charging the atmosphere of a common day,
> Make it the place of confrontation where
>   The dreamer wakes to the categorical call
> And clear cerulean trumpet of the air

the movement serves as a kind of stiffening, not only standing the lines up to the mind but constituting in its own right an aesthetic value, a virility like starch in a formal shirt.

So it is that, in both his relation to his subject and his poetic manner, Tomlinson is an original—and what is more, with an originality that counts, that comes to seem, while we read him, and the more we read him, the very intelligence of the eye, the very rhythm of a chaste beholding. And the mainspring of this originality, it has been suggested, lies in the singleness of Tomlinson's contemplative purpose, the rigour of his attempt to make of the observation of nature through the medium of poetry a shriving of the self—a naked, though not unthoughtful, encounter with appearances.

What makes Tomlinson an important poet is partly his originality; but of course it is not his originality that makes him a poet. If his poetry contained observation alone, it would be of no more interest—though of no less interest, either—than a camera set rolling in a snowy field or by the sea. Tomlinson is a poet, in part, because of a consistent, masculine elegance of language, and also in part because of his feeling for rhythm. But mostly he is a poet because he uses, and excites, imagination, and because this imagination is not of a light or gratuitous kind but steeped in feeling, organic, pregnant with a response to life. Deeply and richly conceived, Tomlinson's poems are neither the mere notations of a stenographic eye, nor cold slabs of reflection; they begin, they vault, and they conclude in feeling. 'That art is selective', writes Dewey in *Art as Experience*, 'is a fact universally recognized. It is so because of the role of emotion in the act of expression. Any predominant mood automatically excludes all that is uncongenial with it.' And the unity of Tomlinson's poems is fundamentally the unity of a magisterial and imaginative mood.

To be sure, no magistrate was ever more humble or amenable while still retaining and exercising his proper powers. Tomlinson's imagination *attends* to observable reality with almost the patience that characterizes and gives distinction to his eye. Like a fine atmosphere, it can be gentle to the point of invisibility, so that objects and places, and not the poet himself, seem to be communicants of feeling. And when it does grow dense, it thickens as light thickens, making its objects as well as itself more vivid.

Impossible to imagine a closer co-operation between the conceiving mind and the receiving eye. Tomlinson's imagination takes its cues, its colours, its composure, from the Persian carpet of the visual world itself.

From what has already been said, it will be seen at once that this delicate co-operation is a matter of strict principle. Indeed, it is largely the imagination—that genie and temptress of the self—that the straps of *seeing* are intended to confine. If Tomlinson's poems are imaginative, it is almost in their own despite. They are imaginative, so to speak, only because they must be in order to qualify as poetry. Granted their way, so it seems, they would be, instead, only a wondering silence. Nor does this principle of imaginative containment—so jealously adhered to—remain implicit. Several of the poems give a sharp rap to the skull of Romanticism, consistently conceived as an egoistic imagination bringing to birth frenzied and false worlds of its own. For example, 'Distinctions' chides Pater for indicating that the blue of the sea gives way to 'pinks, golds, or mauves', 'Farewell to Van Gogh' patronizes that painter's 'instructive frenzy', and 'Maillol' glances at the 'flickering frenzy of Rodin'. Indeed, it is the fault of these, as well as of two or three other poems, that they seem to exist chiefly for the sake of their doctrine. Of course, all of Tomlinson is doctrinal—the bias towards passivity, receptivity, and self-effacement being as overwhelming as it is avowed, determined, and morally aggressive. But for the most part this doctrine proves unobjectionable, for the simple reason that poetry takes it over. In the anti-Romantic poems, however, the doctrine tends to tread the poetry down. And left alone on the field, Tomlinson's vigilance against the self's excess itself emerges as excessive. His strictures are too tight, they hold their breath in prim disapproval. 'To emulate such confusion', he writes of a scuffle between wind and trees,

> One must impoverish the resources of folly,
> But to taste it is medicinal . . .

And just as the first line, here, drops a demolition ball on the point, so the tasting in the second seems a trifle too fastidious. Similarly, 'The Jam Trap', which glances at harmful egoistic hedonism in its picture of flies immersed 'Slackly in sweetness', comes through as so unfairly and extremely reductive that it makes Tomlinson, and not Romanticism, seem wrong-headed.

And yet, unobtrusive and stopped down as it is, Tomlinson's imagination is, as was suggested, precisely the gift and power that makes his poetry poetic. Though obviously far from being ample, headlong, or richly empowering, neither, on the other hand, is it faint or apologetic. It is equally active and attentive, forceful and discreet. As procreative mood, it is the tension and coherence that keeps the poems brimming, and the still depth that moves the detail towards us, magnified. As subjective transmutation, moreover, it is the gold, the glaze, that makes the detail glitter. Subtract it from the poems, and only sorry fragments would remain. Of course, the farther Tomlinson stands off from objects, the more conspicuous the mediation of his emotional and imaginative presence becomes, increasing like the green of deepening waters. Thus bare lines like these from 'The Hill',

> Do not call to her there,
> but let her go
> bearing our question
> in her climb: what does she
> confer on the hill, the hill on her? . . .

are obviously tense with imaginative concentration: with the conceived drama of contemplation, and the conceived mystery of relationship. Yet, whether noticed or not, this controlling and conceiving element is nonetheless almost always present and always felt in Tomlinson's poems. Even the largely 'factual' poems resonate under imagination's bow. Consider, for example, even so unambitious a poem as 'Letter from Costa Brava':

> Its crisp sheets, unfolded,
> Give on to a grove, where
> Citrons conduct the eye
> Past the gloom of foliage
> Towards the glow of stone. They write
> of a mesmeric clarity
> In the fissures of those walls
> And of the unseizable lizards, jewelled
> Upon them. But let them envy
> What they cannot see:
> This sodden, variable green
> Igniting against the grey.

In the knock and juxtaposition of these two glowing and gloomy landscapes, the one dryly sensual, the other soggily spiritual, what a fine effect is produced by the unexpected, proud, and loving preference—so deftly made understandable—for the puritanically passionate English scene. It was imagination that caught and conveyed both the similarity and the deep polarity of these scenes, their different registers in the life of the spirit. And of course it was imagination that produced here and there the fillip of metaphor, adding local intensities to the shaping tension of the whole: a stimulation felt most strongly in the adjectives and in the verbid *igniting*, so boldly yet so rightly qualifying the suggestion of *sodden*. And elsewhere in Tomlinson one finds equal felicities of the imaginative power of augmenting and interpreting appearances without denying them—for example, the rose in 'Frondes Agrestes', seen

> Gathered up into its own translucence
> Where there is no shade save colour . . .

or, in 'Prometheus', the trees that

> Continue raining though the rain has ceased
> In a cooled world of incessant codas . . .

However adverse Tomlinson may be to imagination, clearly there is no lack of it in his poetry.

By now it will have become apparent that Tomlinson is something less of the simple observer and something more of a poet than he himself seems inclined to believe. The view that he encourages of himself, through his poems, is neither accurate nor fully just. Listen to the poems and you will conclude that Tomlinson is but the servant or the guest of appearances. Experience the poems, on the other hand, and you will know that he is something more, and more difficult—namely, their abettor, their harvest, their fulfilment. And this is to say that there is a notable discrepancy, widening at times into a contradiction, between what the poems declare and what they are and do. They speak, as it were, in ignorance of themselves. Thus, though they recommend passivity, it is through their own activity. Though they would teach us to conserve, they themselves are creative and therefore innovative. As they urge us to silence before the multiple voices of space, they impress us with a

distinctively human voice. And as they praise nature as our
replenishment, they replenish us. So it is that what the right hand
gives, the left hand takes away. In 'Observation of Facts', to
cite a specific instance, Tomlinson cautions:

> Style speaks what was seen,
> Or it conceals the observation
> Behind the observer: a voice
> Wearing a ruff . . .

and meanwhile delights us, in the concluding image, by speaking
what has never been and never will be seen.

> . . . I leave you
> To your one meaning, yourself alone . . .

he says of an upended tree in 'Poem'; but what his vehemently
anthropomorphic description actually leaves in the memory is
not a tree but a creature crouching 'on broken limbs / About to
run forward'. 'Only we / Are inert', Tomlinson writes in 'In
Defence of Metaphysics'—and then, in observing that 'Stones are
like deaths. / They uncover limits', himself shows admirably
more than inertia of mind. In 'Château de Muzot', he says of the
stone mass,

> . . . A shriven self
> Looks out at it. You cannot
> Add to this. Footholds for foison
> There are none. Across stoneface
> Only the moss, flattened, tightly-rosetted
> Which, ignorant of who gives
> Accepts from all weathers
> What it receives, possessed
> By the nature of stone.

Yet in so describing it, Tomlinson obviously and wonderfully
adds to it, finding footholds not only for the imaginative 'foison'
of rosetted moss but for the whole parable-conceit of gift,
acceptance, and possession. Examples could be multiplied.

Altogether, then, there is in Tomlinson a rebuke to the active,
creative self that, coming from a poet, seems untutored: there
is professional suicide in the sermon. What other poet is so
insistently and recklessly forgetful of his own gift and its

prerogatives? Virtually taking a giant erasor to his work, Tomlinson will write:

> Those facets of copiousness which I proposed
> Exist, do so when we have silenced ourselves.

Indeed, Tomlinson would thus erase more than his gift; he would erase human consciousness itself. For of course the only truly silenced human being is a dead one. Dewey is again to the point: as he observes, 'nothing takes root in the mind when there is no balance between doing and receiving'; for 'perception is an act of the going-out of energy in order to receive, not a withholding of energy', and though 'the esthetic or undergoing phase of experience is receptive', an 'adequate yielding of the self is possible only through a controlled activity that may well be intense.' Though Tomlinson again and again salutes the 'yielding', the 'activity', as a rule, he leaves out of account. So in 'A Given Grace' he commences:

> Two cups,
> a given grace
> afloat and white
> on the mahogany pool
> of table. They unclench
> the mind, filling it
> with themselves . . .

And several lines later he concludes:

> you would not wish
> them other than they are—
> you, who are challenged
> and replenished by
> those empty vessels.

This is true, but only half true. For it is just as reasonable, and just as partial, to say that it is the empty vessels that have been filled, and filled by mind. Sophisticated poet though he is, Tomlinson yet falls into what Husserl calls 'the natural unsophisticated standpoint' of consciousness, which assumes 'an empty looking of an empty "Ego".' Consciousness can indeed be invested, but only in so far as it invests; as Husserl observes, it is the ego that invests 'the being of the world . . . with existential validity'. Apart from consciousness, after all, the world is but a sweep and waste of energy unseen, unfelt, unheard, and untasted. Of poets, moreover, it may be said that they invest appearances doubly—not only with their mind and senses but with their imagination as well. Thus in 'A Given Grace', while it is Tomlinson's eye that perceives and invests the two cups, it is his imagination that sees them floating in a mahogany pool, making them something other than they are. Facets of copiousness do indeed exist, but only in a dialectic between the self and the objective world.

It should be noted, however, that though Tomlinson has emphasized and done more than justice to the passive aspect of the self's liaison with space, he has managed to strike other notes of his theme as well. In fact, however unequally these may be pressed, the chord of his theme stands complete. Thus in a fairly recent poem, 'The Hill', Tomlinson celebrates at last—quite as if he had never doubted it (as perhaps he had not)—consciousness as itself a grace, a grace of giving. The female figure climbing the hill named in the title is a type of the being-investing consciousness:

> She
> alone, unnamed (as it were),
> in making her thought's theme
> that thrust and rise
> is bestowing a name . . .

A still more recent poem, 'Adam', provides a partial gloss:

> We bring
> To a kind of birth all we can name . . .

So the hill stands forth, rounds out into being, through the generosity of the girl's attention. The grace of consciousness consists in its active intentionality: the girl *makes* her thought's theme that thrust and rise. It is, after all then, stones that are inert. Indeed, a recoiling spring, Tomlinson perhaps goes too far when, in 'The Hill', he adds:

> . . . do not call to her there:
> let her go on,
> whom the early sun
> is climbing up with to the hill's crown—
> she, who did not make it, yet can make
> the sun go down by coming down.

In this instance, of course, the 'making' is only a manner of speaking. And yet here Tomlinson, for one rare and indulgent moment, encourages a solipsistic illusion. Putting by the domestic uniform it usually wears in his poems, the mind steps forward as almost a demiurge, capable of making, by a simple withdrawal of attention, a heavenly body slide out of the sky.

Of course the true grace of any and every relationship is neither a giving nor a receiving, but an interchange and balance of the two. And towards this inclusive reciprocity Tomlinson may be said to have ripened. His early attempts to render it do not quite come off, and are, perhaps, not quite sincere, the self having been made too hollow a counter-weight to space. For example, in 'Reflections' Tomlinson writes:

> . . . When we perceive, as keen
> As the bridge itself, a bridge inlaying the darkness
> Of smooth water, our delight acknowledges our debt—
> To nature, from whom we choose . . .

But this would seem, rather, an instance of being chosen, and the declaration of self-determination does not convince. In some of the more recent poems, by contrast, the self seems genuinely erect before the world it experiences. Perhaps no statement and evocation—for the poem is both—of a pristine and yet not unsophisticated encounter with environment, the mind and space meeting as two equal and mysterious realities, could be at once more justly delicate and soberly beautiful than 'Swimming Chenango Lake'. Here, as in 'The Hill', the anonymous human figure is a type of consciousness—not, in this case, however, of consciousness as the only proud Climber of Creation, but as Creation's Swimmer, active in a dense, merciless element that 'yet shows a kind of mercy sustaining him':

> . . . he has looked long enough, and now
> Body must recall the eye to its dependence
> As he scissors the waterscape apart
> And sways it to tatters. Its coldness
> Holding him to itself, he grants the grasp,
> For to swim is also to take hold
> On water's meaning, to move in its embrace
> And to be, between grasp and grasping, free . . .

Not only the mutuality of two alien orders of being, but the

simultaneous doing and undergoing in human experience, finds
in this poem a crystal paradigm.

So it is that, here and there in Tomlinson, the self has come
into its own. And still more is this true in a few of the poems
addressed to art. Despite his animadversions against Romanticism,
Tomlinson has shown himself quite ready to think of art—
especially music—as a spiritual flowering beyond anything offered
by reality. Thus in 'Flute Music' he notes:

> Seeing and speaking we are two men:
> The eye encloses as a window—a flute
> Governs the land, its winter and its silence . . .

An early poem, 'Flute Music' may perhaps be written off as an
accident of ventriloquism—the result of a saturation in Wallace
Stevens. But in a later and more impressive poem, 'Ode to Arnold
Schoenberg', the same theme sounds again. 'Natural' meaning,
according to the ode, does not suffice: art satisfies by pursuing
'a more than common meaning'. The 'unfolded word' not only
renews 'the wintered tree' of previous art but creates and cradles
space, filling it with verdure.

Is space ordinarily, then, a winter and a silence? Decisively,
persuasively, the other poems answer 'No'. And yet the very
fact that they were written bespeaks a painful and reluctant 'Yes'.
The truth is that, beyond the discrepancy between what the
poems say and what they are, yawns the still greater discrepancy
between what they say and the fact that they are. Let them set
nature before us as a sufficient spiritual end; still, their very existence as poetry, their very excess over nature, suggests that it is
art, and not nature, that cures the ache of being. As both the
beholder and poet of nature Tomlinson is twice the contemplative;
and just in that apparent superfluity, it seems, lies the fullness
that the spirit requires. The poems confess that 'those empty
vessels' of space whet as much as they replenish; and what nature
prompts, art concludes. Not so humble or subservient after all,
the spirit relives its experiences, but recreates them from itself
alone—positing, retrospectively, the space that once had nourished
it. The hill it climbs becomes a subjective space, memory worked
over by imagination. The essential confession of Tomlinson's
art is, I believe, the essential confession of all art: that man is
forced to be, and also needs to be, his own replenishment,

perpetually renewed out of himself. So it is that, merely by existing, Tomlinson's poetry completes the real but limited truth—namely, the gratefulness of the world to the senses—whose thousand faces the poems seek out and draw.

It was in his third volume, *Seeing is Believing* (1958), that Tomlinson first became both the distinct and the distinguished poet that he is today. His first volume, *Relations and Contraries* (1951), is haunted by Yeats and Blake, and though brilliant in patches, is not of much consequence. Tomlinson next moved a good deal nearer to himself in *The Necklace* (1955), which ranks, at the least, as a prologue to his real achievement. It zeroes in on the great Tomlinson theme, but vitiates it by a kind of enamelled elegance; it has Stevens's epicurean quality but not his saving gusto and bravura. Precious in both senses of the word, *The Necklace* is a book to be valued, but—too beautiful, too exquisite —not to feel at home in: you must park your muddy shoes at the door. The very title of the third volume, *Seeing is Believing*, suggests a homely improvement over *The Necklace*. Here the earth takes on some of the earthiness that, after all, becomes it; and the manner is more gritty, rubs more familiarly with the world. In the next two volumes, *A Peopled Landscape* (1962) and *American Scenes* (1966), the same manner—at once meticulous, prosaic, and refined (for Tomlinson's early elegance is roughened rather than lost)—is extended, as the titles indicate, to new subjects if not exactly to new themes. The high point of Tomlinson's career to date came with the first long section of *The Way of a World* (1969), a series of poems dense with his loving intellection, his difficult grace, his strong dry beauty. The comparably ambitious meditative poems in *Written on Water* (1972) unfortunately hamper as much as they restrain the sensuous: here the *display* of contemplation is sometimes more apparent than its joy. Yet *Written on Water*, too, contains a wealth of beautiful writing; it has become hard for this poet to fail.

Tomlinson's dedication to excellence is deep and unmistakable; and joined with his rare if quiet talent, it has led to repeated successes in a period when the successes of more striking poets have seemed haphazard (not those of Stevie Smith and W. S. Graham, it is true, but they have been far less productive). His poems not only survive the rub and wear of repeated readings;

like a fine wood under polish, they improve under such treatment. With his painstaking descriptions, so often hard to seize with the eye, his laconic meditations, his initially uncertain rhythms, his frustrations of various expectations, Tomlinson has taken the hard way around to beauty, and arrived. Though the more recent poems are probably his most accessible, they still constitute a language to be learned, a flavour to be found, and to care about Tomlinson is to approve of this difficulty. Just as the later Yeats makes the early Yeats seem somewhat facile and obvious, so Tomlinson, asceticizing poetry as he has, provides a new sense of what the art can be. His is the sort of modification of poetry that ultimately compels other poets to change, to make it new, to work passionately at their lines.

As for the sensibility that Tomlinson's poetry expresses, its value, I think, should be self-evident. The truth it has seized upon, indeed the truth that seems native to it, is the lesson implicit in art itself—that contemplation is the fulfilment of being. Of course we have always to know what needs to be changed; but we also do well to praise and reverence what is sufficient for the day and the vast design that, though it impinges on us, ultimately lies beyond our human agency.

For without this reverence we can scarcely be committed to the value of being; it is the secret of what Pasternak called 'the talent for life'. Tomlinson is certainly out of season to recall us to the life of the moment conceived as an end in itself; and yet it is just this unseasonableness that puts him in harmony with what is lasting in our relations with the world.

Donald Davie

OF all the first-rate poets of the age, Donald Davie is the most notably reactionary. If only with some strain, we might see him, to advantage, as mining in the great ascetic vein of contemporary art, where the classical spirit thins away—as in Rothko, Bresson, Sarraute, Beckett, Cage—in ever starker forms. And yet Davie stands far to the right of most of his fellow ascetics—indeed, within hailing distance of the eighteenth century. In tone, diction, and verse form, he often recalls the late Augustan poets, of whom he has written well and whom he has anthologized. Above all he has tried, like the Augustans, to be urbane: to voice (in words he quotes from Matthew Arnold) 'the tone and spirit of the centre'. This is reactionary indeed. For of course there is no longer any centre. Or the centre is but a maelstrom, a contention.

Comparing Landor unfavourably with Carew in *Purity of Diction in English Verse* (1952), Davie notes that 'in the latter speaks the voice of Caroline culture, whereas in Landor's verses nothing speaks but the voice of the poet himself'. But Davie himself, as a poet, is in the same position as Landor; it could not be otherwise. The difference is that he chooses not to be in it. 'To make poetry out of moral commonplace', he says, 'a poet has to make it clear that he speaks not in his own voice (that would be impertinent) but as the spokesman of a social tradition.' As Emily Dickinson, Marianne Moore, and others witness, this is not quite true. But it does prompt us to add that 'to make poetry out of moral commonplace', as Davie himself tries to do, when the commonplace is damaged, indeed marooned—indeed, *forlorn*—does require something like impertinence; and rapping on roving knuckles with yardsticks borrowed from old classrooms, impertinently using the word 'impertinence' with its assumption of determinate absolutes, what Davie himself exemplifies, we may feel, is not 'the tone and spirit' of any centre, but something more courageous and significant, not to say lonely: the individual man working out the necessities of his conscience. Moreover, what really fires this conscience, we may feel, is not at all being at the centre, whatever that may happen to be in any age, but being right: right about the need for civilized restraint, for faith in the idea of civilization itself. We hear in Davie's poetry a voice that *will* speak out in spite of its knowledge of the indifference or incredulity that awaits it—a voice consciously coming, not from the centre of contemporary culture, but from out on the edge, in a kind of nagging nostalgia for an austerer day, when men lived and died by Nonconformist lights, or for Reason, Loyalty, Restraint, the Right. It is the voice of a conscience that—protestingly—finds itself left behind.

Davie's conscience is, as we shall see, more complex than I have yet suggested—or than he himself seems quite to have grasped. Almost dramatically self-divided, it contains its own principle of self-correction. It is larger and wiser, as it were, than Davie himself, since Davie, at any one time, embodies but half of it. There is, however, some justice in emphasizing its jaundiced and vigilant side; for there can be no doubt that Davie himself is partial to it. Indeed, it often seems that Davie has taken it as his peculiar role among contemporary poets to be perversely pure and dour—to knock on the ceiling shaken by the reckless goings-on of the present with the broom of the Puritan (or simply the reasonable) past. And if he has made too much of this, cramming himself into a niche that is really too small for him and from which, now and again, he has had to break out and stretch his limbs and take the air, still the niche is of his own carving—is in its measure congenial to him. And, having assumed it so often, he has indeed inclined us to regard him as the poet of 'urbane' and reactionary admonitions, partial as this identity must seem in a final view. And certainly he has assumed it often enough to force us to ask what effect it has had on his art.

We always have need, of course, for rearguard admonitions, for they are the ballast of the day. But poetry, though rear-view by nature, the harking mind of experience, is also celebrative by nature—wants to celebrate even when it can't—and thus is not the best place to fire admonitions. Urbanity, moreover, bears no brief for beauty; its cause is the good. Hence to be an 'urbane poet', if one is indeed a poet, is to be out of line with oneself and with poetry. The chief effect of Davie's attempt to be urbane—and not only in the Arnoldian sense but in the root sense of 'civilized, polished, refined, witty'—has been a waste of his poetic abilities, their silencing while lesser instruments are played. In much of his work, Davie has gone through the motions of poetry, and given the result its name; but the rope he has walked has been utilitarian clothesline, its height but a little way above the ground, and the performance, accordingly, altogether lacking in that power to astonish which poetry displays.

Before taking note, though, of the poorer consequences of Davie's deliberate and even polemical 'urbane' poetic programme, we ought to acknowledge that in one way Davie has indeed achieved, within poetry, a notable urbanity: an urbanity, not of voice or position, but of language. Linguistic urbanity lies (in a phrase Davie quotes from T. S. Eliot) in 'the perfection of a common language'. Here as elsewhere the urbane principle is an enlightened modesty: the intelligence, the social authority in a language seeming so large, the poet's own inventions, his own ego, so small. The urbane mind scorns the folly and fears the vice of all private perspective; it trusts in the justice of the general. Accordingly, the ideal style, to it, is a style without style, as clear, unmarked, and compliant as water—and, like water, wholesome, easy to assimilate, and used by everyone (for as the lines go, so goes the nation).

Doubtless it sounds dull—colourless, much *too* common, not to say too well-intentioned. Yet in Davie's distillations it proves, at best, exquisite. We find, for example, the fresh spring-water transparence of such lines as these from 'Tunstall Forest':

> . . . the tense
> Stillness did not come,
> The deer did not, although they fed
> Perhaps nearby that day,
> The liquid eye and elegant head
> No more than a mile away.

How liltingly social Davie's diction can be, too, how susceptible to warmth for all its impersonality, as in 'The Cypress Avenue':

> My companion kept exclaiming
> At fugitive aromas;
> She was making a happy fuss
> Of flower-naming . . .

And how tightly wound and serious, how finely urgent with realization as well, as in 'After an Accident', where the death that had always seemed remote and deferred—one's own—smashes into the present:

> So Death is what one day
> You have run out of, like
> Luck or a bank-balance.
> In that case, what is
> Coming into it like?
>
> Like coming into money!
> The death we run out of is
> Not the life we run out of;
> The death that we may
> With luck come into, is.
>
> And without money, life
> Is not worth living.
> How did you manage
> All these years,
> Living and not living?

What confronts us in all these examples is language rather than style—the common language filtered and purified. Impossible to parody: it would be easier to take hold of the air. Fleeing from a 'distinctive' voice as from the very principle of evil, Davie, it is true, in a sense achieves one: in the midst of voices with a signature, his stands out by virtue of its choice impersonality. But clearly its intention is otherwise: Davie's is a language, as it were, surprised and found, not forged and made. If his words distinguish themselves, it is not by their manner, but by their 'good manners', their social finality, their intention to communicate. It is, then, from this centre, the heart of the perfected common language, that Davie writes his poetry. And if he fails to make it seem the *necessary* place for poetry, still he proves it to be one of the positions of excellence.

And yet, to repeat, there has also been unhappy waste in this insistence on urbanity—unnecessary limitation and futility. The temptation to slight the real, unpredictable, and slovenly body of experience, to keep it at a polite and useful distance, to talk and civilize and 'purify' the language rather than write poems, has been more than Davie has been able to withstand. Indeed, he has been, on the whole, more eager to embrace it than withstand it. He has even felt it his duty to embrace it. And he has been, in consequence, a poet only when he has escaped from his theories—when he has opened the door, quietly so as not to waken the urbane guards, and stepped out into the surprising world.

An urbane language is one thing, an urbane poetry another. It was with good reason that Arnold, showing his usual sure instinct about poetry, exempted poets from 'the tone and spirit of the centre'. Moderation, sobriety, proportion, right reason—in poetry, Arnold said, these, after all, are 'secondary, and energy is the first thing'. But the English prose writers having left the centre empty, fleeing from that exposed watchtower, so bare, prosaic, and responsible, into the cool of a redolent and secluded poetic style, it has been left to the poets, so Davie has suggested, to occupy, to *man* it. Hence, though one of his books on poetry is entitled *Articulate Energy*, as if in agreement with Arnold, what Davie actually celebrates in it is 'strong sense', which, however energetic, is pre-eminently a *prose* virtue. Towards the primal energy of poetry, which is evolving feeling—imagination intently migrating, arriving, arrived—Davie is in the position of the man who would rather not acknowledge a disreputable family connection. And yet there is, after all, no poetry without it; there is only prose.

The reason poetry cannot be urbane—though with jeopardy urbanity can be imported into it—is that its first and chief centre is its own. With the centre of the real world, as with Johnson's 'extensive view', it can have no essential connection: if it happens to take in a great sweep of it, it is in satisfying its appetite to be itself. Poetry begins and ends in its own precincts; its centre of gravity lies apart from and above the world. It is, in truth, always a new world, evolved unlooked-for out of the energies of the old. Conceived, as Hazlitt says, when a 'flame of feeling' (or of intuition, which is feeling instinct with a certain sense) is 'communicated to the imagination', poetry comes to birth with the incarnation of its own original impulse—a case of the parent having become the child. It is thus enclosed upon itself, as an animal is, though an animal that can act and see and mate. Unlike prose discourse, poetry is not essentially referred away; everything in it is equally 'of the centre', since everything in it is alive with the same self-contemplating, self-nourishing mood.

Reality, let alone the urbane centre of things, is thus necessarily obscured in poetry, as by a painting held close to one's eyes in the midst of a great landscape. As Pasternak puts it in *Safe Conduct*, reality, in art, is always 'displaced' by feeling: 'art is a record of this displacement'. And yet, as in an optical illusion, where front and back appear to change positions, reality, and not feeling, will seem to be forward. Reality does indeed *appear* in poetry, but, as Pasternak says, 'in some new form'. A new quality enters it, a quality of feeling that seems 'inherent in it, and not in us'. This quality 'alone is new and without name. We try to give it a name. The result is art.'

The urbane versifier knocks poetry out of its mesmerizing spin, its life apart and to itself, its life above life, so that it will fall, will come to rest, at the heart of a morally responsible view of things, good money at last. He wants reality to appear in his work, not 'in some new form', but in its most generalized and familiar, its morally guaranteed forms—in fact, as 'moral commonplace'. But the truth is that reality does not appear in his work at all. Seen from 'the centre', reality falls into the blind spot in the middle of the eye. No longer Appearance, it becomes a storehouse of signs, of which the meanings are moral abstractions. The tremendous retort between feeling and reality, and between reality in its known and in its 'new' form, which gives poetry its dramatic and dialectical character, the place where the lightning strikes and plays, yields in 'urbane' work to a stillness in which a monologue of the mind alone is heard, rising thinly in an echoless area of illustrative props.

Such is the monologue we hear in most of Davie's poems of the Fifties, and that lately we have been hearing from Davie again. Of the early work, 'Portrait of the Artist as a Farmyard Fowl' is a typical example:

> A conscious carriage must become a strut;
>   Fastidiousness can only stalk
> And seem at last not even tasteful but
>   A ruffled hen too apt to squawk.

Davie is here so disinclined to make of his poem a new experience, reality breathing and surprised in a 'new form', that he can only point to the real world as one gives directions to a stranger— It is 'over there' from him, just at the distance where its substance disappears and only its laws are legible. Instead of translating us into immediate imaginative experience, he arms us for future moral experience. If we 'see' his images, it is only as moral cutouts. Having been deprived of the weight, necessity, and shimmer of things in their natural place in the intricate world, they have none of the illusionary, substantive character of actual poetic images. They are imposed, not imposing. In 'poetry' of this kind, the mind follows no motive and no will but its own; reality, if an occasion for lessons, is also only a 'show'. Indeed, so very light and detached are Davie's lines in their moral autonomy that they do not escape the foible they satirize. They strut; they display a ruffled caution before the faults of life.

Davie's ambition lies in 'a poetry of urbane and momentous statement'. Yet what Davie actually writes in such a piece as 'Portrait of the Artist' is not poetry, but versified prose discourse— in brief, *verse*. Verse is poetry that we name as such only by grace of its *turning* rhythm and lines: it is the form of poetry without the substance, and so we call it, justly, by its vehicle alone. And surely Coleridge was right to designate 'the recurrence of sounds and quantities' as but the 'superficial' form of poetry. As Emerson said, '. . . it is not metres, but a metre-making argument that makes a poem,—a thought so passionate and alive that . . . it has an architecture of its own' and adds 'a new thing' to nature. And so we must question Davie's wonder—expressed in *Purity of Diction in English Verse*—at 'critics who go out of their way' to deny what Davie calls *his* kind of poetry 'any status as poetry at all'. And all the more when we recall a statement from the second page of the book: 'We cannot help feeling that verse is somehow less important and splendid than poetry. . . .'

The fact is that, where poetry is an art but not a craft, verse is a craft but not an art. As Collingwood has shown, 'As soon as we take the notion of craft seriously, it is perfectly obvious that art proper cannot be any kind of craft.' The realm of the arts, their consanguinity, is beauty; and beauty is born, not crafted. Contrariwise, all verse can do with words is to arrange them craftily; it cannot make them beautiful. Verse is never more than an independent state of the mind, beauty never less than a dependent state of the soul. 'Beauty', as Hegel says, 'is the immediate unity of nature and spirit in the form of intuition'; it is 'the interpenetration of image and spirit.' Yet the goal of verse is precisely the separation of spirit from image, of thought from nature. Lifting directly and deliberately from life in order to survey it, verse finds its order in the realm, not of beauty, but of truth, or at any rate of the notional: the surge, the depths, the soaking element, has long since dried on its wings. It is owing to this spiritual withdrawal, this dissociation of language from reflex and instinct, that verse, for all its potential nobility, is 'less important and splendid than poetry'. In one sense, verse most assuredly *is* pure—but it is just art, just beauty, that it is pure of. If art is praise, as Rilke and others have said, then verse is criticism. It is a rejection of beauty in the interest of moral perfection and truth.

And yet this rejection of beauty is equivocal. Committed to the notional though it may be, verse betrays, by the very fact that it *is* verse, an impotent, a half-hearted desire for beauty. Verse clings to the *form* of poetry as a prelate clings to a mistress—in spite of earnest intentions. Impatient with the 'fiddle' of poetry, verse yet leans longingly over the fence separating truth from beauty, caught by the music, the dancing, going on there—and perhaps by something else, the suspicion of a rite necessary to the soul. As a consequence, verse (in words Davie has applied to himself) is 'in a bind, hung up between / The Aesthete and the Philistine'. But beauty, of course, is all-consuming, or it is nothing; there is no such thing as the half beautiful. And for all its 'poetic' walk, look and sound, its skilful mimicry, what verse exemplifies is not poetic beauty but poetic vanity.

No one, however, is likely to object to the mixed nature of verse as such. What is troublesome is the way it trifles with, and lowers, a form potentially great and beautiful, as one might sew peacock feathers to a kitchen broom. As Walter Bagehot observes, 'People expect a "marked rhythm" to imply something worth marking; if it fails to do so they are disappointed. They are displeased at the visible waste of a powerful instrument; . . . the burst of metre—incident to high imagination, should not be wasted on . . . matters which prose does as well.' And the matters we find in Davie's verse are surely matters which prose does as well. Witness 'Hypochondriac Logic', of which I give the final stanza:

> So poets may astonish you
> With what is not, but should be, true,
> And shackle on a moral shape
> You only thought you could escape;
> So if their scenery is queer,
> Its prototype may not be here,
> Unless inside a frightened mind,
> Which may be dazzled, but not blind.

Nothing here is so delicately conceived or organized, so dependent on feeling for its force, that it needs to be set off from the loquacities of prose. Indeed, Davie's lines cry out for prose—for freedom from their uncomfortable corset, their distracting jingle and bounce.

To be sure, certain uses of verse deliver it from the aesthetic sin of gratuity. If verse form cannot be beautiful outside of poetry itself, at least it can be apt. So it is, for instance, in Pope's great lines on man as 'A being darkly wise, and rudely great: / With too much knowledge for the skeptic side, / With too much weakness for the Stoic's pride', and so on in lines too well known to need quoting. Here large paradoxes, with their stark conceptual division within unity, are terribly fixed in the cement of Pope's couplets, which are austere *formal* divisions within unity (most of the lines, of course, being self-divided as well). Such marriages are rare; but at least one of Davie's pieces, if much slighter than Pope's, shows a similar felicity. This is the sternly charming 'Against Confidences', of which I quote the first and last parts:

> Loose lips now
> Call Candour friend
> Whom Candour's brow,
> When clear, contemned.
>
> . . . .
> Not to permit,
> To shy belief
> Too bleakly lit,
> The shade's relief
>
> Clouds Candour's brow,
> But to indulge
> These mouths that now
> Divulge, divulge.

This crisp indictment seems only to extend—to articulate—the disapproval implicit in the knuckled frequency of the stress, the curt brevity of the lines, the ascetic torturing of the syntax, the hard persistence of the rhyme. The matter having found just the voice it needs, it declaims itself with an easy confidence.

Of course, verse finds the readiest justification of its form in comedy, where it ransoms its trivial use of poetic form by converting it into mockery of its content. When not used for poetry, verse form is already, in effect, travestied poetic form; hence it naturally reinforces any attempt to burlesque. As if realizing this truth about itself, most verse has at least a comic edge. Certainly much of Davie's verse is touched by comedy. It is, however, a touch almost always so light or misjudged ('New Year Wishes for the English' being the chief exception) that it fails to prove redemptive. Indeed, the early verse hardly exerts itself to be comic: it is witty only in the degree that it is dandified —'didacticism', as Martin Dodsworth put it in *The Review* of December 1964, 'dressed to kill with the greatest taste.' 'Portrait of the Artist as a Farmyard Fowl' is a case in point. The comedy of the recent *Six Epistles to Eva Hesse* (1970) is exactly opposite: it is ambitious for a 'vulgar pungency'. But not only is it less than pungent; its vulgarity is of that false and painful kind arrived at through stoop and strain:

> No, Madam, Pound's a splendid poet
> But a sucker, and we know it . . .

The sequence changes in character as it proceeds. At first, the octosyllabics are jaunty, but impatient. 'I want', Davie says, 'to raise no Cain but laughter'. But in fact he does not seem to be enjoying himself at all. Out to cold shower Pound and Charles Olson and their latest champion, Eva Hesse, Davie fumbles rather worriedly at the handles:

> . . . this Byronic
> Writing keeps architectonic
> Principles entirely other
> Than those so sadly missed by Mother;
> Woefully linear, not to say
> Rambling. Now, is this a way
> To write, from now on quite uncouth,
> Not qualified to tell the truth? . . .

Successful comedy is less anxious than this; it rests in ease and triumph on common sense. But here, it happens, Davie cannot bank on common sense. For the truth is that neither Pound nor Olson is a subject absurd enough to call out Comedy's reserves. She can get little leverage against them—can only, as it were, push them about. Beginning with the third epistle, however, the jaunty note fades away, as if Davie had realized that his is not, after all, a soil for raising laughter:

> . . . it was a poor
> Cramped nobility, to be sure,
> That disdainful dourness which
> . . . now, if it survives
> At all, informs the sullen lives
> Of Yorkshire bards who take perverse
> Pride in writing metred verse,
> All their hopes invested in
> One patent, brilliant discipline . . .

At the same time, the verse shakes off its pique and subsides into a mellow celebration of homespun virtues—fidelity, endurance, 'solid service to mankind'—that is rather more pleasing than not. It is still, however, smaller than poetry, and still the waste of a powerful instrument.

All in all, then, there is reason to deplore Davie's conviction— strong at first, then slack, and now renewed—that he is obliged to write verse. In view of what Davie is able to do, he has not done enough, or he has done too much of what is little in itself. When he could have been mining gold, he has been mining coal or, at most, a little silver. Whereas most versifiers strain to become poets but fail to make it, Davie is a poet who chooses, much of the time, to write verse, as a man with two good legs might choose to hop about on one. And when we inspect the reasons for this, we are inclined to be less and not more friendly towards the results. For it would seem that it has all been done at the behest of fallacious theories.

Davie's ruling passion is not for the aesthetic but for the moral— or, more accurately, for the two in one, for a *moral style*: Davie is a man in love with noble restraint. And so long as he has been able to work the 'common language' into something chaste and chastening, it has been almost a matter of indifference to him whether the anvil, much less the result, were poetry or verse.

Nevertheless, his nature—deep, responsive, strong—veers towards poetry; and, left to itself, it might well have worked all its moral passion into poems. But it has not been left to itself. Taking it aside, Davie the critic has assured it that verse is the only channel for purity of language. The course of poetry, he has insisted, is private, muddy, wild: look at Hopkins, he has said, look at Shelley, at Coleridge! And thus persuaded that 'pure diction' is eternally wedded to verse, Davie was led to honour the husband because he adores the bride.

The truth, however, is that poetry may be as chaste as the poet likes. It is fundamentally a phenomenon, not of egoism mixed with language, as Davie seems to believe, but, in Hegel's phrase, of life lifted 'above itself in the very language of life'. And to admit the light of this new experience, chaste words will do as well as licentious ones—indeed, the crystalline language of (say) 'Tunstall Forest' inclines one to think that they will do better. Conversely, there is nothing in the nature of verse as such to ward off the narcissistically cosy or the elbowingly lewd. Purity is in the writer, not the medium.

Or so it is in part. For, the question of language aside, poetry and verse can indeed be compared as to intrinsic purity, if by purity we mean (as Davie does) impersonality; and it is poetry that is the chaster of the two. Davie thinks of verse as wholesomely detached from its author, as 'free-standing in its own right', 'a made thing'—as a bed is only 'made' when there is nobody in it. In fact, however, verse is never any more, if never any less, than a piece of the writer's mind. As a view of life, of course, it may be right; but we have, as it were, only its own word for it: it does not carry its own world of evidence. In consequence, verse is instantly debatable, and we challenge it, not as we question a made or created thing—a cat or a Picasso—but as we challenge a thing *said*. By contrast, poetry, in the first instance, is always a shared experience; it is a world where all may walk. Moreover, if by a free-standing 'made thing' we have in mind something approaching the dignity and independence, above all the mystery, of the Creation, then it is poetry alone that we ought to speak of as 'made'. Within its own created and rounded limits, poetry puts us where life is, so that we may know it again in its—exactly—wonderful immediacy; it enacts a sacrament of experience. Surely the Romantics—Hazlitt,

Shelley, Wordsworth—were right: poetry is moral by nature. In its passion for the 'immediate unity of nature and spirit', it fosters instinctive harmony and atonement; poetry carries with it everywhere, as Wordsworth said, 'relationship and love' (though the more nihilistic it is, the more these freeze, undelivered, in its arms). Thus its moral goodness lies precisely in its beauty: it is the mode where beauty and purity are one. No other form of impersonality, I believe, can compare with it; for at its least inhibited it is an impersonality in eagerness and delight, fraught with an enthusiasm of sympathy.

But enough of what must seem like ingratitude once we acknowledge how much poetry—how much excellent poetry—Davie has written. Perhaps hardly aware of it himself, perhaps even without desiring it, Davie, for all his principled reluctance, has passed again and again from urbanity into beauty, proving himself a poet.

Just south of conscience-stricken urbane verse there lies a temperate region that, following Bagehot, we might agree to call 'pure art'. Here we find art that employs the fewest strokes necessary for its purpose—a nobly restrained art, of jealous economy of means. 'Pure' in the sense that it is lean, trimmed of fat, good value for the price, wholesome, honest, this art is morally on guard against overrichness, yet nutritive. Its proverb: Little with quiet makes the best diet.

It is to art of this chaste and temperate kind that almost all Davie's best poetry belongs. We might take as a minimal example of it—especially interesting because so like and yet so distinct from Davie's verse—the poem 'Creon's Mouse'. What Arnold called the 'application of ideas to life' is as downright in this poem as in Davie's verse; the difference is that 'Creon's Mouse' does not make the mistake—one that Arnold himself would have censured—of omitting the life to which the ideas are applied. Accordingly, the application is indeed, in Arnold's words, 'powerful and beautiful':

> Creon, I think, could never kill a mouse
> When once that dangerous girl was put away,
> Shut up unbridled in her rocky house,
> Colossal nerve denied the light of day.

Now Europe's hero, the humaner King
Who hates himself, is humanized by shame,
Is he a curbed or a corroded spring?
A will that's bent, or buckled? Tense, or tame?

If too much daring brought (he thought) the war,
When that was over nothing else would serve
But no one must be daring any more,
A self-induced and stubborn loss of nerve.

In itching wainscot having met his match,
He waits unnerved, and hears his caverned doom,
The nausea that struggles to dispatch
Pink-handed horror in a craggy room.

The absolute endeavour was the catch;
To clean the means and never mind the end
Meant he had not to chasten but to scotch
The will he might have managed to amend.

You that may think yourselves not proud at all,
Learn this at least from humble Creon's fall:
The will that is subjèct, not overthrown,
Is humbled by some power not its own.

This Creon—so unlike Sophocles' king, who sins through unbending pride, and not thus through humbleness that unbends— is Davie's warning (as he discloses in the October 1969 *Encounter*) against such unnerving recoveries of nerve as Britain's part in the Suez crisis, America's part in Vietnam. The point to note, however, is that the poem is not set within the actual world but, powerfully, within its own. Though indeed addressed to us, it pays us but little mind, sees us but out of the corner of its eye. For something terribly important is riveting its attention: alive in thoughtful immediacy, it is *undergoing* its subject. In the brilliant strategy of the opening 'I think', confessing a reality that lies beyond the mind, confronting it; in the frightening, rapid stepping-up of the first three adjectives describing Antigone; in the way 'Pink-handed horror in a craggy room' moves us at once from awe of her to pity; and finally in the parallel incarceration of Creon within both the responsibility of royal wainscot and the doom of Tiresias's prophecies—in all this there detonates an elliptical drama of sharp impact.

In short, 'Creon's Mouse' is poetry and not verse because it burns with a finite reality. And yet its status as poetry may leave us somewhat uneasy. How close it is, throughout, to the dry bones of verse! How set it is on recoiling from the crush of life to wisdom! The poem seems to begrudge having to glance at a particular reality at all. Giving us only just barely, with not a stroke to spare, the amount and kind of detail necessary to become a unique and absorbing experience, it leaves itself no aesthetic margin whatever, refuses to rest in itself, distrusts and nips its own fierce beauty. Yes, the author of this poem (we might find ourselves reflecting) is certainly a poet; but, a rock skipping over tense water, how little he seems to trust the poetic element!

In view of Davie's enormous respect for verse, his fondness for a 'poor / Cramped nobility', one might conclude that 'Creon's Mouse', gripped on its own poetic influx like a tight bandage on a wound, would be as far as Davie would care or dare to go in conceding what is necessary to art. In fact, however, he has displayed, if only within the pale of pure art itself, a remarkable ease and flexibility, his career presenting a bold, impromptu itinerary, as of a man who, bound to one country though he may be, will yet be on his travels. Thus who would have guessed that the poet of 'Creon's Mouse', so toughly and neatly the moralist, would compose, for example, a poem so achingly exposed, so irreclaimably beyond moral, as 'Pietà', written 'in memoriam Douglas Brown'?

Snow-white ray
coal-black earth will
swallow now.
The heaven glows
when twilight has
kissed it, but
your white face
which I kiss now does
not. Be still
acacia boughs,
I talk with my
dead one. We speak
softly. Be still.

> The sky is blind
> with white
> cloud behind
> the swooping birds. The
> garden lies
> round us and
> birds in the dead
> tree's bare
> boughs shut
> and open themselves. Be
> still, or be
> your unstill selves,
> birds in the tree . . .

In the two remaining stanzas, the poem loses itself, ending very badly. But what could be a more poignant union of the elegantly formal and the piercingly simple than the stanzas quoted? The poet's dialogue with the environment distances very finely his dialogue with his grief, yet without at all displacing it, rather intensifying it unbearably. And the short lines, something of an obstacle at first, come to seem as broken as sorrow. Here—heroically, considering the circumstances—there is no haste, indeed no effort, to seal experience in sense. And yet 'Pietà', too, is pure art. Though somewhat fuller in aesthetic body than 'Creon's Mouse', as if an ascetic had consented to a little repast of wine and bread, its words are just as anonymous, clean, and economical, its touches as light and almost as few for their purpose, as those of 'Creon's Mouse'.

Still, the more one reads Davie, the more the unexpected element rises like a mist and discloses a serene and stable geography, as of an old and well-ordered country: it is just that the country is equally divided between a Northern and a Southern state, and that Davie now tours one, now the other. The fact is that, though almost always one as a poet, namely a pure artist, Davie is of two minds as regards the value of life. Righteously at arms, in some poems, with the way existence falls out, in others he embraces it—and not at all because he is slumming but because he finds it *right* to embrace it. There are, then, two consciences within Davie, antipodean; and each has its own poise, its own authority.

One of these consciences, cold, dour, Northern, we have already seen in full force. For obvious reasons, the verse is its opportunity, its pet. But, as 'Creon's Mouse' exemplifies, its weather blows, it finds its place, in the poetry as well. 'Insofar as we believe in morality', Nietzsche observes, 'we pass sentence on existence'. And with perverse pride, this conscience believes in morality. What else, it might ask, is there to believe in? It rests on itself as the single substance between the void 'God' and the void nihilism. Yet it is not at all metaphysically minded, or even self-reflecting. It simply asks of life, as of style, that it be clean, lifted free from the mess of existence: in truth, it is perhaps more a sensibility than a code. Candour and restraint, austerity, courage, fidelity and conviction—for the most part, it bears these standards without attempting to say why, and without caring to; it is just that they seem right, they make a kind of sense against the grey of an English sky. Of course, pressed to vindicate them, Davie could show (and does in a piece entitled 'Hawkshead and Dachau in a Christmas Glass') how in the perspective of the Second World War, and in particular the death camps for the Jews, they take on, after all, a wide exigency. And yet his belief in morality scarcely waits for a pretext; it exceeds all occasions, amounting to a faith.

To look only at Davie's better poems, it is this conscience that, inspecting St. George's in 'North Dublin', notes, fairly, that it is indeed 'charming in the Church of Ireland fashion', its interior 'sumptuously sober', yet proudly concludes:

> 'Dissenter' and 'tasteful' are contradictions
> In terms, perhaps, and my fathers
> Would ride again to the Boyne
> Or with scythes to Sedgemoor, or splinter
> The charming fanlights in this charming slum
> By their lights, rightly.

'The charming fanlights in this charming slum': in this perfect line of pure art—so little said, yet everything necessary said— the pride is at once explained and justified. In the fist-thrust of 'rightly'; in the play of 'lights' against 'fanlights', the one all energy, the other all acceptance—in these, too, this conscience makes of terseness a pure art. It is this conscience, again, that, catching sight of the sea light scathing the turf in 'Sunburst', directs upon it a sudden fierce wistfulness:

> Light that robes us, does it?
> Limply, as robes do, moulded
> to the frame of Nature? It
> has no furious virtue?

Revolt against the ignobly limp lines of existence could not be expressed with more concentration, nor more disposition to reject them.

Thus exacting of architecture and sunlight, and as in 'Tunstall Forest' of the very air, this conscience is no less stringent towards art, demanding from it, not beauty, but a harder thing, 'excellence'. So in 'Cherry Ripe' it observes: 'No ripening curve can be allowed to sag / On cubist's canvas or in sculptor's stone'; and, seeking 'the ripening that is art's alone', it suggests:

> This can be done with cherries. Other fruit
> Have too much bloom of import, like the grape,
> Whose opulence comes welling from a root
> Struck far too deep to yield so pure a shape . . .

Here, however, the conscience has not been as good as its word: it has itself permitted sagging. For the lines are simply not true. A cherry is fully as sensual as a grape, a cherry tree's root far deeper than a vine's. And yet how masterful the rhythm is! The conscience paused, charmed, and spared the knife. As if ashamed, it rights itself, however, in a later poem, 'Ezra Pound in Pisa'—indeed at first, in its zeal, only too well:

> Excellence is sparse.
> I am made of a Japanese mind
> Concerning excellence:
> However sparred or fierce
> The furzy elements,
> Let them be but few
> And spaciously dispersed,
> And excellence appears . . .

'Sparred', 'fierce', and 'furzy elements' are somewhat *too* sparse; the imagination cannot get hold of them. Yet how 'excellently' the second clause, sparse as it is, follows the first! And though again almost too bare, the last three lines please by their magisterial assurance. The growling music of the *f* and combined *r* and *s* sounds—this, too, is 'excellent'. All together, then, the stanza is pure art but near the edge of aesthetic barrenness. It is in the third stanza that the poem comes to triumphant fruition:

Sun moves, and the shadow moves
In spare and excellent order;
I too would once repair
Most afternoons to a pierced
Shadow on gravelly ground,
Write at a flaked, green-painted
Table, and scrape my chair
As sun and shade moved round.

Here concept disappears into experience as the bed of a river is lost beneath the flow of its waters. How stringently beautiful (for 'excellence', of course, is but the leanest beauty) this scene of spare order is—how deeply it intimates (in part through the richest of the long vowels, *a*) the peace of a necessary submission: chair and shadow obedient to the sun, the mind to art. What Pound himself had required of modern poetry—that it be 'austere, direct, free from emotional slither'—is here achieved nobly in his name.

This Dissenting conscience, so queerly and attractively laced by the cosmopolitan, also turns, of course, to people, to human character—turns on them, as in 'Creon's Mouse'. It even turns on Dissent itself, because it is a church 'based on sentiment'—as, too, on the Evangelist with his

Solicitations of a swirling gown,
The sudden vox humana, and the pause,
The expert orchestration of a frown . . .

It is, as this suggests, a conscience hard to get around—in fact, so very sceptical that, leaving itself nothing to hang on to, its only resource is to be clasped upon itself. Known chiefly by what it does *not* permit, its purpose it to bind human nature. Hence, when it oppresses Davie himself, as now and then it does, his sense of it is understandably rueful, informed by bleak familiarity and by longing to get out:

Not just in Russian but in any tongue
Abandonment, morality's soubrette
Of lyrical surrender and excess,
Knows the weak endings equal to the strong;
She trades on broken English with success
And, disenchanted, I'm enamoured yet.

And when it comes to death, this conscience naturally demands from Davie no less than a gallantry of stoicism. 'Heigh-ho on a Winter Afternoon' begins:

> There is a heigh-ho in these glowing coals
> By which I sit wrapped in my overcoat
> As if for a portrait by Whistler. And there is
> A heigh-ho in the bird that noiselessly
> Flew just now past my window, to alight
> On winter's moulding, snow; and an alas,
> A heigh-ho and a desultory chip,
> Chip, chip on stone from somewhere down below . . .

The stanza coheres in the limpid singleness that is the peculiar strength of pure art and its compensation for what it must eschew—the flash of sequinned detail. As often in Davie's poetry, the lines flow purposefully, pleasingly but without seduction: they mean to bring us to the bank still dry. Yet how much they give us to understand along the way. Think of what can, what *needs* to be said about the inevitability of death, the malign aspect of mortality, the propriety of pluck, the nobility of resignation, and here it has already been said—more, experienced—in the fewest and least self-signalling of words. Unfortunately, part of the rest of 'Heigh-ho' is marred by forced tropes—a frequent fault in Davie. Still, the poem ends worthily:

> . . . some falls are . . . more fortunate,
> The meteors spent, the tragic heroes stunned
> Who go out like a light. But here the chip,
> Chip, chip will flake the stone by slow degrees,
> For hour on hour the fire will gutter down,
> The bird will call at longer intervals.

The other conscience in Davie, distinctively modern, is vital, instinctual—it asks, not 'How can I organize or rectify existence?' but 'How can I protect life, enhance it?' Lawrence had this conscience supremely, Colette and Pasternak had it, and Isak Dinesen took high-altitude draughts of it in Africa; and chiefly to them we owe what knowledge we have of its nobility. It is a conscience that rests on what has been given, judging that it truly is a gift. Almost wholly reverential, it is made up of wondering acceptance, of submission to life's lilt. Even at lowest ebb it finds existence absorbing. It reacts with pain and horror to the waste of life.

And just for that reason it has reserves of reaction, and will quarrel with energy even though it finds an ideality in it.

Such is the conscience that seeks to declare itself, as to someone who has just sensed its existence, in Davie's 'Low Lands', where the poet notes of a river delta:

> How defenceless it is! How much it needs a protector
> To keep its dykes! . . .
>
> But a beauty there is, noble, dependent, unshrinking,
> In being at somebody's mercy, wide and alone.
> I imagine a hillborn sculptor suddenly thinking
> One could live well in a country short of stone.

And this conscience does indeed make itself felt in the noble, unshrinking ease of the lines: lines wide and dependent, like the delta, and, except for their lucidity, very unlike the chiselled rock of 'Creon's Mouse'. In 'Treviso, the Pescheria', the same conscience, now in command, defends the present against the past.

> You are like a ferryman's daughter,
> And I the stream that blurred
> Calls sent across that water,
> Which loyally you have heard.
>
> My lapsings I acknowledge.
> And yet, on either hand
> Combed green, the river's sedge
> Sweetens the fish-wives' island.

Like the close of 'Tunstall Forest' and 'Ezra Pound in Pisa', these graceful lines—smooth, yet brisk with a sense of the moment —beautifully immerse a concept in sensuousness. They are inferior, if at all, only in a slight suggestion of performance: the mind has been a touch beforehand with them. The vital conscience explains itself yet again ('Berries / Ask to be plucked') in what amounts to a complementary poem, 'Housekeeping'—a poem celebrating the joy retained in memory: 'Contentment cries from the distance. How it carries!'

Engaged with life through the passions and senses, thus 'defenceless', this conscience is naturally liable to fear, subject to regret; and several of the better poems catch it as it passes into shadow.

'Across the Bay' records a stinging recoil from 'the venomous soft jelly, the undersides' of mutual human dependence—a jelly touched horribly in a scene of self-surprising rage: 'We could stand the world if it were hard all over.' The poem itself is admirably hard, uncompromising with its own shock and fear. 'New York in August' and 'In California' crackle with a tense exposure that begs protection. And 'Time Passing, Beloved', if still rolling majestically on the nobly dependent breakers of its rhythms, soberly asks in its conclusion:

> What will become of us? Time
> Passing, beloved, and we in a sealed
> Assurance unassailed
> By memory. How can it end,
> This siege of a shore that no misgivings have steeled,
> No doubts defend?

And yet in none of these poems, for all their anxiety and dismay, is there anything like a 'moral' withdrawal or recantation: the sensibility within them clings to immediate circumstance as roots cling to what gives them life.

Not always defining or defending itself, or rueing its vulnerability, this conscience has also, as is fitting, its moments of simple enjoyment. It enjoys itself somewhat guiltily in 'Poreč', perhaps too in 'The Prolific Spell' and 'The Feeders', and to little effect in still other poems—but quite happily, in both senses, in 'A Meeting of Cultures'. The second and third stanzas, it is true, are strained and superfluous; but the rest of the poem is delightful. Of Warsaw Davie says:

> The old town,
> Rebuilt, is a clockwork toy.
>
> I walked abroad in it,
> Charmed and waylaid
> By a nursery joy:
>
> Hansel's and Gretel's city!
> Their house of gingerbread
> That lately in
>
> Horrific forest glooms
> Of Germany
> Bared its ferocity

> Anew, resumes its gilt
> For rocking-horse rooms
> In Polish rococo.

The poem concludes with a visit to a 'D .S .O ./ Of the desert battles', restored by Warsaw's 'sanative' air, 'who for / The sake of England took / Pains to be welcoming':

> More jokes then. And the wasps humming
> Into his lady's jam
> That we ate with a spoon
>
> Out in the long grass. Shades,
> Russian shades out of old slow novels,
> Lengthened the afternoon.

Despite its reminders of the war, then, the poem is joyfully light, with a holiday freedom from anxiety. What it speaks of throughout, its nervous, darting lines and on-springing stanzas convey: life's miraculous ability to renew itself. How, then, should it end, if not in a grateful sensation of the peace of the present—the past no more than the shadows that give depth to the afternoon, or the jam and its tradition, usefulness, sweetness?

Because the conscience of vital engagement finds its truth in the spirit's fleshing, it is not impatient for conclusions: it *abides*. Accordingly, as in 'A Meeting of Cultures', its productions are apt to read—a new genre of poem having sprung out of it—as entries in a poetic diary. Two poems mentioned earlier, 'New York in August' and 'In California', share this effect. The latter (which needs to shed its first two stanzas) concludes:

> By nightfall, to the snows;
> And over the mile on tilted
> Mile of the mountain park
> The bright cars hazarded.

That is, it concludes without enclosing its subject. And yet it does not simply break off; it ends only after it has pushed its theme of 'the risk we sense'—at times, in places—to an aesthetically definitive, because emotionally ultimate, moment. An immanent, elusive danger having become localized and manifest, immediate in the glare of oncoming headlights, the sense of form is subtly satisfied. Though no conclusion can be so deep and liberating as one attained though creative reason, or creation that is also analysis, the fact is that there are harmonies and finalities apart from those of reason, fugitive and fragile as summer clouds; and with luck and inspiration the poet can find them. Thus, nothing could seem more felicitously consummate, more complete as an impression, than Davie's 'The Mushroom Gatherers', naked though it is of all intellectual consequence. Delicately selected from Mickiewicz's *Pan Tadeusz* (as is Davie's much longer work, *The Forests of Lithuania*), 'The Mushroom Gatherers' is set on a country estate in early-nineteenth-century Lithuania, where a visiting count comes unexpectedly on a wandering group whose purpose he does not at first descry. I quote the last two of four stanzas:

> Strange decorum: so prodigal of bows,
> Yet lost in thought and self-absorbed, they meet
> Impassively, without achnowledgement.
> A courteous nation, but unsociable.

> Field full of folk, in their immunity
> From human ills, crestfallen and serene,
> Who would have thought these shades our lively friends?
> Surely these acres are Elysian fields.

Exquisite in its quality of entranced receptiveness, at once mundane actuality and sweet illusion, the poem is at a final limit just as it is. And anyone interested in seeing how much its happy effect is owing to Davie has but to compare it with George Noyes's prose translation of *Pan Tadeusz*, or the inferior short-line version of the same scene in *The Forests of Lithuania*. The artistry is all Davie's own; and in its water-intense mirroring of the subject—through the decorum of the diction, the processional rhythms, the self-absorption of each stanza—it could not be excelled.

Such, then, are the two consciences of Davie's art, each possessing its own territory, indeed its own trophies, among the poems— the one taking life nobly to task, the other nobly surrendering to it. Yet it is only to be expected, too, that several of Davie's poems should be caught in the cross-fire of his opposing attitudes, or constitute strange meetings between them. 'Low Lands', cited earlier, is one such poem. Others—and they are among Davie's best—are 'After an Accident', 'Viper-Man', and 'Wood-pigeons at Raheny'.

Though vitality sweeps unopposed through 'After an Accident', the conscience for life here takes on, magnificently, the force and pitilessness of the moral conscience, in a kind of transubstantiation. Having 'smashed up against last things' in an automobile accident, the speaker sees that *he* is death—that he has been 'living and not living'. He denounces unequivocally the shabby character this sham evinces:

> Death is about my age,
> Smiling and dark, clean-shaven.
> Behind him the valley-floor
> Is ledged in a purple light.
>
> Had I not sought the shade
> Of what is so
> Beneath us as chagrin,
> I had not been afraid
>
> Of his mountainous purple light,
> Nor should I have run out
> Of the soul of gratitude
> Before I ran out of death ...

In these broken lines we hear not only the jolting echo of the crash but a wringing note of severity: they bring a man to judgement with the same righteous energy as 'Creon's Mouse', only in this case in the interest of what we owe, not to others, but to life. The poem tingles all through with the nerves of a vital awakening. Long, it modulates through shock, realization, self-contempt, bemused curiosity, and gratitude, and is alive, honest, and urgent throughout.

In 'Viper-Man', by contrast, we find the two consciences, here distinct, locked in struggle, equal unrelenting powers.

> Will it be one of those
> Forever summers?
> Will the terrace stone
> Expand, unseal
> Aromas, and let slip
> Out of the cell of its granulations
> Some mid-Victorian courtship?

> Never a belle of that
> Lavender century
> But, though so stayed,
> Basked in a settled spell;
> And yet I guard
> Against a change in the weather,
> Snake whipped up in the yard.

Are we, then, as we stand on the terrace—for 'Viper-Man',
being a genuine poem, at once absorbs us into itself—and discover
with surprise what must, we see now, have been true, that the
Victorian belles were also viper-men, their settled spell suggestive
almost of a hibernation; as we both fear and long for the unseal-
ing of pent-up aromas, the snake from its sleep underground—
are we, then, to fulfil our nature or correct it? Expressing conflict
not only through its wavering line lengths but through its brevity,
the poem leaves us suspended, the match an inch from the fuel.

   In 'Woodpigeons at Raheny', there is, by distinction, a succession from one point of view to the other, oneness with the world
giving way to gaunt divorce from it. The poem begins in almost
mesmerized immersion in a scene:

> One simple and effective rhyme
> Over and over in the April light;
>   And a touch of the old time
> In the serving-man, stooping, aproned tight,
> At the end of the dappled avenue
> To the easy phrase, 'tereu-tereu,'
> Mulled over by the sleepy dove—
> This was the poem I had to write.
>
> White wall where the creepers climb
> Year after year on the sunny side;
>   And a touch of the old time
> In the sandalled Capuchin's silent stride
> Over the shadows and through the clear
> Cushion-soft wooing of the ear
> From two meadows away, by the dove—
> This was the poem that was denied . . .

As in 'Time Passing, Beloved'—with one exception, the only
other poem of Davie's to send out Siren appeals to the ear—

Davie here conveys, through an enchanting circularity of sound, a lulling timelessness. In keeping with the touch of the old time in the present, the poem closes on itself in a gentle volley of echoes. A scene luxurious with repetitions has awakened in the poet a desire for that most consummate of repetitions, the reduplication of the world by art—the harmony of the setting seeming to invite, to seek augmentation in, the profounder harmony of poetry. But abruptly this further harmony is denied. The ascetic figure of the Capuchin—a reminder of mortality— breaks the illusion of a *circular* time, shows time to be but death-boned and linear. Estranged alike from time and eternity (a monk without God, a natural creature without a trust in nature), the speaker is overcome by that modern malaise, the experience of *dislocation*:

> For whether it was the friar's crime,
> His lean-ness suddenly out of tune;
> > Or a touch of the old time
> In the given phrase, with its unsought boon
> Of a lax autumnal atmosphere,
> Seemed quaint and out of keeping here,
> I do not know. I know the dove
> Outsang me down the afternoon.

Accordingly, the very music of the poem diminishes, wasting into boniness of syntax, and thudding upon 'I do not know'. If the earlier stanzas outsing the last, it is, then, because they are innocent. Recapitulating English poetry from the age of Keats or the April side of Tennyson to its present day of lean music and still leaner faith, 'Woodpigeons at Raheny' gives us, marvellously, both the poet Davie might have been and the poet he believes he has to be.

As we have seen, Davie was not always to feel—what in the course of this early and perfect poem he comes to feel—a sort of Capuchin out of tune with the natural world. But whether enmeshed with or at odds with life, he was always to sing as one who finds it fitting that a contemporary song be lean. This leanness, this commitment to the pure style and to pure art, may prompt us to conclude that, when Davie does come to praise life, his song is stinted, the 'given phrase' too thin and pale. And yet there is an integrity in his leanness that, the more one reads him, the more one admires. If his work cannot overwhelm us through a powerful excess, neither can it spoil. And how remarkable it is that, for all his leanness, Davie, like a long-distance runner, has covered so much of life. The combination of his spare style and his rich, elastic nature has produced a body of work rare in character: pure art with a broad range.

R. S. Thomas

R. S. THOMAS glories in the Midas touch—and to some degree suffers from it, as the case must be. There are very few poets to whom one could point confidently, helping out some stranger to the earth and its great forms, and say, of almost any one of his pieces, *that* is poetry, and not fear that one had failed to show the thing in its purity. R. S. Thomas is happily such a poet. Though he lacks the big, dredging gift of his countryman Dylan Thomas, though his poetry cannot stir us in our very bones, like new marrow, as 'Fern Hill', 'The force that through the green fuse', and other of Dylan Thomas's poems do, it is yet, unlike his, never lost in the rhythm and the words. It stands out clear, lighter in weight because of its clarity, but with a flame as intense and fine.

R. S. Thomas's poems have an almost visible brilliance and unremitting sensual poignancy. They involve the eye and the feelings equally and strongly. Never, perhaps, has sensory firmness seemed so ready a conductor for emotion. 'Concrete' is too heavy a word for the texture of Thomas's poems. For all their particularization, they are airborne, penetrated with light. Here, in 'Ninetieth Birthday', is Thomas at his best:

> You go up the long track
> That will take a car, but is best walked
> On slow foot, noting the lichen
> That writes history on the page
> Of the grey rock. Trees are about you
> At first, but yield to the green bracken,
> The nightjar's house: you can hear it spin
> On warm evenings; it is still now
> In the noonday heat, only the lesser
> Voices sound, blue-fly and gnat

And the stream's whisper. As the road climbs,
You will pause for breath and the far sea's
Signal will flash, till you turn again
To the steep track, buttressed with cloud.

And there at the top that old woman,
Born almost a century back
In that stone farm, awaits your coming;
Waits for the news of the lost village
She thinks she knows, a place that exists
In her memory only.
                              You bring her greeting
And praise for having lasted so long
With time's knife shaving the bone.
Yet no bridge joins her own
World with yours, all you can do
Is lean kindly across the abyss
To hear words that were once wise.

How direct, naked, human, and sociable this is. Has Thomas not
heard of 'modern' poetry and its difficulty? Has he no embarrassment before the primary emotions? Never mind; nothing vital
is missing from such a poem. Reading Thomas one learns to
endure the glare of emotion; one learns again a kind of innocence.

Not that all ambiguities of response are resolved. When, for
instance, this Anglican priest—so like Hopkins in being hard
smitten by the barbarous beauty of the earth—writes of a moor,

It was like a church to me.
I entered it on soft foot,
Breath held like a cap in the hand . . .

should one cry: Wait, that sort of thing can't be done any more,
it's too like—well, sentiment! or, on the contrary, congratulate
him on the astonishing success of his figure—which has, it is
true, a saving 'metaphysical' daring? In such instances one
becomes hesitant about one's own hesitations. The fact is that
Thomas is an anachronism, a poet of feeling in an age of intellect—
and not the less an anachronism, because the nomenclature of
his feeling is religious. With the exception of 'Green Categories',
which brings Kant and a peasant together, Thomas never really
challenges the mind. His appeal is all to feeling—to compassion,
indignation, awe, the love of beauty.

The great quality of Thomas's work—evident from his very first volume, *The Stones of the Field* (1946)—is thus a passionate naturalness. Thomas makes most other poets seem stale, stuck away in rooms, or carrying *The Oxford Book of English Verse*, if not Webster's *Third*, across a desert. His feeling, his movement, his diction, are light and unlaboured. He seems to enter each of his conceptions as if into a stream that has just sprung out of the ground before him, that takes him abruptly and resistlessly on, and banks him in sight of the sea, the far silence, where all poems end. Though he rides his inspiration, it yet runs away beneath him. He is the current as well as the poised canoe. Of studied progress, of a painful trial-and-error adding on, there is never a note. For all we can tell, of course, Thomas may labour every one of his unfinicky lines, and he has said of being a poet that from the age of forty on you recognize that the Muse's smile is not for you. Yet the poem on the printed page, his gift to us, affords the joy of a passionate and effortless openness before experience.

Dylan Thomas and Hopkins, too, are open and passionate—yet with what a difference. Restless and raging as all three poets are, rattling the gates of earth and sky, eager for a sacramental communion with the world, Hopkins and Dylan Thomas are yet like stained glass windows and R. S. Thomas like a clear one. Their poetry enacts the communion; it shows the ego, the whole body, as irradiated. His only alludes to it, yet with a piercing beauty that convinces. Like most of the better British poets now writing, Thomas puts little between himself and his subject. Except for metaphor and eloquence—important exceptions, to be sure—his poems are ascetic. They seem *out there*, where the lucid phrase meets the world.

In movement, Thomas's poems make a kind of dash up the shore of their subject. They are, as poems go, rapid and sudden, as if to surprise their subject matter, the better to invade or take hold of it. Here is a recent poem called 'The Dance':

> She is young. Have I the right
> Even to name her? Child,
> It is not love I offer
> Your quick limbs, your eyes;
> Only the barren homage
> Of an old man whom time

> Crucifies. Take my hand
> A moment in the dance
> Ignoring its sly pressure,
> The dry rut of age,
> And lead me under the boughs
> Of innocence. Let me smell
> My youth again in your hair.

The only verbal fillip here is 'the dry rut of age'. Yet the poem penetrates. Intricate of movement, following no tune but its own, it displays the floating balance, the dynamic pauses of a classic dancer. Yet the dance is over almost before we have acknowledged its presence, and if we know that it was exactly as it should be, it is only from the unmistakable sensation of having been changed. Not strongly accentual, relying on the delicate water-surface tension of phrase as much as on metre, rhymeless, infrequently end-stopped, and usually in lines of fewer than nine syllables, Thomas's poetry is like a briskly descending brook. Everything about it is bent to a single aim, namely the swift, happy arrival at a mainstream realization.

The same holds true of Thomas's words. They, too, are naked daylight. They have none of the pregnant darkness of things. They refer, they throw up blinds before their subjects. Though eloquently modulated, pleasingly united, they seem scarcely conscious of themselves as sounds. Nor do they jostle their traditional meanings. Sometimes, indeed, especially in figures, they are all too common. When Thomas is not brilliant at metaphor, he is dully conventional; in this regard, there are, in his work, only peaks and slumps. 'The boughs / Of innocence', for example, sends us vaguely into literary sentiment. Yet for the most part Thomas's language is taut. It is form following function. In 'Let me smell / My youth again in your hair', for instance, the words are simple and straightforward. Only the thought is extraordinary. Reading Thomas, we seldom miss newly peeled words, or for that matter formal music, compulsive rhythms, or stanzas and rhymes, because we are too much under the power of his phrase. To seem at once lean and sensuous, transparent and deeply crimsoned, is part of his distinction.

Lean as they are, Thomas's words conduct both strength and subtlety. If he is swift it is not because he has lightened his load; he is swift without leaving anything behind. 'Ninetieth Birthday', for example, delicately rings several contrasts between living history and various eternities that elude it—stone, prolonged isolation, the distant sea, an old mind gone to seed: profound contrasts that are immediate to feeling. Nor is Thomas's tone, as a rule, unshaded. In the same poem, for instance, he is as impatient as he is tender. In fact, almost all his poetry, as we shall see, is a compassionate scolding. How this Anglican priest despairs of leading the old peasant's soul to the great sacramental unity. The sea flashes, but the stone farm is up around the bend, provincial. He is patient, generous, but despondent as he leans across the abyss—she has fallen into the wrong eternity, this lost old child, she is lodged in a crevasse of time. So the poem, for all its swiftness, is deep and full.

Thomas's poetry almost always faces outward. It has just seen someone or something that has brought it to a passionate pause. Often the first lines are hooks thrown out to fetch us to a soul in trouble: 'This man swaying dully before us'; 'Consider this man in the field beneath'; 'Farmer, you were young once'; 'My name is Lowri Dafydd. . . .' '. . . As I go through my day at my desk', Thomas writes in his essay 'Words and the Poet', 'in my contact with others, or out in the world of nature, I see something, begin to turn it over in my mind and decide that it has poetic possibilities. The main concern will be not to kill it. . . .' Poetry such as Thomas's—a poetry of 'the order and beauty of the world', in Simone Weil's phrase—thus begins when the world seizes a passing man and plants itself within him like a seed. This annunciation is a sacrament: Thomas must not 'kill' it. He must look upon himself as a medium.

Of course he must be active, too, an author, the balancing half of the poetic equation. 'The men took the corn, the beautiful goddess, / By the long hair and threw her on the ground': memory or perception proposes, imagination disposes, and such a line comes to be. Poetry is a co-operation between the world and the spirit in the creation of magical appearances. The world draws around, released from itself and lightened, the spirit at last gains density, having put on the world like flesh, and existence is for the moment complete. The poet's imagination grapples with the world in an ecstasy that could be reverence but that could equally be a terrible rivalry to see which will seem the more real.

What helps make Thomas's poetry *poetic* is the grateful dependence of his senses on the world. He needs matter temperamentally as poetry needs it aesthetically: as the blood of his spirit. 'Every true artist', writes Simone Weil, 'has had real, direct, and immediate contact with the beauty of the world, contact that is of the nature of a sacrament.' This sacrament is Thomas's goad. (If often his attention is fixed on the black question mark at the centre of the view, the stooped peasant at his plough, it is in grief that it mars the contact, is marred, mars itself.) The beauty of the world rushes into Thomas's poetry because he leaves himself open as he rushes out to meet it. The universe is, for this artist, itself the supreme work of art. I quote 'The View from the Window':

> Like a painting it is set before one,
> But less brittle, ageless; these colours
> Are renewed daily with variations
> Of light and distance that no painter
> Achieves or suggests. Then there is movement,
> Change, as slowly the cloud bruises
> Are healed by sunlight, or snow caps
> A black mood; but gold at evening
> To cheer the heart. All through history
> The great brush has not rested,
> Nor the paint dried; yet what eye,
> Looking coolly, or, as we now,
> Through the tears' lenses, ever saw
> This work and it was not finished?

So it is that this poet's subject teaches him his end.

A related reason that Thomas's poetry is strong and authentic is that it is inspirited by memory—memory being spirit in its most basic and helpless attachment to the world. 'The humblest function of spirit', Bergson notes in *Matter and Memory*, 'is to bind together the successive moments of the duration of things.' Spirit, then, begins in memory. Nor, much though it is a temporal flowering on the fixed laws of space, can it ever quite escape from 'things' and remain vigorous as spirit. It evolves by looking back. Rising out of matter, as the perception of its duration, it returns to it at length, in works of art, as love.

For a natural poet such as Thomas, memory is the morning air of imagination. Indeed, Thomas is homeward to a fault. He never

tires of speaking of what is around him, though we sometimes
do, for he has told us about it before. We seem often to be passing
the same tree, or seeing the same hills 'buttressed with cloud'. On
the other hand, take him out of his Welsh hills, put him in Spain
or start him reflecting on manned flights to the moon, and his
imagination pales. We must take his excess with his best, nor is
this hard, for it is an excess of love.

One fruit of this love is a magnificent talent for metaphor.
In this Thomas perhaps excels all English poets since Hopkins,
bringing to mind the great, wild outcrop of figurative genius
in the seventeenth century. Here is a Thomas sampler:

> There were larks, too, like a fresh chorus
> Of dew . . .

>   . . . O, hers is all
> This strong body, the safe island
> Where men may come, sons and lovers,
> Daring the cold seas of her eyes.

> You who never venture from under your roof
> Once the night's come; the blinds all down
> For fear of the moon's bum rubbing the window.

>   . . . I blame the earth,
> This brown bitch fawning about my feet.

> I remember also the trapped wind
> Tearing the curtains, and the wild light's
> Frequent hysteria upon the floor . . .

> Prytherch, man, can you forgive
> From your stone altar on which the light's
> Bread is broken at dusk and dawn . . . ?

> Mother, he said, from the wet streets
> The clouds are removed and the sun walks
> Without shoes on the warm pavements.

>   No, no, you must face the fact
> Of his long life alone in that crumbling house
> With winds rending the joints, and the grey rain's claws
> Sharp in the thatch; of his work up on the moors
> With the moon for candle, and the shrill rabble of stars
> Crowding his shoulders.

> . . . sin was the honey
> Bright as sunlight in death's hive.
>
> The fox drags its wounded belly
> Over the snow, the crimson seeds
> Of blood burst with a mild explosion,
> Soft as excrement, bold as roses.

Clean-edged, hard, bright, Thomas's tropes are an enameller's art. They are all firmness, there is never any smear. Yet they are resplendent with the light of actual things; the world seems to press itself into them. What is more, for all their tidiness they have an acrobat's daring. Their forms start from as far away as they can and still meet in the centre without strain. Little miracles of implosion, they hurl two particles of the world so hard upon each other that, for the imagination, they become one. Yet the meeting appears as gentle as the sudden, balance-defying close of a butterfly's wings.

Though metaphor is not essential to poetry, it constitutes nodes, at least in poetry on the beauty of the world, where the purpose of the poem is raised to an electric intensity. Most poetry and most metaphors have the same end: in Frost's words, 'the philosophical attempt to set matter in terms of spirit, or spirit in terms of matter, to make the final unity'. Thomas's poems, pomegranates full of kernels, pack in as much of the infinite beauty of the universe as they can; and metaphors, among other things, are a device for infolding beauty. They form the foothills of the spirit—of spirit that, as Jaspers says, always pushes on towards the whole of Being, seeking relation and the totality of relations. Metaphors are the love forms have for one another. They seduce the unity of things. I quote from 'Farm Wife':

> Hers is a clean apron, good for fire
> Or lamp to embroider, as we talk slowly
> In the long kitchen, while the white dough
> Turns to pastry in the great oven,
> Sweetly and surely as hay making
> In a June meadow . . .

The fire becomes an embroidering farm wife; the farm wife makes, as it were, a meadow; all hint at a common being. Thomas's figures are often signals flashed from a far sea of unity.

Of course they have more limited functions too: clarification, vivification, happy release from the literal. Whatever their purpose, they bespeak a powerful empathy with forms. They give Thomas's poems a rich, impacted beauty.

In truth, however, metaphor is somewhat too prominent in the poems. Because Thomas attempts to catch us with neither lilting rhythms nor lush words, almost the whole burden of arrestment falls on his figures. These pour in as if to fill a gap. But there are simply too many of them. They surfeit. Of course it is hardly Thomas's fault if we read him in the bulk. His poems, after all, were written one by one, in an ecstasy of isolation. And when a poet offers manna, should we hold out for bread? Yet beauty dies of beauty, as Yeats observed; and facility—even the facility of genius—cheapens.

Then, too, as noted, not all Thomas's figures are fresh and right. 'The high pastures of the heart', 'the heart's / Flower', 'the heart's stormier moods', 'thought's bitter blast', 'this bare bone of life that I pick', 'the wind sighs'—these are plucked from familiar sentiment. Nor need he repeat certain figures—the rain's claw, the wind's pane, the stars' shrillness, for instance—as if he were at a loss for novelty or too fond of them.

The truth is that Thomas could throw away half the figures in his volumes and still beglamour us. Yet he does well, I think, to make the most of his gift. Modern British poetry needs it, rather as the eye needs greens and blues. And Thomas's own poetry, for reasons shown, needs it too. When he writes without metaphor he sounds, at best, somewhat like Donald Davie, as in the first half of 'Rose Cottage':

> Rose Cottage, because it had
> Roses. If all things were as
> Simple! There was the place
> With some score or so of
> Houses, all of them red
> Brick, with their names clear
> To read; and this one, its gate
> Mossed over, its roof rusty
> With lichen. You chose it out
> For its roses, and were not wrong...

Friendly and charming, but it lacks the original quality of

Thomas's poems—the hard, vivid surface, as of a painted scene on a burning lamp. The conclusion is more in his vein:

> . . . All summer
> It generated the warmth
> Of its blooms, red lamps
> To guide you. And if you came
> Too late in the bleak cold
> Of winter, there were the faces
> At the window, English faces
> With red cheeks, countering the thorns.

Besides the neatness of wit and the warmth of gratitude and compliment, this has the lift, the intricacy, of metaphor. Thomas's most recent volume, *Not That He Brought Flowers* (1969), is his least moving and absorbing. I, for one, would rather have him at his richest—'an ascetic nature', as Bagehot said of Milton, 'in a sheath of beauty'. But one needs to take him slowly, a few poems at a time. Then he is remarkable indeed.

The moral quality of Thomas's poems is as remarkable as their aesthetic quality—as sharp and unexpected. Nowhere else in English poetry do we find poem after poem directed, in love and anger, at an entire people. There is something of Whitman in Thomas, but a severe, severely tender, hardened, narrowed, and disillusioned Whitman. Thomas is to Wales a kind of Good Samaritan, Mary Magdalen, and fearful Jahweh in one. Turning to his next poem we scarcely know whether to expect a poet blessing or scorning, or steeped in an acid of despair. What we do know is that we will find him as terribly open to his country as a wound.

   Often, conscious of his collar, Thomas writes from the implicit position of God's deputy in Wales. And yet, having entered his bloodstream, his Anglicanism emerges, in great part, not as dogma but as a badgering compassion. 'Creative attention', writes Simone Weil, 'means really giving our attention to what does not exist. Humanity does not exist in the anonymous flesh lying inert by the roadside.' Such is the quality of Thomas's concern. Of course, as a poet Thomas is a Good Samaritan only in the sphere of imagination: it is himself and his readers whom he makes human by his attention. But the atmosphere of generosity

is the same as if he had lifted a peasant bodily from the road.
It may glare:

> I am the farmer, stripped of love
> And thought and grace by the land's hardness;
> But what I am saying over the fields'
> Desolate acres, rough with dew,
> Is, Listen, listen, I am a man like you . . .

It may be subdued:

> You would think sometimes that summer never comes
> To the farmer in his fields, stripped by the wind
> To the blue bone, or impotent with snow.
> You have become used to his ascetic form
> Moving within its cell of leafless trees.
> Not so; his blood uncurls with the slow sap,
> Stretching itself among its sinuous boughs;
> His blood grows hot, the singing cloak of flies,
> Worn each day, bears witness; the stones ring
> Fierce echoes of his heat; he meets himself
> Everywhere in the smell of the ripe earth.

It may crackle with the hail of disapproval:

> And she was fertile; four strong sons
> Stood up like corn in June about you.
> But, farmer, did you cherish, tend her
> As your own flesh, this dry stalk
> Where the past murmurs its sad tune?
> Is this the harvest of your blithe sowing?
>
> If you had spared from your long store
> Of days lavished upon the land
> But one for her where she lay fallow,
> Drying, hardening, withering to waste.
> But now—too late! You're an old tree,
> Your roots groping in her in vain.

But the atmosphere of compassion is continually present—
asserting the human, brightening when it finds it, darkening
when it does not, but always itself a warmth and an illumination.

In Thomas the love of our neighbour (in Simone Weil's
phrase) seems to be an offshoot of the love of the beauty and order
of the world. Thomas wants the peasants to bestir themselves
until, like him, they see the big stars shaking, wildly signalling.

> You failed me, farmer, I was afraid you would
> The day I saw you loitering with the cows,
> Yourself one of them but for the smile,
> Vague as moonlight, cast upon your face
> From the dim source, whose nature I mistook.
> The hills had grace, the light clothed them
> With wild beauty, so that I thought,
> Watching the pattern of your slow wake
> Through seas of dew, that you yourself
> Wore that same beauty by the right of birth . . .

This is from a poem called 'Valediction', which ends:

> For this I leave you
> Alone in your harsh acres, herding pennies
> Into a sock to serve you for a pillow
> Through the long night that waits upon your span.

But in fact Thomas cannot leave the peasants alone. They obsess him; his threats and valedictions are but bravura. He cannot really delight in the wood until he has healed, has tried to heal, the wounded deer within it. Let him name in hard words the peasants' faults; they only endear themselves to him the more. After all, everything about them says, Make allowance: 'The mixen sours the dawn's gold'. So he comes upon their gaunt kitchens, the hens going in and out of the door, the 'stale smell / Of death in league with . . . dank walls', their stinking clothes, eyes 'Fuddled with coldness', 'slow lips' opening 'like a snail', their vacancy as they gob into the fire, their 'beast's gait', their coats like sacks 'pinned at the corners / With the rain's drops'—as he comes upon these his heart sinks, as if through a hole in the beauty of the world.

Often in these poems Thomas is the Word, as it were, standing helpless before a rock. For what can he do, however attentive, to change a life that can be summed up like this?

> Walter Llywarch—the words were a name
> On a lost letter that never came
> For one who waited in the long queue
> Of life that wound through a Welsh valley.
> I took instead, as others had done
> Before, a wife from the back pews
> In chapel, rather to share the rain

> Of winter evenings, than to intrude
> On her pale body; and yet we lay
> For warmth together and laughed to hear
> Each new child's cry of despair.

Here, 'subject to necessity', in Bergson's description of matter, everyone 'repeats the past unceasingly', each generation contributing to the 'accepted pattern', each day emptying the labourer like a sack. Their shepherd in the 'bald Welsh hills', Thomas calls, but they are too far gone in their age-old necessities to hear. He can see them there, the 'nameless and dear', some remote on a hill, hung like a rag on 'a bush of cloud', others nearby in the lane, wearing their cattle's breath 'like a cloak' to hide from him. Then, on Sundays,

> . . . As the melody rises
> From nothing, their mouths take up the tune,
> And the roof listens. I call on God
> In the after silence, and my shadow
> Wrestles with him upon a wall
> Of plaster, that has all the nation's
> Hardness in it. They see me thrown
> Without movement of their oblique eyes.

A few call him in, when dying, to boast of their blood's former heat. For the rest, they are indifferent, 'Caring not whether I praise or blame'. 'I do not fight / You; it is you who fight / Me', he may plead, 'wounding yourself / With blows that I will not give'. Or, vinegared by frustration, he may cry, 'You are condemned / By man's potential stature'. But all to no good. 'Castaways on a sea / Of grass', they cling to their 'doomed farms', and he clings to them. He cannot approve of them, neither can he desert them—not even in his poetry, to which he turns as to a wailing wall. Then the poems rise, full and poignant, a red moon in the night, to protest their long day's decline from beauty.

If he cannot give them God, he offers Wales; for, founded on memory, nationalism is at least a rudimentary form of the spirit. Better to be a 'people' than an anonymous heap by the roadside. Better to be in time than in nothing at all:

> History goes on;
> On the rock the lichen
> Records it: no mention
> . . . of us.

And what a people the Welsh were: the 'warriors / Of a free people' are the sole cause 'the sun still goes down red'. 'You cannot live in the present, / At least not in Wales': 'Above the noisy tractor', hear the old 'strife in the strung woods'. Folding up his priest's gear, walking back through the centuries, Thomas enters the 'vixen-footed / Firelight' a bard, a worshipper of barbarous splendour:

> The stars were hooded and the moon afraid
> To vex the darkness with her yellow braid.
>
> Then he spoke, and anger kindled . . .

But the Welsh do indeed forget the past:

> Four centuries now
> We have been leaving
> The hills and the high moors
> For the jewelled pavements
> Easing our veins of their dark peat
> By slow transfusions.
> . . . .
> We have forgotten
> The far lakes,
> Aled and Eiddwen, whose blue litmus
> Alone could detect
> The mind's acid.

In fact—twisting, bandaging, never giving the arm of his country a rest—Thomas at times *wants* the past forgotten. 'An impotent people, / Sick with inbreeding, / Worrying the carcase of an old song'—this is to be neither a people nor present in history. When 'we have finished quarrelling for crumbs / Under a table', he writes in 'Welsh History', 'or gnawing the bones / Of a dead dead culture, we will arise, / Armed, but not in the old way.'

On the other hand, Thomas wants the peasants to remain up a side path, outside of history. For what is history beside eternity? And what if their inertness is only another name for the peace of God? So, reconstructing them, giving them the benefit of the doubt, making them the resting point of his mind, Thomas sometimes approaches his mute, unchanging, unprotesting parishioners, not with asperity, but with awe, as one moves out on a still lake.

Prytherch, man, can you forgive
From your stone altar on which the light's
Bread is broken at dusk and dawn
One who strafed you with thin scorn
From the cheap gallery of his mind?
It was you who were right the whole time;
Right in this that the day's end
Finds you still in the same field
In which you started, your soul made strong
By the earth's incense, the wind's song.
While I have worn my soul bare
On the world's roads, seeking what lay
Too close for the mind's lenses to see,
And come now with the first stars
Big on my lids westward to find
With the slow lifting up of your hand
No welcome, only forgiveness.

'Which is the greater blessing', asks Teilhard de Chardin, 'to have the sublime unity of God to centre and save the universe? or to have the concrete immensity of the universe by which to undergo and touch God?' Suffering, as he does, the grateful shortsightedness of the artist, Thomas answers, through his poems: Give me the world to undergo. All the same, and for all its 'concrete immensity', it does not weigh him down enough. His mind skitters with the times. He feels impelled to 'seek', as if what he sought had not pinned him down. Or the swelling surface sensuality of the earth distracts him:

> . . . Have I been wise
> In the past, letting my nostrils
> Plan my day? That salt scrubbing
> Left me unclean. Am I wise now,
> With all this pain in the air,
> To keep my room, reading perhaps
> Of that Being whose will is our peace?

So it is that he comes to envy the peasants their awful privilege of self-annihilation. The stoop of their backs is the sign of a stolid but blessed consent. There about the angry, shamefaced priest seething with words are the meekest of Christians, nailed without murmur to the brute necessities of the Creation.

But the pagan in Thomas vies with the ascetic in emulating

the peasants. To the ascetic they have a 'tree's / Knotted endurance', they are 'stern like the soil'; their only knowledge is of God and is the ache in their bones. To the pagan, by contrast, they are a shell in which, could he put an ear to them, he might hear the sea of forgotten lore. After all, their hands have dabbled 'in the world's blood'. Were the peasant to speak, 'would not the glib tongue boast / A lore denied our neoteric sense, / Being handed down from the age of innocence?' And has not every right word on the tongue 'a green taste'?

Or it may be Thomas in his very character as poet who envies the peasants their 'thoughts of no date'. Stanley Burnshaw is one of the latest and best to argue that poetry is an expression of man's 'drive to regain . . . his primary organic unity with the rest of creation: his "seamlessness", which endured through his millions of years, whose heritage is inscribed in his myths, his religions, his arts, his rituals.' Verse, which turns back on itself, as the name suggests, and back on the poet's past, may turn all the way back as well to the 'seamless web' of pre-rational creature knowledge. And, creatures of elemental recurrence as the peasants are, servants of the turning earth, 'scholars / Of the fields' pages', what natural poets they must be—spider-souled, before time. '. . . I know, as I listen', says Thomas, 'that your speech has in it / The source of all poetry. . . .'

Yet poetry enacts seamlessness, I believe, only through a subtle perspective of detachment. By sleight of hand it makes us creatures again, but at the same time as abstract as Plato. If it puts us on a green hill, it also gives us space in which to see the hill rise, horizoned. It allows us to be at once as primal and civilized as the mind can be. Fortunately, at any rate, Thomas does not altogether find his way to the total creature unity he desires, or we should not have his poems. From his dry position as a modern Welsh minister he casts his poems into seamlessness as, from a bank, one drops a line into a pool; he is outside unity yet threaded to it. We are content to let him envy the peasant ploughing against the wild sky, imagining that in that rude life alone is poetry, so long as, in his isolation, he spins out his poems.

When Thomas is not attempting to change the peasants, he is thus aspiring to be what they are. The truth is that he does not know what to make of them. Indeed, they are almost always present in his poems as what forces supposition, interpretation, judgement: they are afield as the problematical.

> . . . I passed and saw you
> Labouring there, your dark figure
> Marring the simple geometry
> Of the square fields with its gaunt question.
> My poems were made in its long shadow
> Falling coldly across the page.

The farmers, notes another poem, are busy 'In ways never to be divulged / To the still watcher beyond the glass / Of their thin breath'.

The central and stubborn meaning of Thomas's work is thus the ambiguity of reflection. Existence and action, as Jaspers remarks, display an 'endless ambiguity': 'anything can mean something else for reflection.' Only eternal knowledge is finite—which helps explain why Thomas, one of the most restless of men, refers himself to it. The peasants, however keenly he observes them, are yet as opaque and unforthcoming as a spot of ink, which he draws out, with his pen, this way then that, in fine lines, in an effort to make the inarticulate speak. Closing their doors to him as the farmers do, they leave him in the hollow vastness of the plausible. Dumb and distant, they perforce become a sounding board for his own changing guilts, humiliations, and arrogances—they are subject to his whims. Yet he experiences this license as anguish. Because they do not come out to meet him, they throw him back on himself. He cannot speak of them without entering himself, second-guessing. He is, when he writes, himself the sum of their changing integers. But it was their own sum, meagre or dear, that he had meant to tally.

So, having hoped to enfold the peasants, Thomas is forced merely to circle about them. Or he goes out to them again and again as if sewn to them but, alas, not sewn tightly enough, nor loosely enough, either. He is litigiously bound to the ambiguity of human experience. 'A reflection which', in Jaspers's words, 'is conscious of being unable to attain any real ground by itself' is not his chosen subject but his predicament.

Yet if poetry is a consciousness of Being that, however complete for the moment, aspires to final permanence only in its form of expression, then Thomas's frustration before the mute men of Wales may be counted a poetic asset, since it keeps his consciousness of life restless and pressing. It has led, at any rate, to poetry finally balanced and alive in its contrary moods and uncertainties.

It is in their common pacing quality that Thomas's manner and matter blend to form a strong and harmonious mood. The lines will not, cannot slow down enough to delight in their own rhythms; nor can the mind at work in them finally rest in any one view of its subject. The open, passionate manner, catching at the world by tufts of metaphor, swiftly climbing, is the aesthetic manifestation of the poet's philosophical quandary, his interpretative eagerness, his need for certainty and its continual frustration.

Doubtless, Thomas's poetry would be still more indelible if its rhythms were deeper set; but perhaps it would be less true to itself. Its lean nervousness is at once attractive in its own right and characteristic of his region and his age; one would not like to see it changed. Unsettled in themselves as his poems may be, they are yet—perhaps partly for that very reason—quick with life, and certain to live.

Besides being internally harmonious, Thomas's poems are also balanced in what Arnold called poetry's two 'interpretations': natural magic and moral profundity. Both qualities are vigorous in his work—the first in the rank strength and quite amazing beauty of his sensuous imagination, the second in his reflection on the lives of the poor and bare, and on his own.

No wonder that in reading Thomas at his best—for instance in 'Green Categories', 'Ninetieth Birthday', 'Walter Llywarch', 'Absolution', 'Portrait', 'The Gap in the Hedge', 'A Peasant', 'The Airy Tomb', 'Death of a Peasant'—one feels a high excitement. In Thomas one can rejoice that another rare poet has come, though as yet scarcely heard of, to the English-speaking world.

Philip Larkin

ENGLISH poetry has never been so persistently out in the cold as it is with Philip Larkin—a poet who (contrary to Wordsworth's view of the calling) rejoices not more but less than other men in the spirit of life that is in him. Frost is a perennial boy, Hardy a fighter, by comparison. The load of snow, soiled and old, stays on the roof in poem after poem and, rubbing a clear space at the window, Larkin is there to mourn once again a world without generative fire. Well, it is just as he knew it would be, though now and then something surprising—a sheen of sunlight, some flutter of life—almost makes him wish for a moment that he could frolic out of doors.

Not that Larkin has wholly a mind of winter. A neighbourly snowman, he sometimes wears his hat tipped jauntily, and smiles and makes you laugh. Notice the drooping carrot nose in the mockingly titled 'Wild Oats':

> About twenty years ago
> Two girls came in where I worked—
> A bosomy English rose
> And her friend in specs I could talk to.
> Faces in those days sparked
> The whole shooting-match off, and I doubt
> If ever one had like hers:
> But it was the friend I took out,
>
> And in seven years after that
> Wrote over four hundred letters,
> Gave a ten-guinea ring
> I got back in the end, and met
> At numerous cathedral cities
> Unknown to the clergy. I believe
> I met beautiful twice. She was trying
> Both times (so I thought) not to laugh . . .

In fact this is more lively than (say) the typical poem in *The Oxford Book of English Verse*. A witty and amiable snowman, then, with a clown's rueful sense of himself, and a clown's way of asking a genial tolerance for, indeed an easy complicity in, his ancient familiarity with defeat.

Yet where the clown, however little and stepped on, is indefatigably hopeful, Larkin is unillusioned, with a metaphysical zero in his bones. Larger than his world, outside it, he bears it before him, in chagrin, like a block of ice. While the clown is merely done to, Larkin in a sense does in the world, denying it every virtue in advance. Behind the paint a countenance of stone . . .

This dismissal of the world, at the same time as it ensures his nullity, is a proud, self-affirming act. Yet at times his complaint against life is precisely that it has never attempted to lure him. Its very indifference, its failure to have any use for him, makes him want to reject it. 'Life is first boredom', he writes in 'Dockery and Son', speaking of his own life but (so overwhelming is the tedium) generalizing, too. And in 'I Remember, I Remember', he elaborates devastatingly:

> By now I've got the whole place clearly charted.
> Our garden, first: where I did not invent
> Blinding theologies of flowers and fruits,
> And wasn't spoken to by an old hat.
> And here we have that splendid family
>
> I never ran to when I got depressed,
> The boys all biceps and the girls all chest,
> Their comic Ford, their farm where I could be
> 'Really myself'. I'll show you, come to that,
> The bracken where I never trembling sat,
>
> Determined to go through with it; where she
> Lay back, and 'all became a burning mist'.
> And, in those offices, my doggerel
> Was not set up in blunt ten-point, nor read
> By a distinguished cousin of the mayor,
>
> Who didn't call and tell my father *There
> Before us, had we the gift to see ahead* . . .

Yet it is just this accident of temperament that brings Larkin into line with contemporary history—not with its actual resilience and stubborn energy but with its contagious fears: his very cells seeming formed to index the withering of the ideal, of romance, of possibility, that characterizes post-war thought. If Larkin is not merely admired but loved, it is partly because, finding poetry and humour even in sterility, he makes it bearable: he shows that it can be borne with grace and gentleness. He arrived at the right time to blend in with the disenfranchised youth of the Second World War ('At an age when self-importance would have been normal', he writes in the Preface to his novel *Jill*, 'events cut us ruthlessly down to size'). And although his depression, like Hardy's, is as if from before the ages, he has continued to seem the poet mid-century England required, his dogged parochialism reflecting the shrunken will of the nation, his bare details the democratic texture of the times.

Larkin's distinction from other nihilists lies in his domestication of the void: he has simply taken nullity for granted, found it as banal as the worn places in linoleum. Other nihilists, by comparison, are full of emotional and technical protest. With frighteningly poised hysteria, a Donald Barthelme dips his readers into a whirlpool of received pretensions that have just been dissolved by parody; a Robert Lowell is tragically grand, a Samuel Beckett savagely sardonic, a Harold Pinter sinister as a toyed-with knife . . . Larkin is plain and passive. Yet these qualities, far from letting him down, prove almost as striking as brilliant inventiveness—striking for their very simplicity. Characteristically Larkin presents not a 'world elsewhere' but life 'just here', denuded of libido, sentiment, obvious imaginative transvaluation. Like Hardy and Frost he uses imagination precisely in order to show what life is like when imagination is taken out of it.

> 'This was Mr Bleaney's room. He stayed
> The whole time he was at the Bodies, till
> They moved him.' Flowered curtains, thin and frayed,
> Fall to within five inches of the sill,
>
> Whose window shows a strip of building land,
> Tussocky, littered. 'Mr Bleaney took
> My bit of garden properly in hand.'
> Bed, upright chair, sixty-watt bulb, no hook
>
> Behind the door, no room for books or bags—
> 'I'll take it' . . .

In everything except effect, Larkin is thus the weakling of the current group of nihilists, or the pacifist, the one who never stands up to the niggling heart of existence, throwing down even the stones of fantasy, technical dazzle, fierce jokes—the devices of an adventurous imagination—as being in any case useless against the Goliath of the void. His achievement has been the creation of imaginative bareness, a penetrating confession of poverty.

This achievement came only with difficulty, Larkin respecting bareness so much and misapprehending the function of imagination so greatly that at first he tried to keep the two apart, like honour from shame. Imagination? The dubious water spilling over the dam the world erects in front of the ego. From the beginning Larkin was the sort of young man, old before his time, whose stern wish is to put aside childish things. 'Very little that catches the imagination', he says in *The London Magazine* of February 1962, 'can get its clearance from either the intelligence or the moral sense.' 'There is not much pleasure', he adds, 'to be got from the truth about things as anyone sees it. . . . What one does enjoy writing—what the imagination is only too ready to help with—is, in some form or other, compensation, assertion of oneself in an indifferent or hostile environment, demonstration . . . that one is in command of a situation, and so on.' The imagination, moreover, is a fetishist, 'being classic and austere, or loading every rift with ore . . . with no responsible basis or rational encouragement.'

Larkin's problem, then, has been to write in the grim countenance of these views, with their pride in naked endurance, their fierce modesty—his limited output no doubt confessing to the difficulty. And if at first he took up fiction as well as poetry, it was because of its traditional alliance with 'the truth about things'. His fiction became the exercise ground of his lucidity. Both *Jill* (1946) and *A Girl in Winter* (1947) creep coldly to their conclusions. Though necessarily works of imagination—works *conceived*—their conceptions are unexcited, even numb. Imagination, they imply, is nugatory, a nail scratching a dream on ice. And so they labour against themselves. Virtually nothing happens to their youthful protagonists; crocuses doomed to fill with snow, they have only to sense futility to give way to it. The pale Oxford undergraduate in the first learns from a visit to his home town, recently bombed, 'how little anything matters', 'how appallingly little life is'. Then a dream tells him that, 'whether fulfilled or unfulfilled', love dies. This is enough to destroy his desire for the innocent Jill. He decides to die, as it were, before his death, so as to die as little as possible. In *A Girl in Winter*, too, wartime lends plausibility to a disillusionment that in fact seems pursued. And again the most ordinary relationships fail, as if there were something radically wrong with the human heart. The heroine, Katherine, finally repudiates 'the interplay of herself and other people'. With resolution, not in self-pity, beyond calling back, even gratefully, she steps out into a lucid solitude. At the close she envisions the 'orderly slow procession', as of an 'ice floe', of her permanently frozen desires: 'Yet their passage was not saddening. Unsatisfied dreams rose and fell about them, crying out against their implacability, but in the end glad that such order, such destiny, existed. Against this knowledge the heart, the will, and all that made for protest, could at last sleep.' And so she chooses to abstain from life, convinced that the fruit is anyway infested.

Given not only these passive protagonists but a starved-sparrow manner and a merely *determined* disenchantment, totally lacking in the passion either of truth or regret, the novels could not help seeming too long, indeed superfluous after the drain pipes, the snow. Larkin had yet to see that his thorough disbelief in adventure—even a Beckett shows a taste for mock adventure—necessitated the briefest of literary forms, and that the surest way to make the humanly sterile emotionally forceful is to place it in the midst of a poem, where, dwarfed by the glorious remembrances of the medium, it can have a shivering significance.

Meanwhile his poetry was the lyrical run-off of his lucidity. The poems in *The North Ship* (1946) treat the same themes as the novels—a world eaten through at the root by time, the wisdom of taking 'the grave's part', the failure of love—with all the runaway outcry that the novels stiffly restrained. Seeking at once the altitudes of the great lyrists of his youth, Yeats and Dylan Thomas, Larkin rises too high for his leaden themes:

> I was sleeping, and you woke me
> To walk on the chilled shore
> Of a night with no memory,
> Till your voice forsook my ear

> Till your two hands withdrew
> And I was empty of tears,
> On the edge of a bricked and streeted sea
> And a cold hill of stars.

And again:

> And in their blazing solitude
> The stars sang in their sockets through the night:
> 'Blow bright, blow bright
> The coal of this unquickened world.'

So Larkin sings as the blade comes down, is ardent about the ice in the fire of youth. Fulsomely embracing poetry as a legitimized form of 'compensation', he wrote as if it were unnecessary to be sensible in it, permissible to speak of 'bricked and streeted' seas or of stars that, while blazing, begged to be ignited. A remarkable discrepancy: the novels prematurely grizzled, the poems puerile.

Larkin had yet to reconcile the supposed unpleasure of truth with the pleasure of imagination. This he was now to do abruptly, being one of those poets who undergo an almost magical transformation between their first and second volume. It was Hardy who showed him that imagination could treat 'properly truthful' themes truthfully yet with acute delicacy, deliberate power. Never mind that Hardy's poems are greyly literal: they get into you like a rainy day. 'When I came to Hardy', Larkin says, 'it was with the sense of relief that I didn't have to try and jack myself up to a concept of poetry that lay outside my own life—this is perhaps what I felt Yeats was trying to make me do. One could simply relapse back into one's own life and write from it.' Again: 'Hardy taught one to feel . . . and he taught one as well to have confidence in what one felt.'

In truth, Larkin's themes belong to that great negative order of ideas that has always proved the most potent in art. We cannot help ourselves: we home to tragedy—optimism in art commonly leaving us feeling deprived of some deeper truth. Nothing is of more initial advantage to a poet than a horizon of clouds. For pathos makes us irresistibly present to ourselves, silhouettes us against a backdrop of fate, renders us final for the imagination. And to achieve it Larkin, as he now saw, had only to 'feel'—feel simply, without exaggeration. This itself meant that he had to measure ordinary life, life as he knew it, with the rigour of regret. In his novels he had passed beyond protest into a limbo of resignation. In *The North Ship*, on the other hand, he had exhibited a preposterous surprise and anguish—as if sterility were not, after all, the scene on which his blind rose every morning. Now he needed to find a manner at once warm and cold, steeped in futility but not extinguished by it. He had to open bare cupboards that would speak of all that might have been in them.

And so he does in his second volume, *The Less Deceived* (1955), and again in his third and most recent, *The Whitsun Weddings* (1964). Here is 'As Bad as a Mile':

> Watching the shied core
> Striking the basket, skidding across the floor,
> Shows less and less of luck, and more and more
>
> Of failure spreading back up the arm
> Earlier and earlier, the unraised hand calm,
> The apple unbitten in the palm.

What redoubtable depths of acceptance in the calm of that unraised hand. Even so, the close-up of the unbitten apple proves affecting: if the poem is stoic about the end, it is without prejudice to the pleasure preceding it; it is stoic with regret. What is more, here Larkin brings the lofty literary sorrow of *The North Ship* down from 'black flowers', 'birds crazed with flight', and wintry drums, to the level of the everyday, where, no longer diffuse, it can be felt like pain in a vital organ. And, neither egoistic nor fetishistic, imagination has now become only a way the truth has of entering us all at once, swiftly and completely, in a context of value. Far from being an evasion of the truth, it is a hammer for the nail, the poignancy secreted in the prosaic.

Larkin's poems now take on the brute force of circumstantial evidence. Like sour smoke, the odour of actual days hangs about them. They have an unusual authenticity; they form a reliving. Even when the naming is general, it can have bite:

> Home is so sad. It stays as it was left,
> Shaped to the comfort of the last to go
> As if to win them back. Instead, bereft
> Of anyone to please, it withers so,
> Having no heart to put aside the theft

And turn again to what it started as,
A joyous shot at how things ought to be,
Long fallen wide. You can see how it was:
Look at the pictures and the cutlery.
The music in the piano stool. That vase.

The final articles are as blunt as pointing fingers and, with the adjective *that*, the series ends in a conclusive jab. It amounts to instant trial and conviction. The vase stands exposed, empty as the atmosphere around it, coldly reduced to its potential function—a failure, a thing without love.

Many of Larkin's poems, however, have the specific density of descriptive detail—often autobiographical. Consider the first portion of 'Dockery and Son':

'Dockery was junior to you,
Wasn't he?' said the Dean. 'His son's here now.'
Death-suited, visitant, I nod. 'And do
You keep in touch with ——' Or remember how
Black-gowned, unbreakfasted, and still half-tight
We used to stand before that desk, to give
'Our version' of 'these incidents last night'?
I try the door of where I used to live:

Locked. The lawn spreads dazzlingly wide.
A known bell chimes. I catch my train, ignored.
Canal and clouds and colleges subside
Slowly from view. But Dockery, good Lord,
Anyone up today must have been born
In '43, when I was twenty-one.
If he was younger, did he get this son
At nineteen, twenty? Was he that withdrawn

High-collared public-schoolboy, sharing rooms
With Cartwright who was killed? Well, it just shows
How much . . . How little . . . Yawning, I suppose
I fell asleep, waking at the fumes
And furnace-glares of Sheffield, where I changed,
And ate an awful pie, and walked along
The platform to its end to see the ranged
Joining and parting lines reflect a strong

Unhindered moon . . .

Here again pleasure and truth meet effortlessly. How casually the lawn and then the moon, both unhindered in beauty, set off hindered humanity. The detail is at once natural (though 'Death-suited' forces perception) and resonant. The poem has the simple fascination of an honestly reported life—even suggesting the moment to moment flow of consciousness. It possesses also a humble appeal of personality, a tone as unpressingly intimate as the touch of a hand on one's arm.

So it was that Larkin took the path of Edward Thomas, of Frost, of Hardy, and became a poet who looks at ordinary life through empty, silent air. His poems now sprang like snowdrops directly from the cruel cast of things, yet in themselves attaining beauty. And just as they now found their pathos in everyday things, so the void now spoke, in part, where day by day Larkin heard it, in the trite though sometimes pert and piquant language of the streets. Here was a language as sceptical as it was hardy, soiled with disappointment. Of a certain billboard beauty, 'Kneeling up on the sand / In tautened white satin', Larkin writes:

> She was slapped up one day in March.
> A couple of weeks, and her face
> Was snaggle-toothed and boss-eyed;
> Huge tits and a fissured crotch
> Were scored well in, and the space
> Between her legs held scrawls
> That set her fairly astride
> A tuberous cock and balls
>
> Autographed *Titch Thomas*, while
> Someone had used a knife
> Or something to stab right through
> The moustached lips of her smile.
> She was too good for this life . . .

By contrast, Larkin's words will not be too good for this life. They make room not only for the colloquial 'Or something' but—sympathetically—for words betraying the fascinated disgust of adolescent sexual emotion. Still, Larkin's regret that anything *should* be too good for this life shines through his contempt for the meretricious poster. He makes the common words sorrier than they know.

Larkin thus renews poetry from underneath, enlivening it

with 'kiddies', 'stewed', 'just my lark', 'nippers', 'lob-lolly men', 'pisses', 'bash', 'dude', and more of the same. And yet his manner rises easily from the slangy to the dignified; its step is light, its range wide. Here it is as vernacular caricature, amused at itself:

> When getting my nose in a book
> Cured most things short of school,
> It was worth ruining my eyes
> To know I could still keep cool,
> And deal out the old right hook
> To dirty dogs twice my size . . .

A degree up from this we find the almost aggressive slang of the poem on the billboard girl. Then comes the perky, street-flavoured simplicity of 'Toads', 'Wild Oats', 'Send No Money', or 'Self's the Man':

> Oh, no one can deny
> That Arnold is less selfish than I.
> He's married a woman to stop her getting away
> Now she's there all day . . .

A step higher and the style rises from self-consciousness and begins to leave the street:

> Talking in bed ought to be easiest,
> Lying together there goes back so far,
> An emblem of two people being honest . . .

This is the plain style of most of Larkin's poems. And this plainness is sometimes heightened by rhythmical sculpturing, syntactical drama, or repetition, as in 'MCMXIV':

> Never such innocence,
> Never before or since,
> As changed itself to past
> Without a word—the men
> Leaving the gardens tidy,
> The thousands of marriages
> Lasting a little while longer:
> Never such innocence again . . .

Whatever its degree of formality, the peculiarity of Larkin's style is an eloquent taciturnity: it betrays a reluctance to use words at all. If, as 'Ambulances' says, a 'solving emptiness . . . lies just under all we do', then Larkin's words, as if preparing

to be swallowed up, will make themselves as lean as they can—
nothingness, they assert, will not fatten on them. Indeed, they
seem to have soaked a long age in a vinegar that dissolves illusions.
Such is the impression they make in 'As Bad as a Mile', and here
again in 'Toads Revisited':

> Walking around in the park
> Should feel better than work:
> The lake, the sunshine,
> The grass to lie on,
>
> Blurred playground noises
> Beyond black-stockinged nurses—
> Not a bad place to be.
> Yet it doesn't suit me . . .

The short lines and clipped syntax suggest an almost painful
expenditure of language. A head with a wagging tongue, they
say, is time's fool. Larkin, of course, also writes in somewhat freer
rhythms, as at the end of 'An Arundel Tomb'. But he always
counts before he pays, and his more expansive effects bank on
their moving contrast with his usual, slightly tough laconicism.

Larkin's laconicism also conveys the poverty of the sayable.
That 'Life is slow dying', it implies, 'leaves / Nothing'—or
almost nothing—'to be said'. He says little because he sees too
much. Like Ted Hughes, he feels pressed back into himself by
a vision of an unjustified and unjustifiable reality, but where this
has finally provoked Hughes into desperate garrulity, it has all
but frozen Larkin's mouth—two slender volumes since 1946;
two interruptions of silence.

If Larkin relies on traditional form, it is partly out of the agreement of numbness and caution that we find in his style. Why
seek new forms, he seems to ask, when there is nothing new under
the sun? In any case, 'Content alone interests me', he says.
'Content is everything'. Like a man freezing to death in a snow-
storm, refusing to be distracted by the beauty of the flakes, he
resolves to be lucid to the last, his mind on the truth alone. And,
paradoxically precisely this is why he writes in form. For, by
virtue of its familiarity, traditional form, skilfully used, is all
but transparent. (Only experimenters, antiformalists, and writers
of verse make an *issue* of form.) At its finest, prosody is anyway
meltingly one with the content; and Larkin is frequently a

fine craftsman. So nothingness stares out of Larkin's poems undistracted, with a native starkness. Even the bodily warmth conveyed by rhythm is often restrained by nicely calculated metrical irregularity.

Yet form has also for Larkin its traditional function: not modest after all, it is an attempt at the memorable. If he writes, the reason is to silence death, if only with the fewest possible words. In a statement contributed to D. J. Enright's anthology, *Poets of the 1950's*, Larkin says: 'I wrote poems to preserve things I have seen / thought / felt (if I may so indicate a composite and complex experience) both for myself and for others, though I feel that my prime responsibility is to the experience itself, which I am trying to keep from oblivion for its own sake. Why I should do this I have no idea, but I think the impulse to preserve lies at the bottom of all art.' Nihilist though he is, he thus raises against nothingness—like every other literary nihilist, if more moderately—the combined plea and protest of his constructions, with their exemplary inner necessity, their perfection.

In sum, his forms are at the same time sorry to be there and insistently there. In his use of words and form alike, Larkin both defies and skulks before his nihilistic 'content', like an animal that, while shrinking back, offers to fight.

So it was that, without betraying his scruples, Larkin became a poignant and cohesive poet, his means the functional intelligence of his ends. More sophisticated writers have chided him for his poetic provinciality, but he is right, I think, to be as simple as he is. His poetry seems not only the necessary expression of his temperament but the very voice of his view of things, the pure expression of his aim—his purpose being not to make sterility whirl but precisely to make it stand still, freed from confusion, from the human fevers that oppose it. Far from adhering piously to English poetic tradition, he uses it for his own ends. The result, in any case, is a poetry of mixed formality and informality, mixed severity and charm, mixed humour and pathos, that carries a unique personal impress—a poetry that, for all its conservatism, is unconsciously, inimitably new.

Even *The Less Deceived* and *The Whitsun Weddings*, however, are somewhat subject to the 'poetic' toning up of *The North Ship*, and poems corrupted by self-pity appear side by side with the mature poems just described. A void with an ashen pallor—how resist rouging it, giving it dramatic visibility? Regret, in any case, touches us so nearly that it slips at the slightest urge into self-commiseration. At his weakest Larkin exploits this readiness for sorrow-suckling, for the histrionic; he tries for pathetic *effects*.

Of course, when a poem is so delightful as 'Days', criticism hesitates:

> What are days for?
> Days are where we live.
> They come, they wake us
> Time and time over.
> They are to be happy in:
> Where can we live but days?
>
> Ah, solving that question
> Brings the priest and the doctor
> In their long coats
> Running over the fields.

But those men in their long coats are too easy to summon over the fields: they border on the animated cartoon. Throwing us on the wretchedness of being passive before them, in need of them, they are more melodramatic than the truth. For all that its subject is 'days', the poem places itself so far from the quotidian that it can say, can picture anything without fearing contradiction from itself. The often admired 'Next, Please' also steps off from life into self-pity. The poem figures expectancy as a 'Sparkling armada of promises' that leaves us 'holding wretched stalks / Of disappointment'. But whatever were we waving at those ships? In the intoxication of its chagrin, the piece neglects propriety and probability. Even the final stanza, though grand, begets uneasiness:

> Only one ship is seeking us, a black-
> Sailed unfamiliar, towing at her back
> A huge and birdless silence. In her wake
> No waters breed or break.

This is a trifle too awesome, Death in makeup. Another admired poem, 'No Road', begins:

> Since we agreed to let the road between us
> Fall to disuse,
> And bricked our gates up, planted trees to screen us,
> And turned all time's eroding agents loose,
> Silence, and space, and strangers—our neglect
> Has not had much effect.
>
> Leaves drift unswept, perhaps; grass creeps unmown;
> No other change . . .

What is really 'unmown' is the conceit—its leaves, grass, bricks, and trees lacking specific reference as metaphors. As in 'Next, Please', the vehicle is too much an end in itself. All three poems are rhetorical, written in emotional generality. Like still other pieces, including 'Whatever Happened?', 'Age', 'Triple Time', 'Latest Face', 'If, My Darling', and 'Arrivals, Departures', they stand at a remove from the literal, on a swaying rope bridge of tropes, dramatic but ill-supported.

Yet virtual fact is liable to the cosmetic impulse, too, as witness so ostensibly autobiographical a poem as 'Church Going'. The first two stanzas, it is true, are everything these other poems are not:

> Once I am sure there's nothing going on
> I step inside, letting the door thud shut.
> Another church: matting, seats, and stone,
> And little books; sprawlings of flowers, cut
> For Sunday, brownish now; some brass and stuff
> Up at the holy end; the small neat organ;
> And a tense, musty, unignorable silence,
> Brewed God knows how long. Hatless, I take off
> My cycle-clips in awkward reverence,
>
> Move forward, run my hand around the font.
> From where I stand, the roof looks almost new—
> Cleaned, or restored? Someone would know: I don't.
> Mounting the lectern, I peruse a few
> Hectoring large-scale verses, and pronounce
> 'Here endeth' much more loudly than I'd meant.
> The echoes snigger briefly. Back at the door
> I sign the book, donate an Irish sixpence,
> Reflect the place was not worth stopping for.

Pungently detailed, this has a wonderful air of verisimilitude and candour. Except for 'Someone would know: I don't', the lines are free of padding, and the symbolism, as in the brownish flowers and 'Here endeth', is like an afterthought to the forcefully literal. Compare the middle of the poem, with its speculation about the time when churches will be out of use:

> Shall we avoid them as unlucky places?
>
> Or, after dark, will dubious women come
> To make their children touch a particular stone;
> Pick simples for a cancer; or on some
> Advised night see walking a dead one?
> Power of some sort or other will go on
> In games, in riddles, seemingly at random;
> But superstition, like belief, must die,
> And what remains when disbelief has gone?
> Grass, weedy pavement, brambles, buttress, sky,
>
> A shape less recognizable each week,
> A purpose more obscure. I wonder who
> Will be the last, the very last, to seek
> This place for what it was; one of the crew
> That tap and jot and know what rood-lofts were?
> Some ruin-bibber, randy for antique,
> Or Christmas-addict, counting on a whiff
> Of gowns-and-bands and organ-pipes and myrrh? . . .

It is hard to say what is more forced here—the questions, or the assertions that 'power of some sort or other will go on' and that the church will be 'less recognizable each week', or the effort to imagine 'the very last' to seek its purpose. Like the consciously colourful detail at the close, all this is essentially idle, a fabrication. The poem picks up again as Larkin confronts the church in discovery and wonder:

> A serious house on serious earth it is,
> In whose blent air all our compulsions meet,
> Are recognized, and robed as destinies . . .

But the effect is partly to make us regret all the more the triviality of the middle stanzas.

The impression of falseness is sometimes just as strong when Larkin sets his imaginative paints aside and attempts serious thought. Indeed, without much exaggeration it might be said that he is only poised and intelligent with particulars—abstractions tend to spill out of his hands. When he thinks, he often seems to be frowningly struggling to create a philosophical intricacy and importance. Here he is in 'Lines on a Young Lady's Photograph Album':

> . . . Those flowers, that gate,
> These misty parks and motors, lacerate
> Simply by being over; you
> Contract my heart by looking out of date.
>
> Yes, true; but in the end, surely, we cry
> Not only at exclusion, but because
> It leaves us free to cry. We know *what was*
> Won't call on us to justify
> Our grief, however hard we yowl across
>
> The gap from eye to page . . .

With 'Yes, true', you can virtually hear his voice leaving its natural home in particulars, growing thin and subject to confusion. As if driven to manufacture complexities, the lines suddenly snarl up what had been plain from the descriptive life of the poem. To say that the past leaves us 'free to cry' is to make a false conundrum of what has already been said simply: that it excludes us. The truly subtle idea in the passage—namely, that the past is forlorn because *excluded from us*—is obscured by the fussy thought. And meanwhile grace and measure are abandoned—'yowl' being especially awkward, an attempt to bring the blanched thought back into poetic animation.

'Dockery and Son' similarly gravels in 'philosophy'. Why, asks the speaker, did Dockery

> . . . think adding meant increase?
> To me it was dilution. Where do these
> Innate assumptions come from? Not from what
> We think truest, or most want to do:
> Those warp tight-shut, like doors. They're more a style
> Our lives bring with them: habit for a while,
> Suddenly they harden into all we've got
>
> And how we got it; looked back on, they rear
> Like sand-clouds, thick and close, embodying
> For Dockery a son, for me nothing,
> Nothing with all a son's harsh patronage . . .

Reasoning this through is at first like trying to put on a shirt with sewn sleeves—and finally we can only *grant* that such assumptions are 'innate' or distant from what we 'think truest'. (Innate assumptions are usually not all we have but what we wish we had: eternal life, supreme importance, a guiltless being. . . .) The simile of the sand-clouds is slipshod also. Until the last line, we are far from the brilliant beginning.

In the final stanza of 'Deceptions', the self-pity that permits such laxity lies still more forward, spoiling an even more exquisite poem. At the same time, it compares weakly with the epigraph from Mayhew's *London Labour and the London Poor*, a statement of bald power almost beyond art itself: 'Of course I was drugged, and so heavily I did not regain my consciousness till the next morning. I was horrified to discover that I had been ruined, and for some days I was inconsolable, and cried like a child to be killed or sent back to my aunt.' The stanza comments:

> Slums, years, have buried you. I would not dare
> Console you if I could. What can be said,
> Except that suffering is exact, but where
> Desire takes charge, readings will grow erratic?
> For you would hardly care
> That you were less deceived, out on that bed,
> Than he was, stumbling up the breathless stair
> To burst into fulfilment's desolate attic.

The final phrase, 'fulfilment's desolate attic', bears a Johnsonian indictment, irrevocably disabused, of the delusions of desire. But even granting the romantic assumption that the seducer made too much of his desire, what is its brief match flame compared to the conflagration of the girl's young life? We can hardly care either that the girl was the less deceived. The poem treats the misreading of desire as a tragedy. But nothing it says or implies supports so extravagant and self-condoling a view.

Yet, serious as they are, Larkin's defects are easily outbalanced by his virtues. Thus, though he may abandon an imaginary scene for questionable thought, he is also likely to have put us into that scene with as piercing a dramatic immediacy as any poet now writing. We have witnessed this in 'Church Going' and 'Dockery and Son'; and here is the first stanza of 'Deceptions':

> Even so distant, I can taste the grief,
> Bitter and sharp with stalks, he made you gulp.
> The sun's occasional print, the brisk brief

> Worry of wheels along the street outside
> Where bridal London bows the other way,
> And light, unanswerable and tall and wide,
> Forbids the scar to heal, and drives
> Shame out of hiding. All the unhurried day
> Your mind lay open like a drawer of knives.

Imagination, said Emerson, is a sort of seeing that comes by
'the intellect being where and what it sees', and this happy
definition highlights what is remarkable in the stanza. For the
lines virtually *are* the original moment, as well as a beauty
beyond it and compassion for it. 'Print', it is true, is lost in
ambiguity (footprint? a picture-shape on the wall?) and indefinite
in relation to the light described later; and 'scar' rather rushes a
fresh wound. But almost everything else tells keenly—'The brisk
brief / Worry of wheels' poignantly commenting on the girl's
inconsolateness, 'bridal London' on her social ruin; 'Light,
unanswerable and tall and wide' being unimprovable; and the
simile of the drawer of knives, though risking melodrama,
properly savage.

We touch here on gifts more specialized than the dramatic
imagination, gifts for epithet and metaphor. Of course, in their
own way, these too are dramatic, restoring a primal power to the
language. We are all bees trapped behind the spotted glass of
usage till the poet releases us to the air. And so Larkin releases
us in these lines of 'Coming':

> On longer evenings,
> Light, chill and yellow,
> Bathes the serene
> Foreheads of houses.
> A thrush sings,
> Laurel-surrounded
> In the deep bare garden,
> Its fresh-peeled voice
> Astonishing the brickwork . . .

'Chill and yellow' and 'fresh-peeled' are especially happy inventions. So again at the beginning of a recent poem, 'Dublinesque':
'Down stucco side-streets, / Where light is pewter. . . .' In
another recent poem, 'The Cardplayers', the trees are—magnificently—'century-wide'. Spring, in the poem of that title, is
'race of water, / Is earth's most multiple, excited daughter'.

Delightful in 'Broadcast' is the 'coughing from / Vast Sunday-full and organ-frowned-on spaces'. And what could be at once more homely and endearing than the 'loaf-haired secretary' of 'Toads Revisited'?

Larkin's imagination has also, of course, a turn for wit. At times he instinctively inhibits the sobbing in his strings by playing staccato. Consider the lover in 'Lines on a Young Lady's Photograph Album':

> From every side you strike at my control,
> Not least through these disquieting chaps who loll
> At ease about your earlier days:
> Not quite your class, I'd say, dear, on the whole . . .

Or take the comic candour of 'Annus Mirabilis':

> Sexual intercourse began
> In nineteen sixty-three
> (Which was rather late for me)—
> Between the end of the *Chatterley* ban
> And the Beatles' first LP . . .

Next time around the parenthesis reads, 'Though just too late for me', which gives the playfulness a fine grimace. These poems have the good grace of self-irony, a civilized lightness. Better still is the comedy—vigorous with universal truth—in 'Toads' and 'Toads Revisited'. With rising bravura the first begins:

> Why should I let the toad *work*
>   Squat on my life?
> Can't I use my wit as a pitchfork
>   And drive the brute off?
>
> Six days of the week it soils
>   With its sickening poison—
> Just for paying a few bills!
>   That's out of proportion . . .

The second, with toad-eating helplessness, concludes:

> No, give me my in-tray,
> My loaf-haired secretary,
> My shall-I-keep-the-call-in-Sir:
> What else can I answer,

> When the lights come on at four
> At the end of another year?
> Give me your arm, old toad;
> Help me down Cemetery Road.

Entertaining though they are, these are works of the full imagination, more quickened than compromised by caricature. They are true and touching as well as spirited. One would be tempted to call the poisoning toad and the pitchfork the best comic conceit in modern poetry were not that of the old toad on Cemetery Road consummate to the point of tears. We are not far here from the world of fairy tales and have only to hear of Cemetery Road to fancy that, like the way through the woods to Grandmother's house, it has existed in the imagination for ever.

An unusual poet, reminding us on the one hand of the grand classical tradition and on the other of Beatrix Potter and Dorothy Parker, and all the while sounding like no one so much as himself! And Larkin has still other virtues. To begin with, there is, as we have seen, the instinctive adjustment of his means to his end, so that, for instance, he is one of the most pellucid of poets because nothing to him is more self-evident than nothingness. Then the unconscious rightness of his forms, 'Toads' being, for example, appropriately restless in alternating uneven trimeters and dimeters, 'Toads Revisited' properly more settled in its trimeters; 'Toads', again, troubled with alternating off-rhyme and 'Toads Revisited' calmer in off-rhymed couplets, full rhyme kept in reserve for the *entente cordiale* of 'toad' and 'Road'. There is the frequent perfection of his metrical spacing; the easy way his words fall together; the tang and unsurpassed contemporaneity of his diction and imagery; the fluent evolution of his poems. There is also his beautifully mild temper and his tenderness for those pushed 'To the side of their own lives'. Nor finally should we fail to add his facility at opening that scepticism about life which everyone closets in his bones.

Still, only at his best does Larkin make us grateful for what a human being can do with words. It is above all in 'Coming', 'Toads', 'Toads Revisited', 'At Grass', 'Here', 'The Whitsun Weddings', and 'An Arundel Tomb' (with two fairly recent poems, 'High Windows' and 'To the Sea', pressing near) that he puts experience under an aspect of beauty, gracing and deepening it with the illusion of necessary form and producing the privileged sensation—perhaps illusory, perhaps not—of piercing through to a truth. It is in these poems, too, that, at once detached and concerned, he most frees us from self-pity without destroying feeling.

With the exception of 'Here' and 'Toads', these pieces display an exquisite stoic compassion for the littleness, the fragility, indeed the unlikelihood, of happiness. Even in 'Here', however, tenderness is implicit in the perception, the diction, the syntax. For instance, in 'Isolate villages, where removed lives / Loneliness clarifies', the lives are considerably enfolded by the clause at the same time that the line break removes and isolates them. But such tenderness is like water under ice. Where life is as raw, insufficient, and essentially lonely as it is in 'Here', better (so the poem implies) keep yourself inwardly remote, like the 'bluish neutral distance' of the sea. Though 'Here' is all one travelling sentence till it brakes in short clauses at the end, 'Swerving east, from rich industrial shadows' out finally to the 'unfenced existence' of the sea, emotionally it is one continuous 'freeze', since each successive 'here' is as barren, as without self-justification, as the rest. 'Here' leads us as far from ourselves, as far into objective reality, as we can go—to the sea that has nothing for us, 'Facing the sun, untalkative, out of reach'—then leaves us there, all but freed from desire and too well schooled by the accumulated evidence, too guarded, to be appalled. The poem is a masterpiece of stoicism.

The equally fine 'Coming' is as remarkable for its original conception as for the felicity (already sampled) of its similes. Indeed, the two prove inseparable in the second half of the poem:

> It will be spring soon,
> It will be spring soon—
> And I, whose childhood
> Is a forgotten boredom,
> Feel like a child
> Who comes on a scene
> Of adult reconciling,
> And can understand nothing
> But the unusual laughter,
> And starts to be happy.

Throwing us back into the vulnerable heart of childhood, into an ignorance not ignorant enough, the simile redeems an inevitably romantic subject by abrading it, complicating it with domestic truth. Nor could any comparison be at once so unexpected and convincing, giving exactly, as it does, the situation of being drawn into an emotion neither understood nor trusted yet beyond one's power to refuse, since the moment it comes it reveals itself as all, nearly all, of what was needed. The poem, if complete in itself, is also an expressive elaboration of its most poignant word, 'starts'. Too doubting and perplexed for rhyme or a long line, as slender as the inchoate joy it evokes, it is like the 'chill and yellow' light described at the outset, lyrically lovely yet inhibited—its recurring two beats like a heart quickened but still at the tentative start, the mere threshold, of happiness.

There is nothing tentative about 'At Grass', which celebrates the profound peace, the cold joy, in the relinquishment of labour and identity. The retired racehorses in the poem have stolen death from itself:

> The eye can hardly pick them out
> From the cold shade they shelter in,
> Till wind distresses tail and mane;
> Then one crops grass, and moves about
> —The other seeming to look on—
> And stands anonymous again . . .

The early, strenuous days of the horses, full of 'Silks at the start' and 'Numbers and parasols', are later evoked with the same classical directness as this shaded scene, which has a clarity that leaves nothing between us and the subject. Like the horses the poem exists quietly, is envyingly 'at ease' in a pace slowed often enough by stressed monosyllables to seem tranced beyond all care. The rhyme, too, is spaced out placidly, making the stanzas like the 'unmolesting meadows'. (It does, however, cause an awkward syntactic inversion at the close: 'Only the groom, and the groom's boy, / With bridles in the evening come.') Because of its distanced subject and because the horses have both lived out and outlived their swiftness, the poem takes the sickness out of the desire for oblivion, offering in place of weariness a paradise of shade.

An even more exquisite poem is 'An Arundel Tomb', which begins:

> Side by side, their faces blurred,
> The earl and countess lie in stone,
> Their proper habits vaguely shown
> As jointed armour, stiffened pleat,
> And that faint hint of the absurd—
> The little dogs under their feet.

The lines rise to the ceremony of their occasion. So 'Side by side', each syllable royally weighted, is balanced by the four syllables of 'their faces blurred', the two phrases equal and graceful in their partnership but immobile as the effigies they describe. Through rhyme, the third line offers its arm to the second as they move in iambic procession. Then the time-softened long *i* stiffens into the short one, and the little dogs break into the sentence like an afterthought (which in fact they may originally have been). Modelled and exact in its rhythms, lovely, fresh, and affecting in its detail, tender in its deeply deliberated tone, holding the slow centuries in its hands, the poem is indeed very lovely, very moving. Unfortunately, it has need to be in order to humble its one defect: its manipulation of the subject for the sake of pathos. Noting 'with a sharp tender shock' that the earl and countess are holding hands, the poet says:

> They would not think to lie so long.
> Such faithfulness in effigy
> Was just a detail friends would see:
> A sculptor's sweet commissioned grace
> Thrown off in helping to prolong
> The Latin names around the base . . .

But why would they not think to lie so long? If Larkin denies them intention, it is evidently to press his own, which is to view faithful love through the ironic and brittle glass of accident. One balks at this, censures it, and at the same time acknowledges, 'This is Larkin's most beautiful poem'.

Less exquisite but more substantial than 'An Arundel Tomb', 'The Whitsun Weddings' is distinguished for ease, poise, balance, and inclusiveness.

It has even more of England in it than 'Here', similarly taking us by train through the country and making its breadth and variety, its unfolding being, our own. The very movement is that of a leisurely if inexorable journey, the lines frequently pausing as if at so many stations, yet curving on in repeated *enjambements* past scenes swiftly but timelessly evoked, as though the stanzas themselves were the wide windows of a moving train:

> All afternoon, through the tall heat that slept
>   For miles inland,
> A slow and stopping curve southwards we kept.
> Wide farms went by, short-shadowed cattle, and
> Canals with floatings of industrial froth;
> A hothouse flashed uniquely: hedges dipped
> And rose: and now and then a smell of grass ˙
> Displaced the reek of buttoned carriage-cloth
> Until the next town, new and nondescript,
> Approached with acres of dismantled cars . . .

This is deft, light in depiction but strongly evocative. And the English themselves are as vividly present as their towns and countryside, indeed man himself is here in his several ages: the children in the platform wedding parties frowning as 'at something dull', the young men 'grinning and pomaded', the brides' friends staring after the departing trains as 'at a religious wounding', the married couples themselves boarding the carriages in distraction, the uncles shouting smut, the fathers looking as if they had 'never known / Success so huge and wholly farcical', and the mothers' faces sharing the bridal secret 'like a happy funeral'.

And the poet? By chance, he himself is there on the train that Whitsun as the eternal witness of the contemplative artist, inward with what he sees yet outside it precisely to the extent that he sees it. Single amid the married couples in the carriage, he is yet caught up by them, caught up *with* them ('We hurried towards London'), quickened into a sense of physical existence in time. On the other hand, with his indisplaceable knowledge of failure, absence, endings, he is the loneliness of contemplation lucid before the happy blindness of the body and its emotions. He knows he might well envy this happiness and yet he dwarfs it:

> Now fields were building-plots, and poplars cast
> Long shadows over major roads, and for
> Some fifty minutes, that in time would seem

Just long enough to settle hats and say
    I nearly died,
A dozen marriages got under way.
They watched the landscape, sitting side by side
—An Odeon went past, a cooling tower,
And someone running up to bowl—and none
Thought of the others they would never meet
Or how their lives would all contain this hour.
I thought of London spread out in the sun,
Its postal districts packed like squares of wheat:

There we were aimed. And as we raced across
    Bright knots of rail
Past standing Pullmans, walls of blackened moss
Came close, and it was nearly done, this frail
Travelling coincidence; and what it held
Stood ready to be loosed with all the power
That being changed can give. We slowed again,
And as the tightened brakes took hold, there swelled
A sense of falling, like an arrow-shower
Sent out of sight, somewhere becoming rain.

The poem throughout links beginnings to ends, ends to beginnings—as in its wedding parties 'out on the end of an event / Waving goodbye', its mingling of generations, and the stops and starts of the journey itself. And here at the close, at the same time that it gives the energy of life and the fruition of time their due, even as arrows speed and rain promises germination, it also makes us aware of inevitable dissolution, as arrows fall and rain means mould, dampness, the cold, the elemental. Like certain romantic poems—'The Echoing Green', 'Kubla Kahn', 'Intimations of Immortality', 'Among School Children'—the poem thus brings together, irreducibly, life in its newness and power and life in its decline and end. Nowhere else in his work (though 'To the Sea' marks a near exception) is Larkin so irresistibly drawn out to observe with an emotion close to happiness the great arena of life in its diversity and energy, undeluded though he is, doomed though he feels the energy to be.

'Poetry', St.-John Perse remarks, 'never wishes to be absence, nor refusal'; and certainly in 'The Whitsun Weddings' Larkin grants it the presence of the world, as he grants the world its presence. Yet even apart from 'The Whitsun Weddings' we would be without Larkin's poems the poorer by that much presence and that much love. Poet though he is of the essential absence of life from itself, he yet makes himself present as regret that it must be so; and for all his defeatism it is easy to find him a sympathetic figure as he stands at the window, trying not to cloud it with his breath, mourning the winter casualties, concerned to be there even though convinced beyond all argument that, like everything else, his concern is gratuitous.

Ted Hughes

TED HUGHES is our first poet of the will to live. Lawrence wrote of animal joy, a lighter, perhaps more fanciful thing. Robinson Jeffers picked up the topic occasionally, a hawk on his wrist, but was too eager, too clumsy, to master it. Hughes is its master and at the same time is mastered by it. The subject owns him, he is lord of the subject.

The will to live might seem the first and healthiest of subjects; in fact it is almost the last and most morbid. Men come to it after the other subjects have failed. It is the last stop—waterless, exposed—before nothingness. Civilization blows off, love and utopia evaporate, the interest the human mind takes in its own creations washes out, and there, its incisors bared, stands life, daring you to praise it.

Curiously, in an interview with Egbert Faas in *The London Magazine* (January 1971), Hughes speaks as if he were not at the very end but instead at some new beginning. Other poets, he says, suffer the disintegration of Christianity; he, by contrast, celebrates demonic force. More, he calls for a new ritual, a new whirring of 'the elemental power circuit of the Universe'. But we look at him and shy at the brutal light and conclude that he himself—he above all—is beyond the help of ritual. His hand is on the naked wire and he is held there helpless, a celebrant of a sort but a grimly desperate one. '. . . The whole and every individual', writes Schopenhauer, 'bears the stamp of a forced condition. . . .' It is Hughes's distinction to be the poet of this truth. As a thinker he is a hangman, not a priest.

Schopenhauer, Hughes notes, is the only philosopher he 'ever really read'—a case, no doubt, of bringing coals to Newcastle. Hughes would have come round to the same glowering pessimism on his own (and perhaps did), his school the animals. His work gives the impression—A. Alvarez notes the same of his presence—of a being congenitally indifferent to humanism, a mind on the outskirts of civilization, like a boy who skips school and spends the day, even the night, in the woods. That leaves the stars above, gleaming like the barrels of guns, and the animals below, jumping as if at the sound of shots.

In the beginning it was love—a boy's eager love, compounded of curiosity, possessiveness, and adventure. '. . . My interest in animals began when I began', Hughes writes in *Poetry Is* (a series of B.B.C. lectures originally published under the title *Poetry in the Making*). 'My memory goes back pretty clearly to my third year, and by then I had so many of the toy lead animals you could buy in shops that they went right round our flat-topped fireplace fender, nose to tail. . . .' Later, at threshing time, Hughes would snatch mice from under the lifted sheaves till he had thirty or forty crawling inside the lining of his coat. Squirming life! Yet the animals—'the magpies and owls and rabbits and weasels and rats and curlews' his older brother shot—were just as exciting dead. 'He could not shoot enough for me.'

Then it was partisanship and envy, the steaming appetite cooling into respect. In the poems the animals re-emerged not as playthings but as the lords of death and life. In memory and imagination they were gods—or demons, no matter. In what did their superiority consist? In nothing so much as their lack of self-consciousness, of the sicknesses of the mind. No hesitation, no remorse, a mind all reflex, streamlined as a trigger—it began to look like the state before the fall.

In discovering his own death—so it would seem—Hughes concluded that the one thing that mattered was life: he became a worshipper of the claw. An animal's organs represent purely, as Schopenhauer said, 'the will to live in [its] particular circumstances'. Quick eyes, the trap jaw, the noose of the talon—these are forms of vital genius. The creature may be a poor thing of 'forced condition', but it is also a wire that will destroy, if it can, the first mouth that chews it. 'The universal desire for life' is a thing both driven and terrible. No poems so grim and airless, so remote from joy as Hughes's. But if this is life, so be it, he seems to say. Better to fight than die.

Signalling all to come, Hughes's first collected poem, the

title piece of *The Hawk in the Rain* (1957), places man both literally and vitally below the hawk:

> I drown in the drumming ploughland, I drag up
> Heel after heel from the swallowing of the earth's mouth,
> From clay that clutches my each step to the ankle
> With the habit of the dogged grave, but the hawk
>
> Effortlessly at height hangs his still eye . . .

The hawk is 'a diamond point of will', the speaker is turning to mud. So runs the refrain of Hughes's poems, all written in furtive or open contempt for the human as the paltriest instance of the will to live, hence also of 'reality itself', as Schopenhauer would put it. We are all, says another poem, 'held in utter mock by the cats'. Nine to one.

Hughes is primarily a poet of the will to live at the phenomenal level of the leaping blood—which is almost to say at the poetic rather than the philosophical level of his theme. Only infrequently has he descended with Schopenhauer into the darkness below. Once in the somewhat Yeatsian 'Crow Hill':

> What humbles these hills has raised
> The arrogance of blood and bone,
> And thrown the hawk upon the wind,
> And lit the fox in the dripping ground.

Here he invites a glimpse into the vast desire that, in Schopenhauer's words, 'presses impetuously into existence under a million forms . . . eagerly grasping for itself every material of life'. In 'The Bull Moses', he goes down farther still:

> The brow like masonry, the deep-keeled neck:
> Something come up there onto the brink of the gulf,
> Hadn't heard of the world, too deep in itself to be called to,
> Stood in sleep . . .

He thus embodies, again in Schopenhauer's words, 'that which is no longer phenomenon, but thing in itself': the will as pure Cause, in trance at the centre of the world.

If Hughes scorns life, scorns it secretly, in part it is because this radical perspective lingers even in his daylight consciousness, like the black in a coal miner's skin. But he must live in the sun like everyone else; besides, his poet's senses pertinaciously buoy him up there; and there he feels forced to choose between the cat and the man.

To Hughes, the more terrible the beast the more admirable. The stabbing thrush, the slavering wolf, the meat-eating dragon-fly that 'stands in space to take aim', the hawk whose 'manners are tearing off heads', the pig whose 'bite is worse than a horse's', the jaguar waddling 'like a thick Aztec disemboweller', the rat with 'incisors bared to the night spaces, threatening the constellations', the tom that 'Will take the head clean off your simple pullet', the stoat 'Drinking the staring hare dry', the 'carrion-eating skate' with 'cupid lips in its deathly belly'— these are the heroes of his world, his fierce bulwark against nothingness.

To Hughes the human has nothing whatever to recommend it: to be human is to start out *behind* the animals, like a one-legged man in a race. The human mind, for instance—what is it but a kind of missing leg, an ache where the amputated part had been? Not even in Lawrence does the intellect appear so repulsive as in 'Wings', Hughes's poem on Sartre, Kafka, and Einstein. Sartre 'regrows the world inside his skull, like the spectre of a flower', his hands meanwhile sinking 'to the status of flies'. As for Einstein, he has thought himself right out of being:

> The tired mask of folds, the eyes in mourning,
> The sadness of the monkeys in their cage—
> Star peering at star through the walls
> Of a cage full of nothing . . .

'Poetry is nothing if not that', Hughes says in the Faas interview, 'the record of just how the forces of the Universe try to redress some balance disturbed by human error.' So 'Wings' would redress Einstein—rather like the robin that glimpses him walking ('—that was exciting!'). The poem is brilliant with negative grandeur. All the same, one wishes it were not trying so hard to snatch these pale worms from the ground. It wants to punish, to gobble. It is a gesture of contempt.

So mind, in Hughes, takes the sting out of a man. Women, too, incapacitate. They are formidable even though weak. Hughes seems to fear and hate them, like all would-be strong men—like the early Brecht, for instance. They are presented as stale, overpowering wombs, as in 'Crow and Mama', 'Revenge Fable', and 'Song for a Phallus'—mamas squatting on their little boys. Or they are head-swallowing vulvas:

And Crow retched again, before God could stop him.
And woman's vulva dropped over man's neck and tightened.
The two struggled together on the grass.
God struggled to part them, cursed, wept . . .

Nothing more dangerous to an independent man. At their safest,
in Hughes, women are grovelling whores, gravel under the male
heel. In the radio play *The Wound*, the licentious queen and her
ladies have 'faces like ear-wigs', they are 'maggots, writhing,
squirming to split their seams—[a] carnivorous pile of garbage'.
In truth this notion of female vileness is itself vile and we may
be glad Hughes's world is ordinarily reserved for beasts and men.

Only two types of men survive Hughes's pitiless need for
strength, the he-man and the artist. The first boasts what Norman
O. Brown calls the 'simple health that animals enjoy, but not
men'. The Vikings in 'The Warriors of the North' thaw 'at
the red and black disgorging of abbeys, / The bountiful, cleft
casks, / The fluttered bowels of the women of dead burghers'
and Hughes cannot admire them enough. Then there is Dick
Straightup—like a Western hero, too manly even to be sexual,
despite his name:

> Past eighty, but never in eighty years—
> Eighty winters on the windy ridge
> Of England—has he buttoned his shirt or his jacket . . .

'When I imagine one of those warriors in the room', Hughes
writes almost girlishly in 'The Ancient Heroes and the Bomber
Pilot', 'And hear his heart-beat burl . . . my heart / Is cold and
small.' Or take Hughes's retired colonel, his 'face pulped scarlet
with kept rage', a 'man-eating British lion / By a pimply age
brought down':

> Here's his head mounted, though only in rhymes,
> Beside the head of the last English
> Wolf (those starved gloomy times!)
> And the last sturgeon of Thames.

A patriotic toast to a red neck.

For Hughes the he-man's shadow extends into the caves of
sleep. To be able to curl up beyond all danger, to snore fear-
lessly—this is to be like the bull Moses, heavy and dark, a stone
sunk beneath the frantic waters of conscious life. 'The unconscious part, the vegetative life with its ganglion system, into which

in sleep the brain-consciousness disappears', notes Schopenhauer, 'is the common life of all.' Here there is safety, a red strength. Dick Straightup, a local legend, once

> fell in the sleet, late,
> Dammed the pouring gutter; and slept there; and, throughout
> A night searched by shouts and lamps, froze,
> Grew to the road with welts of ice. He has chipped out at dawn
> Warm as a pie and snoring . . .

Other poems sound the implications. In the masterpiece 'November' Hughes writes of the sleeping tramp: 'I thought what strong trust / Slept in him. . . .' Death would not think to stoop so low as that rainy ditch—think to descend there into 'the common life of all'. 'I swell in there, soaking', says the sleeper in 'Wino', a babe in the veined hot interior of the grape, his 'mulatto mother'. Then there are Hughes's witches, demonic queens of night and the common life,

> Nightlong under the blackamoor spraddled,
> Back beside their spouse by dawn . . .

—women to whom the poet pays all the deference gentlemen once showed to ladies.

As for the artist, he has the steel of Nature's involuntary will, he drops on the word, the note, the colour, as the hawk drops on the mouse. Like the thrush, he displays 'bullet and automatic / Purpose': 'Mozart's brain had it, and the shark's mouth / That hungers down the blood-smell even to a leak of its own / Side . . .' The artist works in a fearless, instinctual region of attack where no one heeds 'the minimum practical energy and illumination'— that curse of civilization. Here pleasure is like breakage, Dionysian. Dick and Jack and Dan, drunk themselves, 'sing, / Rightly too, the drunkenness of time'. And Beethoven, whalish of appetite, ugly of mug, laughs with 'black-mouth derisive' at nibbling and pretty aesthetes. '. . . I think of poems as a sort of animal', says Hughes, their stalker.

Though certainly it is easy to see why Hughes is criticized for violence, it isn't really violence he celebrates but an energy too strong for death. Hughes has even written one poem against violence, as if to clear his good name. In 'Wilfred Owen's Photographs' Parliament refuses to abolish the navy's cat-o-nine-tails until 'A witty profound Irishman calls / For a "cat" into the House, and sits to watch / The gentry fingering its stained tails.' True, the poem conveys contempt for the good men's queasiness. Yet its title, with its queer optimism, seems in earnest.

The closest poem to 'Wilfred Owen's Photographs' is 'Crow's Account of the Battle', which, however, is cynical about peace:

> This had happened too often before
> And was going to happen too often in future
> And happened too easily
> Bones were too like lath and twigs
> Blood was too like water . . .

Yet even in its regret over war the poem slings blood and anguish like a clown slinging pies. The truth is that Hughes cannot avoid violence because life to him is a violent conception. And he wants to be on the winning side. His weakness is not violence but the absolute egotism of survival. It is the victor he loves, not war. He thrills to strength with all the envy, the trembling, of a mortal man.

But what is there to either win or lose? In truth, nothing: Hughes is a total nihilist. To keep death from drawing a black line and adding every effort up to zero is, for him, the whole sum of life. It is all a struggle against debit; the credit side is a blank.

Hughes is a nihilist on the scuffling, muscled side of nothingness, the opposite kind from, say, Philip Larkin, who has long since become a wise ghost. Larkin observes life half wistfully, half coldly, as if from the farther side; Hughes is in the midst of the battle, relishing its proof of the will not to die—the correct name of the will to live. Where Larkin has taken 'the grave's part', Hughes is terrified of 'the earth's mouth'. The latter fights shy of the border across which Larkin, glad to be reprieved from eating ash, has slipped almost gratefully.

The logic, of course, lies with Larkin. Hughes's 'wild rebellion' against nullity is, as Schopenhauer would put it, an 'irrational tendency'. It has no 'sufficient reason in the external world'. Driven out of the womb, it is our fate, according to Hughes's 'Existential Song', to run 'for dear life'—but not because life is dear, the running itself prevents that. In 'The Contender' the hero nails himself to life 'Though his body was sweeling away like a torrent on a cliff / Smoking towards dark gorges'. Nothing can budge him. Even 'through his atoms and decay' he grins into 'the ringing nothing'. What a hero! What a fool. For of course his trial of strength is 'senseless'. Several of Hughes's recent poems are full of grinning and black laughter. It is the sound of the will in the void.

Yet there is no telling life (at least not in Hughes) that it has nothing to lose. Waking up to itself in the middle of a race, it means to 'win'. So Hughes sides with the runners out front. Increasingly, though, he seems to have found himself among the losers—to have fallen behind with the weak who eat the dust.

His first two volumes vigorously champion animal wile. They represent a vomition of the human, of death. Hughes perches and gloats with the hawks, runs with the eaters not the eaten. To be sure, even so he cannot outrun himself. His human weakness nags like a tearful child stumbling behind. He is only a partisan, not one of the elect. In an unguarded moment, he even turns up his love of will and discloses its masochistic underside:

> And we longed for a death trampled by such horses
> As every grain of the earth had hooves and mane . . .

All the same, life in these poems keeps its pride. Life is the side to be on. In 'November' even some of the gibbeted animals

> . . . still had their shape
> Had their pride with it; hung, chins on chests,
> Patient to outwait these worst days that beat
> Their crowns bare and dripped from their feet.

In Hughes's two most recent volumes, by contrast, the pride has given way. Rigid and unliving, it was never more than a support to hold up the tunnel while the creature passed. Now the creature halts, terrified of the weight overhead. Living things begin to feel small. Even savage animals no longer save Hughes from himself; rather, his own frailty seeps into them. Hughes has gradually given himself up to his human problems, rather brilliantly.

In the first of these recent volumes, *Wodwo*, the poems about animals are few. It is as if Hughes no longer knew how to pick the creatures up. More, when he does grab hold they are apt to turn and look at him with human eyes. Thus, where the wolf in the preceding volume, *Lupercal*, embodies feral energy, here it represents tormented mind: 'the wolf is small, it comprehends little', it goes 'to and fro, trailing its haunches and whimpering horribly'. The tracks of Hughes's animals now cross the inapprehensible. Metaphysical shock—Pip's madness—has broken their minds. Something like a rage of helplessness, of frustrated consequence, seems to set his skylarks 'Squealing and gibbering and cursing / Heads flung back . . . Like sacrifices set floating'. Something like a metaphysical masochism makes his gnats dance 'A dance giving their bodies to be burned', though 'their mummy faces will never be used'. Hughes's animals have discovered a world that doesn't need them.

In both *Wodwo* and the still more recent *Crow*, the principle of individuation thus does its work only too well. Anxiety begins to radiate from finiteness of being. The source, the mother, all comforting reason or ignorance of unreason, are lost. The nearly human wodwo observes: 'I seem / separate from the ground, and not rooted but dropped / out of nothing casually. . . .' All in all, it is as if the fountain of universal desire had been extinguished and the last drops were descending in isolation down the air.

Yet Hughes will resist this mood, will make or find life ebullient again. His gnats may complain that 'the one sun is too near / It blasts their song', but they add with braggadocio,

> That they are their own sun
> Their own brimming over
> At large in the nothing
> Their wings blurring the blaze . . .

And though the skylark may gibber and scramble 'In a nightmare difficulty / Up through the nothing . . . As if it were too late, too late', it disappears heavenward all the same, leaving the sky 'blank open': 'Only the sun goes silently and endlessly on with the lark's song'. The bird, after all, is

> . . . shot through the crested head
> With the command, Not die
> But climb
>
> Climb
>
> Sing . . .

Even the wodwo, with all his dullness, says, 'I'll go on looking'. Hughes's dependence on will is thus not altogether defeated. If Heidegger has begun to claim him, Schopenhauer claims him still. He is now metaphysically buoyant, now metaphysically low and fearful—a spurt of animal energy, or a mind deflating with a hiss of stale air.

Crow, especially, is a reel of attitudes. The title figure, nimbly embodying opposite extremes, is mythological in the sense that he is a vital yet fantastic being, at once animal and human. Hughes can colour him Schopenhauer, then Heidegger, or middle class, or elemental, or plain crow, and he will remain the same disturbing, curiously indismissible creature. He is Hughes's animal defiance and human jitters in one.

Because he is all the compulsion of instinct, Crow is 'stronger than death'—'evidently'. He is unthinking animal energy, as reflexive as water spat off a stove. He is also helpless animal appetite, unapologetic. 'In the beginning was Scream', and Crow, from the moment of his own beginning, screams for 'Blood / Grubs, crusts / Anything'. A blaze of animal egotism, he is the only creature in the world:

> His wings are the stiff back of his only book,
> Himself the only page—of solid ink . . .

He gazes into time 'Like a leopard into a fat land'. Then he is animal agility—cunning, amazing. Once Stone lumbered towards him, a mistake, for Stone has since 'battered itself featureless' while Crow has become a nimble monster. He can even outskip the flooding 'word'. Admire him, he will endure.

All this was implicit earlier in Hughes's roosting hawk:

> The sun is behind me.
> Nothing has changed since I began.
> My eye has permitted no change.
> I am going to keep things like this.

But the hawk was a hero and Crow . . . Crow is a necessary evil. Since he is its raw material, life, of course, cannot do without him; but that he should be the whole of it, as he threatens! He is matter inadequate to the good. He tries, oh how he tries, but he is—black. A further difference from the hawk: he knows shame. His every feather is 'the fossil of a murder', he feels 'Clothed in his conviction'. True, his guilt is mercifully un-localized; but he is all the more disquieting for that: what he would do to the real Black Beast if he could find him!

When his anxiety deepens, Crow, without losing his crow's

features, embodies empty human consciousness. '. . . the will to live does not appear in consequence of the world', said Schopenhauer, 'but the world in consequence of the will to live'; and perhaps this is echoed in 'Lonely Crow created the gods for playmates'. But for the rest lonely Crow is Heideggerean. For, having created the gods, he becomes the emptiness of the knower as against the fullness of the known. 'The mountain god tore free / And Crow fell back from the wall-face of mountains / By which he was so much lessened.' In the end he is 'his own leftover'. 'Mind is the negative', as Sartre put it. Knowledge is smoke, *being* the fuel. The knower walks out to the end of himself and then is only the distance between himself and what he knows. Hughes's 'Robin Song' laments:

> I am the lost child
> Of the wind
> *Who goes through me looking for something else*
> *Who can't recognize me though I cry. . . .*

Another twist and Crow is the finite beset by the Infinite. Now the sun is not behind but before him, burning. Like the wolf in *Wodwo* he is too little to understand:

> His utmost gaping of brain in his tiny skull
> Was just enough to wonder, about the sea,
>
> What could be hurting so much?

Great ego, famished spirit that he is, he resents being left out:

> Yet the prophecy inside him, like a grimace,
> Was I WILL MEASURE IT ALL AND OWN IT ALL
> AND I WILL BE INSIDE IT
> AS INSIDE MY OWN LAUGHTER . . .

At other moments, however, he pulls back:

> Crow saw the herded mountains, steaming in the morning.
> . . . .
> He saw the stars, fuming away into the black, mushrooms of
>   the nothing forest, clouding their spores, the virus of God.
>
> And he shivered with the horror of Creation. . . .

It is better to be left out. . . .

Of course this very human Crow is a victim—the purest case. Like the next little 'man', he is fool enough to dream: 'Crow thought of a fast car— / It plucked his spine out, and left him empty and armless'. His mama holds on, holds on. His words won't keep things down. Manhattan buys out his song. And though God certainly loves him, 'Otherwise, he would have dropped dead', what then loves 'the shot-pellets / That dribbled from those strung-up mummifying crows?' No, the world's not right, at least for a crow. Fly, evade, still death will trip you up and dangle you from your one remaining claw, 'corrected'.

The theme of Hughes's recent work is, then, the dual horror of existence—that of the monstrous rage for life and that of being small, left out, emptily included. Double-barrelled, it hits a wide target and a poet who had once seemed limited to being the laureate of animals has developed (has suffered to develop) a significant scope. Not that his mind ranges free: it is part boot, part worm. Yet at least the brutal will to live, on the one hand, and the fear of both life and death, on the other, have the virtue of being essential truths. They comprehend, they are respectively, the first impulse and the first hesitation, the sun and the vapour of being. And of this frightening portion of existence—the struggle to live and the nothingness of life—Hughes is a jolting and original poet.

Hughes's style has changed almost from volume to volume. The reason is that his apprehension of his subject has altered also. His manner has bloated or grown lean, smoked up or illuminated, entirely as this changing apprehension has prompted. It could not have been otherwise: poetry is poignant understanding first, words second—though the words will seem always to race the understanding to the goal and get there in advance. The manner is a device for feeling the subject so fully, so precisely, that we will never forget it. But if it succeeds we will not forget the manner, either: it will cling to the subject, or to the memory, like a robe in the wind.

As it turned out, any early faith in Hughes's poetic ability was more than justified. And yet the praise that greeted his first volume, *The Hawk in the Rain* (1957), was not. Critics flocked to the book like ghosts to a pit of blood. Having been starved for violence, they found Hughes's violence—in Edwin Muir's word—'admirable'. The truth, I believe, is that nothing in the book could have turned out admirable, least of all the violence, because of Hughes's relation to his themes.

That relation is one of a sniggering voyeurism—a voyeurism of various forms of sensational extravagance. In fact the book can scarcely be said to have a subject, for extravagance is a romantic refusal of a subject, an excitation of the nerve ends. Here everything—war, childbirth, the weather, laughter, love—is galvanized into the improbable; even the prodigious wears a fright wig. Lovers like 'slavering' wolves yearn to 'sob contentment toward the moon'. A tight-buttocked secretary, if touched by a man, 'would shriek and weeping / Crawl off to nurse the terrible wound'. Jack Horner's 'hedge-scratched pig-splitting arm' grubs its nasty 'get' among the Virgin Mary's 'lilies'. Sympathies fasten 'like flies' to a crashed airman's blood but desert at the sight of his eye staring up from a handkerchief. In short, a puerile, dark titillation is the recurring note. The poems seem dreadfully knowing without displaying the least real knowledge of life.

Following suit, Hughes's manner is strained, pretentious, overexcited—a famine. Occasionally the phrases are welded in a series like brass knuckles: 'and I, / Bloodily grabbed dazed last-moment-counting / Morsel in the earth's mouth'. This leaves the mind stunned but empty. At the same time, the style affects elevation. For instance, 'Fair Choice' tells of 'Suave / Complicity with your vacillation / To your entire undoing'. A stanza in 'Egg-Head' runs:

> Brain in deft opacities,
> Walled in translucencies, shuts out the world's knocking
> With a welcome, and to wide-eyed deafnesses
> Of prudence lets it speak . . .

The egg seems addled. All in all, it is as if Bully the giant had chosen to speak with the lexical mincingness of an Elizabethan page. The sensational embraces the precious, fulsomely. The language attempts to squeeze every thrill out of its subjects and yet be priggishly superior to them. It turns to Shakespeare as to stilts: 'Stamp was not current but they rang and shone / As good gold as any queen's crown'; 'Where admiration's giddy mannequin / Leads every sense to motley'. Here the barbarous aspires to the disquisitional.

Because of his false exploitative relation to his subject, Hughes can neither put word to word with any necessity nor make his poems pace, like animals, involuntarily. Concrete and abstract often mix *against* each other, like salt and sugar: 'blackouts of impassables'; 'their limbs flail / Flesh and beat upon / The inane everywhere of its obstacle'. Nor does concrete meet any more happily with concrete—a hammer 'knits', a jaguar hurries 'after the drills of his eyes / On a short fierce fuse'. As for the rhythm it is subject to cramps: '. . . Here's no heart's more / Open or large than a fist clenched'. At the other extreme it simply flops down: 'Love you I do not say I do or might either.' The volume is, all round, a disaster.

How remarkable that Hughes's next book, *Lupercal* (1960), should have proved an undeniable triumph. Like Larkin, Hughes is one of those poets who grow up miraculously between their first and second volumes. The second breaks like a new day and the old folly is abandoned.

If Hughes is a voyeur of violence in *The Hawk in the Rain*, in *Lupercal* he is a fearful lover of the will to live—a far profounder thing. Wading out at last beyond the froth of violent escapism, he is abruptly stunned by the elemental severity of his subject. His manner contracts at once, thoroughly penetrated by the ancient cold. Now he knows—where before he had been too glutted with sensation to inquire—that the tooth is the clue to existence. He hardens himself, he prepares for battle. Better to speak of *this* subject, he seems to have told himself, in a style as sharp and naked as an incisor.

The better poems in *Lupercal* have the waxy distinctness formed when the imagination presses down hard on actual things: they are taut and clean. In extreme contrast to the first volume, there is now no 'falsifying dream', no fancy or sensational indulgence, between 'hooked head and hooked feet'. The rhetorical fumes have lifted, revealing a world pristine and from the beginning, a world before which Hughes stands and looks, and looks again, matured by awe.

Where nothing in *The Hawk in the Rain* seems seriously observed, here no one can doubt that, if only within a narrow range, Hughes is an incomparable observer—that, for instance, he has seen pike more fully, boldly, and simply than anyone else:

> Pike, three inches long, perfect
> Pike in all parts, green tigering the gold.
> Killers from the egg: the malevolent aged grin.
> They dance on the surface among the flies.

> Or move, stunned by their own grandeur,
> Over a bed of emerald, silhouette
> Of submarine delicacy and horror.
> A hundred feet long in their world . . .

Or doubt, either, that he has seen otters:

> Underwater eyes, an eel's
> Oil of water body, neither fish nor beast is the otter:
> Four-legged yet water-gifted, to outfish fish;
> With webbed feet and long ruddering tail
> And a round head like an old tomcat . . .

or water lilies, or cats, or hawks, or pigs, or the 'month of the drowned dog', November:

> . . . The wind hardened;
> A puff shook a glittering from the thorns,
> And again the rains' dragging grey columns
>
> Smudged the farms. In a moment
> The fields were jumping and smoking . . .

Or finally, his wonder edged with amusement, a bullfrog:

> . . . you pump out
> Whole fogs full of horn—a threat
> As of a liner looming. True
> That, first hearing you
> Disgorging your gouts of darkness like a wounded god,
> Not utterly fantastical I expected
> (As in some antique tale depicted)
> A broken-down bull up to its belly in mud,
> Sucking black swamp up, belching out black cloud
>
> And a squall of gudgeon and lilies.
> A surprise,
> To see you, a boy's prize,
> No bigger than a rat—all dumb silence
> In your little old woman hands.

In all these instances, observation and imagination are so subtly merged that it would be arbitrary to separate them: their beauty is equally objective image and feeling. They display the unfaltering steps of a poet who has at last caught the scent of his destined subject. Now Hughes's words know how to act, where to strike, what to tell; now, it seems, everything is possible to him. To begin with, precision, as in 'submarine delicacy and horror'. Effortless grandeur: 'This evening, motherly summer moves in the pond'. Dramatic *frisson*, as when Cleopatra enjoins the asp, 'Drink me now, whole / With coiled Egypt's past; then from my delta / Swim like a fish toward Rome.' Telling metaphor: 'owlish moons', 'the welding cold', rain plastering the land 'till it was shining / Like hammered lead'. Haunting sensuousness: 'And lit the fox in the dripping ground'. Graceful plainness: 'the blue eye has come clear of time'. Quiet profundity of image, as in 'November', where, once again, the gibbeted owls, hawks, cats, weasels, and crows are 'Patient to outwait these worst days that beat / Their crowns bare and dripped from their feet'. Vocalic and alliterative music, as in the same lines. Imitative rhythm, as again in the persistent drip of these lines. Sybilline statement: 'The crow sleeps glutted and the stoat begins'. Merciless directness, as in 'View of the Pig': 'pink white eyelashes. / Its trotters stuck straight out.' And still other effects, a whole poetic cornucopia.

The richest poems of *Lupercal*—'An Otter', 'Pike', and 'November'—are boldly organized. Though they may seem random, in fact they possess a delicate and contingent unity. Each impression faces the same way, is part of a quivering shoal pointed towards some fountainhead of miraculous adaptation, or horror, or patience, as the case may be. Indeed, this method shows up throughout *Lupercal*, as if after *The Hawk in the Rain* Hughes had determined to throw out the brutal cables of discourse for more subtle and vibrant threads. The result is a remarkable increase in strength—poems lithe and swift and sinewy.

In *Lupercal* Hughes tightens himself like a spring; in his third volume, *Wodwo* (1967), he lets the spring go. He alters, not in his truths, but again in his relation to them: now he throws himself on universal will, riding, not simply observing, energy. The stanza as a contracted ordering of lines gives way to the poem as a free space where life may run—the poems of *Lupercal* look neat on the page, many of those in *Wodwo* sprawl over it and leap down. The new space is almost frightening in its freedom: there seems to be nothing at all just beyond the lines, and nothing, too, in the frequent abrupt gaps between them. Still, having decided what is real, Hughes boldly runs with it. Here his imaginative awe is less contemplative than dramatic. Living things are seen often as from their struggling midst, in a flurry of perceptions.

The rhythm, generously empathic, seems regardless of itself. It is the shadow flying after the subject. It is notable less for exactitude than for a kind of frantic keeping up, as in 'Gnat-Psalm':

> Dancing
> Dancing
> Writing on the air, rubbing out everything they write
> Jerking their letters into knots, into tangles
> Everybody everybody else's yoyo . . .

If the movement ever *becomes* the subject, it is in the third section of 'Skylarks' and in 'Second Glance at a Jaguar'. The first could not be more exact, more inspired:

> I suppose you just gape and let your gaspings
> Rip in and out through your voicebox
> > O lark
>
> And sing inwards as well as outwards
> Like a breaker of ocean milling the shingle
> > O lark
>
> O song, incomprehensibly both ways—
> Joy! Help! Joy! Help!
> > O lark

We take our own breath with each 'O lark' and pause in admiration. The second poem, as it paces on and on menacingly in thirty-three consecutive lines, is perhaps too much of a *tour de force*. Still, its mimicry of its subject seems effortless, an instinctual meeting of poet and jaguar:

> Skinful of bowls, he bowls them,
> The hip going in and out of joint, dropping the spine
> With the urgency of his hurry
> Like a cat going along under thrown stones, under cover . . .

The general effect of *Wodwo* is thus that of the will to live turned up to fever pitch. Even where energy is distanced, as in 'Stations' and parts of 'Scapegoats and Rabies', the irregular lines, the rubbed-out punctuation, the sudden drops, create an impression of near delirium, of a poetry and life more lost in space, with fewer bearings, than any poetry or life heretofore.

The cause of this change in style, apart from the exploding empathy, is what we earlier spoke of as a new element of anguished consciousness. Even the empathic poems betray a scarcely containable anxiety. They jump and dart like animals, but like animals trying to outrun the end.

Much is sacrificed, something gained. Beauty is no longer (in Yeats's phrase) like a tightened bow. One delights in sweep and energy, not in delicate, indelible forms. Detail is lost, as in the whirr of the humming bird. Stop the poem, moreover, to look at the parts and they often seem less than choice, as in 'Ghost Crabs':

> All night, around us or through us,
> They stalk each other, they fasten on to each other,
> They mount each other, they tear each other to pieces,
> They utterly exhaust each other.
> They are the powers of this world.
> We are their bacteria . . .

Hughes seems to lay about for phrases, not to care much about the words themselves. Hence the poems depend in large part on their surge and brilliance of conception; they must come down as wholes, like surf, if they are to move us at all. The exceptions are short pieces similar to the *Lupercal* poems: 'Thistles', 'Still Life', 'Wino', and 'Full Moon and Little Frieda' are perhaps the best of these, each being beautiful throughout. Still, the longer poems, however lacking in exquisiteness, are unlooked-for and compelling adventures. If often prose, they are *bursts* of prose in the stellar regions of poetry. There are few poems so headlong in our literature. Lawrence, Whitman, Williams—the points of comparison are few.

In truth, even the poems most like the *Lupercal* poems are a little sprung: the new virus, which undoes form, has just attacked them; they relax beyond the earlier elliptical brevity. For instance, 'Full Moon and Little Frieda' begins:

> A cool small evening shrunk to a dog bark and the clank of a
> bucket—
>
> And you listening.

The first line liberally gives the evening all the space from which it shrinks; the second confirms the shrinking, the intentness of the ear. Yet, as this example also shows, the poems have their economy, they are canny in form. 'Full Moon and Little Frieda', 'Wino', 'Thistles', 'Still Life', and 'Mountains' (except for its superfluous first three lines) are intelligently brief and almost tangibly rounded, and it would be difficult to say which of them ends the most wonderfully.

Certainly they differ enough from the longer poems—from 'The Howling of Wolves', 'Skylarks', 'Second Glance at a Jaguar', 'Gnat-Psalm', 'Wings', 'You Drive in a Circle', 'Ghost Crabs'— to make it wrong to weigh them together in the same basket. Are they superior to these? How easy to feel that Hughes's full energy and brilliance are not in them. Their form is consummate, but they are not his longest throw. His later style, though it stirs up more than it settles and elbows aside containment, yet spoils us a little for his earlier one—at least if we return to it still reeling from the wilder manner. The truth is that the poems have to be kept apart, like cats and dogs.

The poems in *Crow* (1970; Harper and Row published a slightly expanded edition in 1971) develop from the newer style, being slapdash, forceful, a little noisy and deaf in the ear, breathless. Now, however, the energy has largely dwindled to a nagging thing of the voice:

> There was this hidden grin.
> It wanted a permanent home. It tried faces
> In their forgetful moments, the face for instance
> Of a woman pushing a baby out between her legs
> But that didn't last long the face
> Of a man so preoccupied
> With the flying steel in the instant
> Of the car-crash he left his face
> To itself that was even shorter . . .

Hughes's new poems, like his first, are talk. 'They were usually something of a shock to write', he notes: but they sound like discourse all the same. As experiences most are no more dramatic than the Disney cartoons to which David Lodge has accurately compared them (*Critical Quarterly*, Spring 1971). They are flat if vehement, with only a murky profundity, like that of black marble. And sometimes Hughes has to drop the slab on your foot, at the end, to ensure a strong effect.

Yet what talk this is! It is so pell-mell, so bizarre, so knowingly black, that the reader cannot help but attend. One readily believes

Hughes when he says that 'mostly they wrote themselves quite rapidly'. They are like fat thrown on the fire: ugly to both eye and ear, they yet spit and sizzle, are frantically there. They are fully as discordant and provoking as a crow's call—which, of course, is precisely their intention. And Hughes keeps throwing them out as if Crow were indeed real and sat hugely on the back of his chair, dictating.

Where the *Wodwo* manner confesses anxiety, the new manner reeks of disgust, races with horror. There is great cynicism in the style, which is slung out like hash. At this stage of case-hardened disillusion, so Hughes seems to say, words will all taste the same anyhow. The very indifference of the language is thus expressive. 'The first idea of *Crow*', Hughes observes, 'was originally just to write his songs, the songs that a Crow would sing. In other words, songs with no music whatsoever, in a super-simple and a super-ugly language which would in a way shed everything except just what he wanted to say without any other consideration. . . .' Thus, while the style of *Lupercal* is an attack of beauty on nihilism, the style of *Crow* is the croak of nihilism itself. Impossible to guess from these poems that Hughes could write such a line as 'Reeds, nude and tufted, shiver as they wade' (except for the beginning, here, of 'Dawn's Rose': 'Dawn's rose / is melting an old frost moon').

So this latest manner has its rationale, the spill of the words its compulsion. Still, in most of these poems Hughes wastes himself. A master of language who tosses words on the page—can any aesthetic justify this? Hughes explains that he relinquished the 'musically deeper world' of formal patterning 'to speak a language that raises no ghosts'—but in fact he mostly speaks prose, which is *all* ghost. Fresh and aggressive as his slants on his themes may be, his words themselves are frequently stale:

> He wanted to sing very clear
>
> But this tank had been parked on his voice
> And his throttle was nipped between the Roman's Emperor's
> finger and thumb
>
> Like the neck of a linnet
> And King Kong in person
> Held the loop of his blood like a garotte
> While tycoons gambled with his glands in a fog of cigar
> smoke . . .

This is to jumble old prose queerly rather than select words that will listen to themselves anew. The lines are striking, but in the manner of a deformed hand. Certainly there is nothing in them to make one wish to come back; they lack local genius. The same is true, we said, of the longer *Wodwo* poems, but in fact these last are somewhat happier in detail, less strained and grotesque, more often piercing, and more dramatic and deeply empathic besides. They have more sensual and formal richness than the poems in *Crow*.

Not that all is a loss here even as language. The detail in the first and better half of the volume comes forward a little further with each reading, winning one over. Even a wasted Hughes can prove very good. Consider 'Crow on the Beach':

> Hearing shingle explode, seeing it skip,
> Crow sucked his tongue.
> Seeing sea-grey mash a mountain of itself
> Crow tightened his goose-pimples . . .

If these phrases do not exhilarate, neither do they bore; they have humour, freshness. Better still is 'Dawn's Rose', with its surprise and subtlety, its virtuoso comparisons:

> Desolate is the crow's puckered cry
> As an old woman's mouth
> When the eyelids have finished
> And the hills continue.
>
> A cry
> Wordless
> As the newborn baby's grieving
> On the steely scales.
>
> As the dull gunshot and its after-râle
> Among conifers, in rainy twilight.
>
> Or the suddenly dropped, heavily dropped
> Star of blood on the fat leaf.

Here each word counts. Other poems, too, revert to economy. 'Crow Sickened', 'Oedipus Crow', and 'Crow Blacker than Ever', for instance, are stripped-down narratives. The first even drops the nominative pronoun, so ready a presence is Crow in these poems:

> Unwinding the world like a ball of wool
> Found the last end tied round his finger.
>
> Decided to get death, but whatever
> Walked into his ambush
> Was always his own body . . .

Perhaps the best poem of all is 'Crow's Elephant Totem Song', a queer, delicious fable. It neither flags in tartness and beauty (ugly-beauty), nor violently plops, like many of these poems, on the decayed floor of nihilism:

> They Hyenas sang in the scrub   You are beautiful—
> They showed their scorched heads and grinning expressions
> Like the half-rotted stumps of amputations—
> We envy your grace
> Waltzing through the thorny growth
> O take us with you to the Land of Peaceful . . .

Though this is grotesque, it is not with a vengeance. All these poems avoid the chief bane of the book, namely the list—a fatal device where brilliance of detail has been denied.

> Who owns these scrawny little feet? *Death.*
> Who owns this bristly scorched-looking face? *Death.*
> Who owns these still-working lungs? *Death.*
> Who owns this utility coat of muscles. *Death.*
> Who owns these unspeakable guts? *Death.*

Etc., etc. The attention soon stops dead like chalk hitting a wet spot on the board.

Just as Hughes's words repeatedly sag into prose despite the lines on which they are hung, so his conceptions fall a little too readily into the mean slots of nihilism. In truth he now knows his own mind too well. He needs to pray, like Frost, to have some dust thrown in his eyes. And this is true even though the *Crow* poems crisscross one another. Both the nihilism of the tearing mouth and that of the 'nothinged' mind have become Hughes's familiars. How jolting were he now to write a poem as flexibly free of existential categories as 'An Otter'. He is in the double jeopardy of calling his shots beforehand and of shooting wildly for fear that he will. Often in *Crow* the intention is either patent, as in 'Examination at the Womb-Door', or frantically obscure, as in 'The Smile'. Most of the poems fall to either side of the richest poetry—poetry of conceptual but unconsummated imaginative experience.

Yet, raise objections against the *Crow* poems as we will, the volume itself, Crow-like, remains insistently standing before us, waiting to get its due. And perhaps the truth is just this, that it has to be read and considered as a whole. The poems, good and bad, add to one another; and Crow himself is somehow larger than their sum, so that the subtitle seems exact: 'From the Life and Songs of the Crow'.

In truth, the accumulative virtues are many: the subtle varieties of approach, the dogged essential probing, the metaphysical hopping about, the clever and fresh adaptation of cartoon techniques, the savage humour, the startling obliquities of attack, and, not least, the bristling fascination of Crow himself, the wealth of his black adventures and situations. Then, too, there is the new fearful beauty so randomly struck off, as in the lines on 'the herded mountains, steaming in the morning', or on strange unknown 'littleblood, hiding from the mountains in the mountains'; again in

> So Crow found Proteus—steaming in the sun.
> Stinking with sea-bottom growths
> Like the plug of the earth's sump-outlet.
> There he lay—belching quakily . . .

and again in:

> The grass camps in its tussock
> With its spears and banners, at nightfall.
> . . . .
> And I too am a ghost. I am the ghost
> Of a great general, silent at my chess.
> A million years have gone over
> As I finger one piece.
>
> The dusk waits.
>
> The spears, the banners, wait.

In sum, though the contents of *Crow* are far from being realized past change, the volume itself goes beyond what anyone else would be likely to conceive, let alone bring off. It has an impact that only a very remarkable and inventive talent could create.

What will Hughes do now, having worked his subject so near

the philosophical bone? It is impossible to say; it cannot be an easy position to be in. Yet he has it in his favour that he has already displayed, several times over, a cunning for changing and still surviving as a poet—as if some aesthetic form of the will to live were ruthlessly pushing him on.

Thomas Kinsella

PERHAPS the most seriously talented Irish poet since Yeats, Thomas Kinsella gives us (like glimpses of a shabby backyard) the expectable battered grief over his country's failing heroic spirit. At the same time he displays a steadily increasing scepticism about life itself: an appalled perspective from which even heroism is just tearing. Life for Kinsella is both a moral hell of blind eating, of eating 'pain in each other', and a metaphysical void consisting of the treacherous anterior negation of natural hopes. He thus comprehends the opposing nihilist realms of Hughes and Larkin; but where the other poets colonize them, he simply finds himself from time to time in each. He has little philosophical ambition or curiosity; he rather takes off and unpacks what he feels, itemizing the heavy load. Doubly cursed, an Irishman, a modern man, he walks the earth—guilt and weariness freezing his animal faith—as if it were an overnight moon.

> There is nothing here for sustenance.
> Unbroken sleep were best.
> Hair. Claws. Grey.
> Naked. Wretch. Wither.

Naming the first and last things in their inexorable order, the final six words, hopeless in parataxis, are Kinsella's latest Summa. If they form a graph of the essential Victorian nightmare, it is a nightmare seen now in the grey light of day, without believing resistance, as the ageing view their face in the morning mirror.

The interest—certainly the *achievement*—of Kinsella's work lie in his resistance to this scepticism. Viewed so much from inside, his 'nightnothing' has, as was said, little intellectual consequence. But in countering it he exemplifies—not least in his carefully wrought poetry—the strength and resourcefulness of the constructive will. He has even sought heroic images of a being at once passionate and ordered—images of secular and vital grace. These have not survived in his poetry, nor were they necessary to it, but the will which underlay them was. Making use of his bile, the same will has also informed his attacks on Ireland.

Kinsella's problem as a poet has been to weigh his depression honestly against the truth that, without an animal adherence to life, however wrathful, balked, pained, poetry has no reason to exist. His difficult achievement has been the creation of a dozen or more poems of vital necessity, poems passionately ordered without special pleading on the part of the will.

Like Larkin and Hughes, Kinsella spoke straight out of his own necessity only after masking and ventriloquizing in the necessities of others; he too was one of those contemporary poets who walk about on elegant stilts until, descending, they discover their authority as denizens of gravity. The poems in *Another September* (1958) are so accomplished that they are bad; they have no individuality. The poet's technique acts as a substitute for personality. Here are two examples:

> Weakened with appetite
> Sleep broke like a dish wherein
> A woman lay with golden skin.

> In hospital where windows meet
> With sunlight in a pleasing feat
>   Of airy architecture
> My love has sweets and grapes to eat,
> The air is like a laundered sheet,
>   The world's a varnished picture . . .

Poetry like this comes into being only because a young man has decided to be a poet. It is all familiar surface, so full of 'effect' that it has none. Even the exceptions in the volume—'The Monk', 'Baggot Street Deserta', 'Clarence Mangan', and the beginning of the title poem—are only partial exceptions; the tinkle of the literary exercise still hangs about them.

Then in *Downstream* (1962) Kinsella emerged as a master not of slick verse but—more saddened, more naked, more groping— of a poetry of subdued but unrelenting power. And so he continued to prove in the short sequence *Wormwood* (1966) and the cumulative volume *Nightwalker and Other Poems* (1967). Here surfaced a poetry that, if almost completely without a surprising use of words, all being toned to a grave consistency, has yet the eloquence of a restrained sorrow, a sorrow so lived-in that it seems inevitable. With its sensitive density of mood, its un-self-conscious manner, there is nothing in this poetry for other poets to imitate. Its great quality is the modesty and precision of its seriousness.

Consider 'Tara', in which this modesty is the more apparent because the subject itself is all mist and quietness. Alluding to, rueing, accepting Ireland's extinguished glory, the poem imitates as well the smoking transitoriness of all things. Here the past seems to survive as the debris of a dream:

> The mist hung on the slope, growing whiter
> On the thin grass and dung by the mounds;
> I hesitated at the dyke, among briars.
>
> Our children picked up the wrapped flasks, capes and baskets
> And we trailed downward among whins and thrones
> In a muffled dream, guided by slender axe-shapes.
>
> Our steps scattered on the soft turf, leaving
> No trace, the children's voices like light.
> Low in the sky behind us, a vast silver shield
>
> Seethed and consumed itself in the thick ether.
> A horse appeared at the rampart like a ghost,
> And tossed his neck at ease, with a hint of harness.

The poem shows an art beyond and indifferent to surface excite-ment. Everything here is 'muffled', even the metre, which, despite the stresses, seems softened, diffused by the long clauses. The very absence of rhyme enforces the impression of obscured forms and fastenings. The gentle way the words and lines are bound intimates acquiescence in decay. The alliteration, at the same time that it holds a few of the words together, also enacts disintegra-tion, as when the *s* in 'sky', after extending the shield to vastness by continuing through 'vast silver shield', makes it simmer in 'Seethed and consumed itself' until lost in the thick *th* of 'thick ether'; and at the end its principle of repetition itself hints of harness. So too the diction, precise but not uncaged, not striking, without ambition to stop time, to move or amaze it into amnesty. All in all, here where axe-shapes give directions, where the heroic shield of time itself looks fatally compromised by the mist, the lines trail with the picnic party down the obliterating path of history.

This is a depression so calm, so stable, that it is something new in poetry in English, newly beautiful, newly quiet. All Kinsella's finest poems are written in partial forfeiture to the inevitable destruction of life and pleasure. His art is like the wintered grapevines that growers sheathe in ice to keep off the still colder frost. Thus not only the subtle linkage of his sounds but his imagery has the beauty of stolen fruit—is precious because limited, taken at risk. Here is the close of the long, austere elegy for a fisherman, 'The Shoals Returning':

> The shale-grass shivers around him.
> He turns a shrunken mask
> Of cheekbone and jawbone
> And pursed ancient mouth
> On the sea surface.
> A windswept glitter of light
> Murmurs toward the land.
> His eyes, out of tortoise lids,
> Assess the crystalline plasm,
> Formations of water
> Under falls of air.

The writing is as reticent as the elegized subject, here recalled like a revenant to the 'ravenous element', the scene of his life and death. Difficult not to imagine his eyes, however reptilian, however claimed and changed by his work on the sea, humbly, humanly delighting in the beauty even of the realm in which his spirit will be, has been, 'eaten / In the smell of brine and blood'— the very beauty so cautiously intimated by the lines, as a child gives but a glimpse of a possession he fears to lose, of a possession he fears. Here again is the astringent sensuousness found so often in contemporary British poets—poets as sensitive, as poignant as any but more canny before the threats of pain than most, more concerned to get themselves through. So the lines invite just so much joy in appearance as we can stand to lose, if we must lose it. For instance, 'crystalline' evokes sparkling light and voluptuous glassiness but also the minerally cold and static, which leaves us estranged. And 'plasm' speaks not only of rich glutinous substance but of living material horrifyingly uncontained. Again, 'Formations of water' is determinedly abstract while 'falls of air' activates and beautifies the most abstract of elements—the second phrase supplying what the first withholds and supplying it, moreover, as an unlooked-for gift, the kind we can afford to do without.

At the same time that Kinsella's art claps a stoic hand to the mouth of grief, stands aloof from defeat, proves reticent almost beyond resistance, the salvage work of his images, his craftsmanship, the elegant immaculateness of his style, his meticulous if severe structures, imply a protest against the waste, any waste, of existence. This protest is the pale light shed by the pewter of his lines. '"To Autumn"'—which also recalls to life one who could look on death with measuring eyes—is an excellent example of this ambivalence, this meeting of contrary intentions:

> Insect beads crawl on the warm soil,
> Black carapaces; brittle harvest spiders
> Clamber weightlessly among dry roots
> In soundless bedlam. He sits still writing
> At the edge of the wheatfield, a phantasm of flesh
> > *while thy hook*
> > *Spares . . .*
> Ripened leagues, a plain of odorous seed,
> Quiet scope, season of mastery,
> The last of peace. Along ethereal summits
> A gleam of disintegrating materials
> Held a frail instant at unearthly heights.

Almost reduced to silence as the poem is by its knowledge of destruction, its self-protective taciturnity, still it encircles with the parapet of its words Keats's ripest moment. Forlornly suspended between black carapaces and disintegrating materials, Keats's words seem here to come haltingly from a failing mind; yet it was tenderness that sought them out, so as to make their object, what death spares, what the *poem* spares, Keats himself. The closing image is a tribute to genius as generous and poignant as anything in Keats. And the immense care of the writing looks at once to Keats's mastery and to the pervading fear of disintegration. Only consider the way the absence of a finite verb in the lines on the 'season of mastery' lends at one and the same time a reprieve from death and a disquieting fragility. Nor could 'ethereal' and 'unearthly' be used with more tact, balanced as they are by the laboratory severity of 'disintegrating materials'. The ethereal *l*'s in the final lines, the momentarily held nasals, the breathless aspirates at the beginning and end of the last line, the grasping, assisting stress on 'Held', help make the close a verbal enactment so empathically precise yet so self-possessed that it can both carry and outlast the instant.

Just as Keats's painfully lovely homage to fruition—the plumped images, the seasoned sibilance, the *o*'s round as apples and rich as hazel nuts, the dreamy, humming resonance, the juicy *l*'s, the full rhymes—just as all this has been abstracted into the spare middle of the poem, Keats himself being reduced to a 'phantasm' disturbingly one in sound with 'Clamber' and 'bedlam' as well as 'mastery', so the expansive structure of Keats's poem, its syllogistic poise, has shrunk to a procedure so taciturn as almost to be disjointed: the ode has dwindled to an aside. The sentences refuse to comment on each other; they speak and turn to stone. The poem omits connectives as if fearing that, should it attempt to build a form, it would fall, mere cards. And yet, brilliantly economical, no structure could in fact be more solid, less embarrassed by weak links. At the same time that it lies low, is reticent to escape vulnerability, exposure, naïveté, it is planning all the while how best to survive, and surviving. It avoids the narcotic of repetition as if determined not to be taken unawares. Everything that needs to be said is said, said well and briefly, and in the right order. The poem even manages to ease the anguish latent in all perspective by quickly assuming several in succession, withdrawing from the close-up of the insects to include Keats against the wheat and then widening further to admit the snow-topped summits. Supporting if also tempering this effect, the brittle spiders imply disintegration without beauty, the unearthly heights the disintegration *of* beauty, a more exalting if more painful thing.

Still other poems seem to unhinge themselves before time, the collapse of reason, the reader's indifference—*any* eventuality, all fears—can undo them; yet their odds and ends, too, are masterfully and almost helplessly united. 'Ritual of Departure', for instance, seems both visually and structurally to be coming apart, in keeping with the absence of a binding principle in Irish life, the implicit reason for the speaker's departure. I quote the end of the final section:

> Landscape with ancestral figures . . . names
> Settling and intermixing on the earth,
> The seed in slow retreat, through time and blood,
> Into bestial silence.
>   Faces sharpen and grow blank,
> With eyes for nothing.
>   And their children's children
> Venturing to disperse, some came to Dublin
> To vanish in the city lanes.
>   I saw the light
> Enter from the laneway, through the scullery
> To the foot of the stairs, creep across grey floorboards,
> Sink in plush in the staleness of an inner room.
>
> I scoop at the earth, and sense famine, a first
> Sourness in the clay. The roots tear softly.

Almost line by line the poem decomposes on the page. More, the asterisks between its four sections are like nails fracturing a mirror. And yet the effect of the form, its agreement with the subject, its *completeness*, show that it is right. The poem has the comprehensive discontinuity of successive photographs of a slipping hand. It 'moves' by rejecting one standstill scene after the other—contracts from the reverential opening of 'A dozen silver spoons', 'brilliance in use that fell / Open before the first inheritor', and a pictured Dublin 'More open in an earlier evening light', and the open country, to thoughts of an 'inner room'; degenerates from the 'perfectly' matched spoons, their crested stag rearing at bay, rattling 'A trophied head among . . . gothic rocks', to the 'bestial silence' of contemporary Irish peasants; falls from the panelled 'theatre of swift-moving clouds' and 'pleasant smoke-blue far-off hills' to grey floorboards, the staleness and sourness of modern Ireland—and all as subtly and pitilessly as history itself has pinched the faces of the country people, famished Irish life: a life now as stubbornly wrong as the *o* in 'Sourness' in the final line, an *o* puckered to the front as if in dissent from the sweeter sounds of the nearby 'scoop', 'roots', and 'softly'. The poem is sunk in a hopelessness beyond any effort at diagnosis. Nothing remains, not even to rear at bay—nothing except the enactment of a ritual, the poem itself as a formal valediction, as if at least this much were owed to the 'brilliance', the openness, of the past.

'The Shoals Returning' is equally modernist in its crafted dereliction. Composed in forlorn sections, its structure is a metaphor for human blindness, the labyrinth of experience. The fisherman Gerry Flaherty *'comes from the sea'*, *'sings'*, *'returns'*, *'disappears'*—so say the headings, as remote as a newspaper's except for the concentration implied by their italics: one scene then another and another, until space seems fragmented, time disjunctive. The narrow columns of the poem are like distant doorways through which little can be seen, though that little intensely:

> The boats waited at Smerwyck,
> Black-skinned, crook-backed,
> On the grass by the drying boat-slip;
> The rocky knife-sharp shore
> Drained bare: crayfish stared:
> Brutal torso of conger
> Slid through a choked slit—
> Naked savagery
> On which, when the eyes lift,
> An infinite sheen alights,
> A sheet of blinding water
> Pierced by black points of rock.
> By nightfall the bay ran cold
> With the distant returning tide
> Under the wall of Mount Brandon.
> The clefts brimmed in darkness . . .

A blinkered view, straight out and without relief, a view to be *suffered*. The writing is magnificent, yet magnificently sensuous or magnificently cold? The smaller structures within the larger ones, the short, choppy, unevenly syllabled lines, both protect us from the sea and seem completely at one with it, similarly indifferent to their own movement, their own beauty. This is beauty like the netted fish, gathering weight 'shudder / By shudder', turning 'to unbearable stone'. In both structure and feeling the poem advances bulking, insensible horn, hidden softness and intelligence. Again reticence is eloquence, the fragmentary the full.

In 'Nightwalker', by contrast, the structure mirrors 'madness within' and 'madness without'. The fourteen-page monologue of an official in the Department of Finance (as Kinsella had been) out exercising 'Shadowy flesh', walking the streets of Dublin under the 'fat skull' of the moon, seeing television watchers 'snuggle in their cells / Faintly luminous, like grubs', recalling 'Bruder and Schwester—Two young Germans' wanting earlier in the day 'to transfer investment income', their faces 'livid with little splashes / Of blazing fat', and spinning stunningly bilious fables of Ireland's destiny of self-sabotage, the poem is powerfully harsh with contemptuous hopelessness, regret for lost heroism, loathing for 'Massed human wills'—its moon a horrifying 'hatcher of peoples'. Here, with aching lungs, Irish poetry comes abreast of 'The Waste Land' and 'Hugh Selwyn Mauberley'. It has been thrown with the centrifugal flight of a culture losing its provincial integrity, its safety, into that modern space in which, however populous, the individual finds himself receding from everyone. In particular, Kinsella, like his predecessors, looks on his own culture as a moral catastrophe, an alien unreason that, since it contaminates him, is not alien enough. His poem has the extreme bitterness of a man who finds that the last refuge of his virtue is his despair. If more continuous, less allusive and difficult than 'The Waste Land', its structure similarly expresses, through slips and shifts, both uncontrollable cultural disintegration and personal misery, the spirit writhing to find a tenable position. It, too, alternates with disconcerting unpredictability—with intent method—between objectivity and subjective theatre, nightmare, jagged emotionalism. The fuses overload, the truth flashes, is a truth grown monstrous.

In one sense 'Nightwalker' is even more 'modern' than 'The Waste Land', forty years more advanced in despair. And yet, probably for the same reason, it is aesthetically wearier. Like Robert Lowell's poetry it brings out by contrast the experimental brightness, the sophisticated buoyancy of Eliot's great poem. With its cool, modelled precision and showmanship, 'The Waste Land' now looks like the work of a lively young poet (convalescent though Eliot may have been, and assisted by Pound) completely on top of his material and out to dazzle the wizened eyes of English poetry—and Pound's poem has the same Yankee energy. 'Nightwalker' is certainly deft and, for a work coming out of the English tradition (Eliot's poem rather broke into it), undeniably bold. And yet properly, given the defeatist mood it assumes, its manner is less invented than that of 'The Waste Land' or even 'Hugh Selwyn Mauberley'. It is a masterful constellation of familiar styles, restively twisting from one to the other, finding none sufficient, ringing each with parody—now bitter-sweetly lyrical, now prosaic, now metatheatrical, now luridly expressionistic, now satirical. Moreover, the same grey tone prevails throughout, so that the various styles all but blur into one. The language, though characteristically meticulous, shaped, poised, is not exquisite. It is sculptured from dour pumice stone, not Poundian 'alabaster', and is too morose for the '"sculpture" of rhyme'. The words seem dragged down by the lagging blank verse. And the verse itself, if formal, scarcely credits measure. As *traditional* form it is as perfunctory, as much a habit no longer believed in, as exercise for 'Shadowy flesh' or government service. In all, the poem is stalled between anxiety and saturnine resignation, aesthetic adventurousness and aesthetic doldrums—but powerfully stalled, like a dream from which the dreamer wants to wake.

The triumph of 'Nightwalker' as a construction is that, for all its splintered logic, its associative jerks between narrative and hallucinatory fantasy, the pressure never lets up, everything having equally a note of corrosive misery, the terror of an abscess that is too full. Endlessly resourceful, thoroughly worked out and worked over despite its lived-out nausea, *felicitously* flaring, like the final, futile straining of the stork's wings as it alights, the odyssey over, it stands as a rebuke to the country its author loves, scorns, regrets: the country that has, in its ill fortune, the good fortune to arouse so *much* regret.

So it is that, whether on the fields of his sounds, his diction, his images, or his structures, Kinsella's love of heroic human character, of natural beauty, his love-hatred of Ireland, above all his love of the blown glass of words, wars with his scepticism and depression. And so it is that the poems face at once towards their own extinction and towards a defiance of human defeat. This is art at the crossroads, going out, turning back, ambiguously arrested like a raised arm that could either be greeting or fending off. Yet we cannot really regret a poetry able to discover, in its straits, such lines as 'Formations of water / Under falls of air', such structures as those of '"To Autumn"' or 'Ritual of Departure', such new mottling of familiar resources as moves us in 'Nightwalker'. The poems display the poet's *traditional* ability to join words with the intelligence, the just-born, unguessably old infusing spirit, the care and control, that the rest of the world seems increasingly without.

And yet, as was observed, Kinsella does not leave it to his art alone to exemplify the passionate order that is at once his answer to scepticism and, in its absence, the greatest reason for it. Several of his poems, among them some of his best, are intent to conjure into existence, or to happen upon, to seize, instances and models in life itself of vital poise.

The best, longest, and most ambitious of these are 'Downstream', 'A Country Walk', and 'Phoenix Park', and perhaps it is no accident that all three—together with Larkin's 'Whitsun Weddings' and Graham's 'The Nightfishing'—illustrate a new kind of reflective poem, the modern poem of travel. Like certain earlier poems—Gray's 'Eton Ode', for instance, or Wordsworth's 'Tintern Abbey'—these face a solitary consciousness towards place and time yet do not, as it were, sit still, are not even ostensibly at rest, but move through the world, continually stimulated to new observations, reactions, associations. Cast through space, these poems bring a flutter to the tentativeness of consciousness, which they heighten. They ride on motion the way, and at the same time as, the mind floats on duration. Informed by our contemporary hypersensitivity to the moment, they say that life is only here and now, and fleeting, a thing that *cannot* stand still; and more, that space is as unfathomably deep as time, is time's body, but at least outside ourselves, both mercifully and cruelly outside. The poems increase the sense of exposure to existence as actual travel renews and magnifies the sensation of living.

And in so doing they seem to draw Kinsella out to the front of himself in expectation, curiosity, involvement in life—an involvement lacking energy in the other poems, discouraged, but here released as if by the momentous motion of the poems. In consequence Kinsella's personal presence proves surprisingly pressing and immediate. He is there before us as a chaos in search of an order. Indeed, his poems, being singlehanded attempts to haul his existence into unity, seem more American than Irish and by the same token more Irish than English. They rise from a nearly insurmountable interior isolation, from a scepticism of the social world so total that the poet seems all but lost in himself; and yet he comes out, all the same, to forge or claim as his own some image of order in the world. (All this is true of 'Night-walker', too, except that it is heroic only in its craft and residual wrath and that, instead of seeking passionate being, it digs into life, in its own passion, with the nails of despair.)

In 'Downstream' and 'A Country Walk' the one answer to the devastations of history—an answer so slight as to be pathetic, so beautiful as to steel hope—is the sight of, a momentary empathy with, an instance of vital serenity in nature. The speaker in the first poem, rowing with an unidentified companion through a narrowing channel full of the sly intimidations of dusk, a channel spectral, besides, with recollections of the Second World War, finds himself downstream indeed from 'the primal clarities' of the Greco-Christian past; and finally his skiff is sped into the Mill-Hole, 'a pit of night'—an emblem of modern history, 'the cold fin / Turning in its heart'. For him (as for most modern artists) the centre of gravity has shifted downward into terror:

> . . . The river bed
>
> Called to our flesh. Across the water skin,
> Breathless, our shell trembled. The abyss . . .

It is just here, however, beside what the first, longer version identifies as a former religious retreat 'Where teacher and saint declined in ghostly white, / Their crosses silent in a hush of wills', that the speaker discerns, drifting in living white on 'pure depth' itself, an emblem of vital order:

> . . . A milk-white breast . . .
> A shuffle of wings betrayed with feathery kiss
>
> A soul of white with darkness for a nest.
> The creature bore the night so tranquilly
> I lifted up my eyes . . .

For a moment the old stability of nature, the unconscious trust achieved through ages of struggle, quiets the human will. Here, without sacrificing itself, life attains grace. Opposites kiss, fear sleeps. Vitality and order have been reconciled.

In 'A Country Walk' the example of ideal order, more

obviously dynamic, more troubled in its serenity, is the river to which the speaker comes after escaping 'the piercing company of women': a river that, 'Under a darkening and clearing heaven', its 'face a-swarm', its 'thousand currents . . . Kissing, dismembering', sliding in 'troubled union', giving and swallowing light, relieves the great sickness from his feeling. Poetry recognizing its own in this passionate dispassion, this restless calm, 'Heart and tongue were loosed: / "The waters hurtle through the flooded night. . . ."'

Here is the releasing order missing from the 'gombeen jungle' of the proximate town square, from turbulent sexual relations, from historical Ireland, whose monuments to violence the speaker has passed, and finally from the town as seen earlier from a hill top, 'mated, like a fall of rock, with time'. Here, on the other hand, is the stir and impulse missing from the priest glimpsed a moment before, his 'eyes / That never looked on lover' measuring the speaker's 'Over the Christian Brothers' frosted glass', and from the three cattle seen at the outset, soothing as they were, indeed in another world, as they

> . . . turned aside
> Their fragrant bodies from a corner gate
> And down the sucking chaos of a hedge
> Churned land to liquid in their dreamy passage . . .

Here in the river under Hesperus in 'green and golden light', not human and yet not in another sphere, here in the river running like the thousand currents of a man's life, is the identity of power with form, the rare and wonderful balance that satisfies flesh and spirit alike, killing the misery in the excess of either, one with the reason of the soul.

These poems are wholly in accord with themselves, their conscious appreciation of united flow and pattern, impulse and rest, being implicit, evident, admirable in their very procedures—certified by them, emulated. Even as 'Downstream' sends the speaker out in search of order—readying him through the enchantment of movement, half mesmeric, half anticipatory, for an image that will strike with the enlarged force of the images in dreams yet not endure because, like a dream image, an effect of time and need—all its fears and horrors prepare and unconsciously call out for the moment when the swan startles with its almost perfect, its vitally stirring, peace. And then when the rock where the speaker seeks a landing place towers and blots the heavens, to which the sight of the swan had involuntarily directed his eyes, order alluding to order, the poem is over, ending as it has to in the actual darkness here below. The poem never fixes on anything and yet it is all as continuous and determined and beautiful as the unwinding of a lustrous grey cloth, a cloth that darkens, like the twilight, as it unfolds. Just as the movement of the poem merges the interest of the local and fugitive with the fascination of movement itself, so the implicit life of every image is one with the import of the poem as a whole. And 'A Country Walk', through the protagonists' furious or envious notice of objects, picks up and bears along the outer world as casually yet peremptorily as a river gathers debris, and at the end, having swollen to its utmost capacity, seems to pour in silence past its own last words. Neither poem wills its order, or they will it without willfulness. Everything in them coheres yet not as if by conscious effort.

Meanwhile, their style, classical in its gravity and poise, itself reconciles emotion and order. The blank verse of 'A Country Walk', disturbed yet distinct as a pattern, is at once intent and dreamy, exact and elegant, vigorous and serene, as in these lines on the town,

> Below me, right and left, the valley floor
> Tilted in a silence full of storms;
> A ruined aqueduct in delicate rigor
> Clenched cat-backed, rooted to one horizon . . .

or these,

> . . . A line of roofs
> Fused in veils of rain and steely light
> As the dying sun struck it huge glancing blows . . .

or here,

> Then came harsh winters, motionless waterbirds,
> And generations that let welcome fail . . .

or (it is hard to stop quoting from this immaculate poem) the exquisite line,

> The littered fields where summer broke and fled . . .

The style of 'Downstream', less concentrated, without angry

edge, is detached and yet mimetic in its flow, line by line, stanza
through stanza. Indeed, perhaps never has *terza rima* been given
such a 'liquid grip':

> Again in the mirrored dusk the paddles sank.
> We thrust forward, swaying both as one.
> The ripples scattered to the ghostly bank
>
> Where willows, with their shadows half undone,
> Hung to the water, mowing like the blind.
> The current seized our skiff. We let it run
>
> Grazing the reeds, and let the land unwind
> In stealth on either hand . . .

Few of the lines, few of the stanzas, are stopped; the verse flows,
yet not evenly, halting again and again internally, as if in sudden
and momentary releases from the current. The writing is eloquent without being luxurious, with merely the rich sufficiency
that flowing water itself seems to possess. The metre adds sway,
the rhymes sink 'as one', like the paddles. And the stanzas themselves are held together in one stream by the interlinking rhymes
as well as by *enjambement*. The style kisses, dismembers; bears
tormented consciousness tranquilly along.

'Phoenix Park' is less happy, if more ambitious, than these two
fine poems. Here Kinsella's repressed 'racked heroic' nerve is
deflected from Ireland on to love; the river floods a furrow.
Married love as 'ordeal', as a furnace for the 'designing will',
as a system for turning selfish flesh into 'crystalline' understanding,
becomes for a poet frequently nauseated by appetite (in 'At The
Crossroads' even the moon stares 'from the void, tilted over /
her mouth ready'!) the 'one positive dream', replacing the great
orders of the past. Here is at once a crucible for vitality and a
dignified support for animal faith, a defiance of the nihilistic
'phantasm' that aches 'to plant one kiss / In the live crystal' of
forgiving love. The speaker and his wife, making a farewell
drive through the environs of Phoenix Park, preparing to leave
Ireland, are like nomads whose only tent, tattered as it is, is each
other.

Here, by contrast with the other poems, the movement is not
identical with a need for order but an indication that the little
order for two that lies in marriage is independent of the
world, though both elegiac and seeking all the same a less 'sour

present' than Ireland's. Putatively a pattern already existing in a relationship, this fragile, difficult order is articulated over the nostalgic drive like talkative hope over an acknowledged, not quite decisive discouragement. The problem is that it is too much mere talk. Neither the menace the flesh poses to understanding nor the 'increase' imputed to love as 'ordeal' is apparent in this apologetically discursive poem. Its central conceit of an 'ordeal-cup', in which the mineral and the biological mix awkwardly, forms an image so remote from actual experience that none gets into it. And when the conclusion tells us that 'Loneliness' also draws important emotional events 'into order'— the very events love is said to organize—love comes to seem less than the 'one' positive resource and the speaker uncertain of his experience. In 'Phoenix Park', as though reacting against the galled defeatism of 'Nightwalker', as though trying to rise like a phoenix itself from the angry flames of that earlier, more convincing poem, Kinsella has exerted his will all too strenuously, if also wearily. The 'positive dream' is at once too desperately positive, too much a mere dream.

In proportion as the poem wills order (the order *of* the poem is also infelicitous, the poem ending behind itself on a period already outgrown), the writing is woolly, similarly giving the wish for the deed. In places it has too little flesh, too little passion:

> *Fragility echoing fragilities*
> *From whom I have had every distinctness*
> *Accommodate me still, where—folded in peace*
> *And undergoing with ghostly gaiety*
> *Inner immolation, shallowly breathing—*
>
> *You approach the centre by its own sweet light.*
> *I consign my designing will stonily*
> *To your flames. Wrapped in that rosy fleece, two lives*
> *Burn down around one love, one flickering-eyed*
> *Stone self becomes more patient than its own stone . . .*

Somewhere behind '*Fragility echoing fragilities*' is a living woman and her provocations to a man's self-understanding; but the language seems to want to obscure this. Moreover, to speak of being accommodated by distinctness is perhaps not to speak distinctly enough. The writing is poised but 'ghostly', rather private, unforthcoming. And if it were more fully awake would it conceive a 'Stone self' as being capable of degrees of patience?

Yet 'Phoenix Park' is not easily dismissed. Not only is it rich enough in thought, subtle enough, serious enough, to repay rereadings; whenever it ceases to philosophize and *observes*, it is wonderful, as in the stanzas in section IV on distant Dublin, 'An eighteenth century prospect to the sea' and 'wicked laughter' rising, and perhaps even more in this earlier passage, almost a poem in itself:

> You are quiet and watchful, this last visit.
> We pass the shapes of cattle blurred by moisture;
> A few deer lift up their wet horns from the grass;
>
> A smoke-soft odour of graves . . . our native damp.
> A twig with two damp leaves drops on the bonnet
> From the upper world, trembling; shows us its clean
> Fracture and vanishes, snatched off by the wind:
> Droplets of moisture shudder on the windscreen.
>
> —You start at the suddenness, as though it were
> Your own delicate distinct flesh that had snapped.
> What was in your thoughts . . . saying after a while
> I write you nothing, no love songs, any more?
> *Fragility echoing fragilities . . .*

Here the final line collects and focuses all the fragilities of the hour—the blurred cattle, the apprehensive deer, the native odour of graves, the trembling and snatched twig, the shuddering droplets, the woman's delicate flesh, her anxiety over the passing of love—and is not so much an abstraction, as in its later use, as the closing of a circuit, a consummation. The woman's fragility is brought forward by tender perception not as a ghostly influence but as her own life-quality. How finely, too, the motif of fragility is counterpointed by the steady tone and composure of line, by the wet horns and windscreen and the watchfulness of both husband and wife, all signalling possibilities of strength even amid the 'odour of graves'. That measured line of almost placid monosyllables, 'A few deer lift up their wet horns from the grass', gives the most delicate hint of each, balancing against a pictured anxiety an aural stability.

With its intelligent flesh, its vital spirit, its subdued living order, such writing prevails both as a model and as an expression of love, of a crystallizing relationship between life and form.

The spirit is almost happy in it, is at rest, because, as in the descriptions of the floating swan and the light-giving, light-swallowing river, it has found for the moment a scene, the words, by which to know and accept itself. This poet who seldom writes from and about ideas is really more felicitous without them. His most natural subject is the silent clasp when a torn man—whether a fisherman, a Romantic poet, a patriot, or a lover—makes peace with the world that has torn him.

Unfortunately, what Kinsella's most recent volume, *New Poems* (1973), reveals is that the death of the will to order is just as likely as its excess to lead to washed-out, unwilling writing. The new poems evince an extreme depression of his art and spirit. The dejection once held back by the poet's pride in his own mastery now meets with little resistance, seems to have soaked right through the forms and language. After his effort in 'Phoenix Park' to rise from despair, Kinsella has slumped back into defeatism with a vengeance. Discouraged by the world, the new poetry stagnates in tired literary fantasy ('I saw, presently, it was a cauldron: / ceaselessly over its lip a vapour of forms / curdled, glittered and vanished . . . I confess / my heart, as I stole through to my enterprise, / hammered in fear'), or revisits actual scenes with the bleary eyes of a malcontent. Though the volume contains effective lines and passages, notably in 'The Liffey Hill', 'A Selected Life', 'Touching the River', 'The Route of the Táin', the poems on childhood, and the uncharacteristically graphic 'Crab Orchard Sanctuary: Late October',

> The lake water lifted a little and fell
> doped and dreamy in the late heat.
> The air at lung temperature—like the end of the world . . .

still as a whole it seems the work of a poet for whom no strong sensation remains.

Indeed, in opening at last the trunk of his childhood, Kinsella seems to have discovered, like Larkin, an *initial* void: 'Not even in my mind / has one silvery string picked / a single sound. And it will never.' His animal faith—so he now interprets it—was all along like wet wood that the world failed to ignite. Dour adults towering about him like headstones, he could not see *life* except as the little that waited, grumbling, on this side of death, the visible, grievous side. Precocious at despair, he says of the death of his infant sister,

> . . . My own
> wail of child-animal grief
> was soon done, with any early guess
>
> at sad dullness and tedious pain
> and lives bitter with hard bondage . . .

His grandmother—in life a black-aproned Fate, 'lines of ill-temper' round her mouth—proved in death a terrifying Siren of decay:

> I couldn't stir at first, nor wished to,
> for fear she might turn and tempt me
> (my own father's mother)
> with open mouth
>
> —with some fierce wheedling whisper—
> to hide myself one last time
> against her, and bury my
> self in her drying mud.
>
> Was I to kiss her? As soon
> kiss the damp that crept
> in the flowered walls
> of this pit . . .

In brief, childhood in these poems is a dumbly frightened 'hand of solo': 'Jack Rat grins'.

The poet of *New Poems* is even less animally secure than this child, scattered as he is 'in a million droplets of fright and loneliness'.

> The sterile: it is a whole matter in itself.
> Fantastic millions of
> fragile
>
> in every single

'All Is Emptiness / and I Must Spin' runs one of his titles—and in parts of these poems Kinsella is in truth reduced to writing for the mere form of it. Beyond every emotion that attaches to the world—beyond even nostalgia and anger, the respective last stands of Larkin and Hughes—he seems unable to judge his own creativity, so that he can end the poem 'Tear', for instance, with lines hard to credit to the master of, say, 'The Shoals Returning':

> Old age can digest
> anything: the commotion
> at Heaven's gate—the struggle
> in store for you all your life.
>
> How long and hard it is
> before you get to Heaven,
> unless like little Agnes
> you vanish with early tears . . .

Yet even in *New Poems*, however unsure and intermittent, one passion in Kinsella remains: the passion for selectivity and movement, for 'putting together'. It has gone pale, you may think—and certainly the passages of fantasy are sickly. But reread the poems, make yourself as patient as water on a windless day, and you find that, for the most part, the passion has only grown more delicate, gaining in refinement what it loses in force. Kinsella is still an artist, his poems 'a labour', as he says of his rescue-work translation of *The Táin*, 'of some kind of love'. Suffocating under his depression but still alive is the desire to pay homage to art, nature, courage, love—to everything great. 'Certain gaps in ourselves', he remarks in his superbly intelligent and sensitive lecture 'The Irish Writer', 'can swallow up all the potentiality in the world', and though Kinsella is in danger of leaving nothing *outside* himself, still he haunts the edge of potentiality, observant if no longer hopeful. If his new art, for instance 'The Liffey Hill', really *is* new—at least as new as Lowell's *For the Union Dead*—the reason lies in his spiritual extremity. His tenuous structures are the metonyms of a spirit on the verge of disintegration. All the same, our wish for Kinsella as a poet must be that the protesting animal in him will regain its strength; the security of his touch depends on it, as does the vigour of his art, its bruised bloom.

Stevie Smith

STEVIE SMITH had a wonderfully various mind and her work is a forest of themes and attitudes. In large part it was her intelligence and honesty that led to this—to the protean, compound substance we all are. She was rather fierce about the truth—a modern peculiarity. The encouragement the age gives to both acceptance and doubt, the way it leaves us with the museum of everything without much trust in any of it, made her at once diverse and sardonic. '. . . we are born in an age of unrest', observes Celia, the narrator of her third novel, *The Holiday* (1949), 'and unrestful we are, with a vengeance.' Evidently Smith was prone to be sardonic anyway. Perhaps because her father had deserted to a life on the sea when she was young, she was quick to turn 'cold and furious' about anything selfish or unjust. Calling the heroines of her novels after Casmilus, 'shiftiest of namesakes, most treacherous lecherous and delinquent of Olympians', she seems also to have been nagged by a sense of unworthiness that may have gained strength from the same experience. In any case, fatherless, she would be 'nervy, bold and grim'; she would fend for herself. And clever as the next person, in fact cleverer, she would be nobody's fool, nor suffer foolishness. All this gives a wickedly unstable and swift slashing quality to her work. She herself is not to be trusted—except to be formidable, unpredictable, remorseless.

To a degree, however, Death stood in for Smith's father; she looked up to it, ran to it when she was hurt, needed its love. In *Novel on Yellow Paper* (1937), the heroine, Pompey, is sent to a convalescent home at age eight and there appalled by a maid's 'arbitrary' motherly feeling; 'it was so insecure, so without depth or significance. It was so similar in outward form, and so asunder and apart, so deceitful and so barbarous in significance.' Soon after, she becomes afraid for her mother, who suffers from heart disease—and terrified once again for herself, since there is nothing she can do: she is reduced to 'fury and impotence', 'a very hateful combination'. Thus startled into distrust of life, she discovers the great trustworthiness of death. 'Always the buoyant, ethereal and noble thought is in my mind: Death is my servant.' Let life do its worst, the black knight can be summoned. Indeed, what could be more liberating for the mind, keep it 'so quick and so swift and so glancing, and so proud'?

Thus allied, this clever poet was free to dance around life rather mockingly. Of course if she mocked certain things it was because they deserved it. 'I certainly have a flippant and frivolous mind,' says Pompey, 'I certainly get worse having this flippant and frivolous mind the older I get.' She enjoys this wickedness, then, she proclaims it: the sentence has the delicious emphasis of a boast. But what the context reveals—the subject being Christianity—is that she is really too serious to be serious about some things. (Smith kept up a running fire on 'this Christian religious idea', which is 'too tidy, too tidy by far. In its extreme tidy logic . . . a diminution and a lie'.) If the poet mocks life itself—life on the loose—it is only because she fears it: her flippancy is a defence against its gravity. 'But it is not necessary to dwell on these horrid, horrid things, when there is so much in life that is pie-eyed and daisy-sweet. Is it? Are there not?' There (from *Novel on Yellow Paper*) is her delightful, disturbing ironic note, sardonic yet curiously high spirited.

Smith's combination of honesty and 'wicked bounce' makes her work a tonic. Considering the risks she ran, she wrote remarkably few poems that are clever or zany for their own sake. If her novels are too clever by half, the poems are as clever as they should be—clever beyond reasonable expectation. Much as she plays with her moods and insights, much as she remains sprightly and astonishingly inventive in poem after poem from the first volumes of the late Thirties to the posthumous *Scorpion and Other Poems* (1971), her work has almost always the dignity of disciplined seriousness. Of course like the sketches that often accompany them, many are slight—but they are frankly *hors d'œuvres*, and justified by their unique tone or epigrammatic incisiveness.

Nor did Smith's secret betrothal to death keep her from delight

in life—from loving friends or the earth with 'the waters around
[it] curled'. Indeed, she was blessed with a capacity for careless,
innocent joy—an 'instinctuality', in words from *The Holiday*, that
brought 'with it so much glee . . . so much of a truly imperial
meekness'. The child in her, prematurely replaced by the adult,
seems to have followed her like a shadow through her days, as
a memory, a promise, of unlimited pleasure. It was not, in fact,
Death she revered but the fountaining impulse of being. Indeed,
she proved in certain poems—several of them among her best—
one of the rare celebrators of what Blake called 'Eternal Delight'.
If her bounce was often 'wicked' it was only because and in so far
as this essential, transcendent joy was thwarted by circumstance
or some inherent curse, some Original Contradiction.

But certainly it *was* thwarted and perhaps no poet's work
has ever seemed so much a quarrel of classical scepticism and
romantic liberation. Smith was open to every likelihood and
perhaps finally partial to none. Few so skilful at opening a crevasse
between two truths. Is it wise to abandon hope wholly? 'No,
it is not wise'. Is it wise to endure when Death's a prize easy to
carry? 'No, it is not wise.' Certainty of this kind is worse than
the uncertainty it resembles; it is wisdom past cure.

Just as the truth is mixed for Smith, so her poems are frequently
startling and seemingly extempore mixtures of elements. She
likes particularly to combine the archaic and the contemporary,
the measured and the runaway. Often she brings a breezy or
nervously colloquial manner to old-fashioned themes or traditional stories; so a poem on Rapunzel ends,

> What's that darling? You can't hear me?
> That's odd. I can hear you quite distinctly . . .

and a river god speaks with disarming, updated frankness:

> And I like the people to bathe in me, especially women.
> But I can drown the fools
> Who bathe too close to the weir, contrary to rules.
> And they take a long time drowning
> As I throw them up now and then in a spirit of clowning.
> Hi yih, yippity-yap, merrily I flow,
> Oh I may be an old foul river but I have plenty of go . . .

Where archaic measure avers assurance, Smith's rapid contemporary line, often long and unbound, dashes through silence

as if uncertain of its right to interrupt it. Occasionally it rattles
dramatically, abruptly, impatiently, out of a metrical opening,
and then it may simulate the brusque, offhand dealings of life
itself. 'My soul within the shades of night', begins 'The Recluse'
harmoniously; 'O too little wisdom and too much compunction',
the same poem ends, its rhythm 'undone' like the soul of the
recluse, a woman foolish enough to allow a girl to break her
'chain of delicious / Melancholy' and draw her briefly into the
sun. Another poem begins:

> I am a girl who loves to shoot,
> I love the feathered fowl and brute,
> I love them with a love as strong
> As ever there came from heaven down . . .

But this is bravado, an attempt to out-sing question; and imme-
diately the poem landslides towards prose and self-justification:

> Why should I not love them living as dead?
> As I shoot, as I shoot, and as my fine dog Tray
> Brings the shot one to hand, he is I, I am they.
> Oh why do my friends think this love is so questionable?
> They say they love animals but they do not love them as I am
>   able . . .

Smith sometimes uses metre as a foil, to show where we have
been or would like to be before showing where we are.

Occasionally after wrapping the cloak of archaic verse about
her she simply leaves it on, enjoying its weight and feel. Here
is the conclusion of 'Edmonton, thy cemetery . . .':

> I love the dead, I cry, I love
> Each happy happy one.
>
> Till Doubt returns with dreary face
> And fills my heart with dread
> For all the tens and tens and tens
> That must make up a hundred,
> And I begin to sing with him
> As if Belief had never been
> Ah me, the countless dead, ah me
> The countless countless dead.

She seems to delight in the metronomic rhythm, the sappy,
effective antithesis of 'happy happy' with 'countless countless',

the patina on 'dreary', 'fills my heart', and 'Ah me'—to enter
wholeheartedly into the crooning melancholy of the verse.
Yet surely the tearful eye of the poem is about to wink. 'As if'
Belief had never been indeed! But the mockery—as in the
toddler's rhyme of 'hundred' and 'dread' or the lisping 'tens and
tens and tens'—means no harm, nor need it when 'Doubt' is as
negative as any mockery. Smith characteristically looks on the
past with an ambiguous expression, at once nostalgic and dis-
believing.

On the other hand, Smith's poems are often solely in her
contemporary voice, as here in the beautiful beginning of
'Black March':

> I have a friend
> At the end
> Of the world.
> His name is a breath
>
> Of fresh air.
> He is dressed in
> Grey chiffon. At least
> I think it is chiffon.
> It has a
> Peculiar look, like smoke.
>
> It wraps him round
> It blows out of place
> It conceals him
> I have not seen his face . . .

If this is typically rapid, it is, of course, not from anxiety but from
eagerness: the short lines and stanzas suggest a haste to be gone.
One of the advantages of Smith's almost chattering manner is
that it allows stretch and snap to the verse, as here in her most
familiar poem, 'Not Waving but Drowning':

> Nobody heard him, the dead man,
> But still he lay moaning:
> I was much further out than you thought
> And not waving but drowning . . .

Disabused beyond the naïve, musical air of 'poetry', her colloquial
line often insists on its plain truth-telling, as in this toughly
poignant quatrain. And of course it lends itself especially well
to moods inclining to speed and impatient of controls. 'My

friend, if you call it a friend, has left me', says the delightfully smug neurotic in 'The Deserter':

> he says I am a deserter to ill health,
> and that the things I should think about have made off for ever, and
>   so has my wealth.
> Portentous ass, what to do about him's no strain
> I shall quite simply never speak to the fellow again.

In truth, greatly serviceable, the line will do almost anything except report that the world, the mind, the heart, are tidily bound.

About all we can count on in reading Smith is that she will be as surprising as she is skilful, her finesse equal to her boldness. And we can also count on hearing a voice—a 'talking voice', as Pompey says, pointed 'with commas, semi-colons, dashes, pauses', a voice held 'alive in captivity'. Indeed, Smith is so instinctively a dramatist of voice that she endows even the verse essay with necessity. And this is all the more remarkable in that her language is anyway that of a writer of verse. She remains almost always outside and above her words; they are smaller than she is, her instruments. And yet they are not only exact, they live, because they are quick with voice. It is in entering delightedly and inventively into idiom, rhythm, attitude, intonation, that Smith's imagination is most alive. Hence where most versifiers merely deck their morals in metre, Smith, cadenced and dramatic, converts hers into personality:

> Is it not interesting to see
> How the Christians continually
> Try to separate themselves in vain
> From the doctrine of eternal pain?
>
> They cannot do it,
> They are committed to it,
> Their Lord said it,
> They must believe it . . .

Though these lines come from 'Thoughts about the Christian Doctrine of Eternal Hell', they are more than thoughts, they are acts. Here is an adversary who delights in her own force and voice, in the mind at joust. 'Is it not interesting'—'amusing', hints the euphemism. 'Continually' and 'in vain' perpetuate the gloating, unChristian tone. And how the emphatic staccato of the second stanza routs the deceptive flowing mildness of the first. In those brutally abrupt, rigidly parallel, flatly declarative sentences the Christians are as effectively imprisoned as in the doctrine of eternal pain; the lines seem audibly to nail them in. Later, with a fine new note of urgency the poet will say, 'Oh, oh, have none of it, / Blow it away, have done with it'. The poem changes in expression like a living face.

Still, authoritative and captivating as Smith's voice usually is, it is never so impelling as when it invests an immediate situation or world. If the poet cannot put her imagination of voice aside, she can put both imagined space and the moment into her voice, as iridescence is in the bubble, as a mirrored face or world is there. Here is the last part of 'Scorpion':

> I should like my soul to be required of me, so as
> To waft over grass till it comes to the blue sea
> I am very fond of grass, I always have been, but there must
> Be no cow, person or house to be seen.
>
> Sea and *grass* must be quite empty
> Other souls can find somewhere *else*.
>
> O Lord God please come
> And require the soul of thy Scorpion
>
> Scorpion so wishes to be gone.

Here, as against the voiced opinion, the thematic nakedness, of 'Thoughts about the Christian Doctrine of Eternal Hell', is all the poignancy of a voice's rage to be silenced. It is still the complex, shifting intonation to which we respond—the blend of spite, longing, and fondness, the uncompromising emphases (how the sharpened tail jerks about!), the wry intensity of *so* in the final line. But the poem fills out, as well, with the pressure of undeniable reality, the immediacy of an individual fate. And though sea and grass are subordinate to the speaker's impatient need for them, they are nonetheless there at the periphery, adding a horizon of appearance, a sense of the earth.

On one side of poems like 'Scorpion', 'Black March', 'O Pug!', and 'Farewell' are brilliant poems in *other* people's voices—voices slid under a merciless microscope. On the other are a few poems in which the voice nearly forgets itself. Perhaps the most remarkable of these last is 'Pretty'. Beginning like a school essay, 'Why is the word pretty so underrated?', it first gives a conventional response, 'In November the leaf is pretty when it falls / The stream grows deep in the woods after rain', then bewilders:

> And in the pretty pool the pike stalks
>
> He stalks his prey, and this is pretty too,
> The prey escapes with an underwater flash
> But not for long, the great fish has him now
> The pike is a fish who always has his prey
>
> And this is pretty. The water rat is pretty
> His paws are not webbed, he cannot shut his nostrils
> As the otter can and the beaver, he is torn between
> The land and the water. Not 'torn', he does not mind . . .

Pretending to befriend a down-at-heel word, Smith is in fact remaking it: just so, however, will she save it. And meanwhile she leads us a pretty chase indeed. 'Aristotelian virtue', we surmise in our curiosity, our haste, 'this is the pretty'. And can we be blamed if we soon abandon Aristotle for a theory of Platonic ascent?

> The owl hunts in the evening and it is pretty
> The late water below him rustles with ice
> There is frost coming from the ground, in the air mist
> All this is pretty, it could not be prettier.
>
> Yes, it could always be prettier, the eye abashes
> It is becoming an eye that cannot see enough,
> Out of the wood the eye climbs. This is prettier
> A field in the evening, tilting up.
>
> The field tilts to the sky. Though it is late
> The sky is lighter than the hill field
> All this looks easy but really it is extraordinary
> Well, it is extraordinary to be so pretty . . .

By this point the word 'pretty' has proved nearly hypnotic by dint of repetition—we begin to delight in it no matter *what* it means. Yet the speaker's concern for precision ('Yes, it could always be prettier') reassures, and in fact Smith knows just where she is going and now swiftly arrives:

> And it is careless, and that is always pretty
> This field, this owl, this pike, this pool are careless,
> As Nature is always careless and indifferent
> Who sees, who steps, means nothing, and this is pretty.

So a person can come along like a thief—pretty!—
Stealing a look, pinching the sound and feel,
Like the icicle broken from the bank
And still say nothing at all, only cry pretty.

Cry pretty, pretty, pretty and you'll be able
Very soon not even to cry pretty
And so be delivered entirely from humanity
This is prettiest of all, it is very pretty.

So the pretty is finally revealed as the elation of insouciance, an essential carelessness bewitchingly reflected by nature. The end of the poem bites deeply into the inhuman; it chills.

Now the poem declares its unity. Now we can see why the punctuation, syntax, and metre were nonchalant, why the delineation was casual, the rhyme infrequent. And now we understand why the poem showed no haste to delimit its ruling idea. We grasp, too, that compelling but puzzling ascent from the wood to the field to the sky; for of course the field is prettier than the wood, being barer, and the sky prettier still, being not only self-sufficiently lit from within but also the ultimate vastness and plainness for an 'eye that cannot see enough' of what does not care to be seen. It is even fitting that none of the words should hold us by an exquisite appositeness; that would be beautiful, not 'pretty'. No, only the voice should hold us, as it does, directing us to the world through a concept, to a concept through the world, while bearing us along on its note of pleasure, its light ripples; for this is its paradox, that it cannot care enough for the careless, empathize enough with the deliveringly indifferent.

Yet just as the poems of immediate scenes and situations touch us more nearly than those of sharply voiced thought, so they pale, in turn, beside the finest poems in still another group, those of magic and romance: poems not only luminous with personality and weighted by matter but also dipped in the fabulous. Here the ordinary world, struck by a haloed moon of transcendental fantasy, lies under a spell, whether lovely or troubling. For finally Smith could not be held down and, in escaping the limitations of the earth, took it with her. Like Forster, Yeats, Dylan Thomas, and Isak Dinesen, she raised it felicitously into the marvellous. The author of the grim

> Sin recognized—but that—may keep us humble,
> But oh, it keeps us nasty . . .

the author of the austere,

> Prate not to me of suicide,
> Faint heart in battle, not for pride
> I say Endure, but that such end denied
> Makes welcomer yet the death that's to be died . . .

this author, so strong and stern, is also the author of

> In the quiet waters
> Of the forest pool
> Fafnir the dragon
> His tongue will cool . . .

and this is itself quite marvellous. True, Fafnir is hounded—
the fate, it would seem, of all lofty and happy creatures. Certain
knights kill him for their merit and—a telling and topical touch—
burn the grass on which he feeds. Yet the innocence in 'Fafnir
and the Knights' is the kind that overrides all furious knowledge
of the world. Springing, perhaps, from loyalty to her childhood,
which had been violated too soon, there was in Smith a 'Childe
Rolandine' who championed self-forgetting, intrinsically blessed
innocence. Like her league with death, this was her way of saying
that 'The cruelty and blindness of the world and of history' are
not all, there is refuge.

If 'Fafnir and the Knights' is not equal to, say, 'The Blue from
Heaven' or 'The Ass', the reason is largely that it lacks the
complexity of ambivalence or dialectic: the 'Happy simple
creature' is so enshrined in its superiority to the knights that there
is nothing for the reader to do but look on. In the other poems,
by contrast, transcendent innocence is like the magical, bubble-
footed shadow of the meagre water-strider—the same happiness
as seen by doubters. The poems so chequer innocence with
their own sophistication that we must ourselves help draw an
inference of blessedness over the heads of mockery and disbelief.
Smith's manner declares that *she* is no fool, and her casual tone
disarms us:

> King Arthur rode in another world
> And his twelve knights rode behind him
> And Guinevere was there
> Crying: Arthur, where are you dear?

Why is the King so blue
Why is he this blue colour?
It is because the sun is shining
And he rides under the blue cornflowers.

High wave the cornflowers
Thad shed the pale blue light
And under the tall cornflowers
Rides King Arthur and his twelve knights.

And Guinevere is there
Crying: Arthur, where are you dear? . . .

Charming, superbly calculated, happy. The poem has a juggler's grace of balance. The humour of Guinevere's bafflement, the rising, suspended pitch of her question, its timeless domestic idiom, set off the archaic verse, the magical scenery, and the supernal theme. So does the mock-dumb question, 'Why is the King so blue . . . ?' The brocaded ballad form is made a tatters by the forgetful rhyme and stress count: the lines and stanzas (and grammar) seem as dithered as Arthur by the blue. And if the great cornflowers are themselves peculiar, so is it peculiar to find a king happy among them. This is a king in whom the child has grown tall. The cornflowers combine the huge world of childhood dreams and the ethereal religious world into one. Here the antitheses fathered by the native gap between Arthur and Guinevere are counterpointed by a comically sublime and unexpected synthesis.

The twelve knights soon dwindle to one, then Arthur is alone:

That Arthur has fallen from the grandeur
Of his powers all agree
And the falling off of Arthur
Becomes their theme presently.

As if it were only temporarily
And it was not for ever
They speak, but the Queen knows
He will come back never.

Yes, Arthur has passed away
Gladly he has laid down his reigning powers
He has gone to ride in the blue light
Of the peculiar towering cornflowers.

Here, as before, the movement is subtly mimetic. For instance, the second and fourth lines of the first of these stanzas, being brief and uncertainly stressed, enact Arthur's supposed falling off. 'As if it were only temporarily' sounds makeshift and hasty. 'He will come back never' is dolefully emphatic. If the Queen and her court have the worldly grandeur and the words, they have also the agitation, and the last stanza rides off in beatitude on strong and measured stresses.

In 'The Ass', too, Smith encircles and throws into relief a dumb transport with every articulate resource, so that cleverness and innocence, narrative and rapt stasis, are curiously and winningly combined. She rallies humour and irony to redeem an unfashionable supernaturalism. Here the witch is as uncomprehending as Guinevere. 'Finding no pleasure in her tyranny' over the holy simpleton Eugenia, she gives her exasperated release:

> She is an ass, she cried, let her pass
> And perish in the soppy morass.

Eugenia, as childishly happy as Fafnir and Arthur, journeys on, wrapped round by story though herself transcending time: like most of the better poems of fantasy, 'The Ass' blends action with supernatural implication, in a strong dual appeal. Proving too smart for the fiend who tempts her into the morass ('But she said, No, / She was not such an ass . . .'), happy on the causeway among the beetles, gnats, and mosquitoes, singing 'Baabaa-ba-bay' for seven happy years, Eugenia arrives at last at the sea. Here is the end of the poem, one of Smith's most beautiful surprises:

> Oh my poor ass
> To run so quickly as if coming home
> To where the great waves crash.
> Now she is gone. I thought
> Into her tomb.
>
> Yet often as I walk that sandy shore
> And think the seas
> Have long since combed her out that lies
> Beneath, I hear the sweet Ass singing still with joy as if
> She had won some great prize, as if
> All her best wish had come to pass.

The narrator is herself confounded (such is the ploy) by the apparent cosmic profundity and immortality of the ass—'apparent' because the consummation is of course left to delicious hypothesis. Her scepticism struggles audibly with her wonder: 'as if' being twice suspended at the end of lines, saying it is all too much to believe, belief must stop, yet also conveying a raised and covetous note of longing. Then 'wish' enters as a kind of flowering of the sound and meaning of 'if', and the Biblical 'come to pass' closes the poem in a final ennoblement of the harsh little syllable 'ass'.

In still another poem of transcendental fantasy, 'Watchful', strangeness replaces humour as a screen for innocent delight. The heroine, called by Watchful when still a child, is finally lured from her accustomed life—playing with her brothers at Northumberland House, making money on the Stock Exchange, giving parties in London—out over the saltings past the 'high crests of the golden sea', also past mournful birds in a gamekeeper's gallows and a dying old badger, to the dark house of Watchful, whom she revives from weakness, cold, and sleep as if reviving her own soul. 'Oh Watchful, my darling', she complains as she enters his door, 'you have led me such a dance.' For she had to be watchful indeed to see that she did not really want money and to note the 'wild' and 'laughing' eyes of the people at her parties, still more to perceive that the leaping waves were also too hectic, their gold perhaps reminiscent of wealth, and too flashing, and anyway lit by a changing sun—watchful, too, to hurry by the animals whose fate it is to die. But now she is away from the world while still within it, and

> We need not dance any more
> He said, Only the fire dances on Northumberland Moor
> The fire you have lighted for me dances
> On Northumberland Moor.
>
> Then winter blew away, a sweet sea ran pretty
> And in this new world everything was happy.

So she forsakes the frantic waves for this noncommittal joyous distance where the sea can be grasped as a whole, and is sweet, and in motion like a living thing, as free of its own mass as the watchful soul of its flesh, the earth of its empty moors.

This 'new world' in which the earth is identical with a simplifying transcendental end is the paradise typically intimated by

Smith's art—an art swift, light, and deft, running with simple ease. The lines describing it are only, as it were, those that come upon the window that all the lines, knowingly or not, seek out. Smith's delineations are typically spare, brisk, decisive—appealing as little to the reader's imagination of substance as do her thin-lined sketches. The effect is chaste and freeing, sparely precise. There is never any clutter; the bones lie stripped in the light and as if by the light itself. Smith enters each object just long enough to feel it, then moves on. She registers objects less through the eye than the ear. In 'The Ass' the waves 'roll in pleasure to be so a-wash', and we hear their pleasure more than we see it. And if 'the great waves crash' the impression is almost entirely aural, the stresses on the long *a* (a vowel full of body) convincing us of their greatness, as the subsequent short *a* helps them crash. Yet this auditory realization, too, is rapid. In all, Smith's delineations are so spare as to imply a wish to be gone from the embroiling earth and so exact as to imply an attachment to it. They are the 'new world' where it falls into language.

If the new world of 'The Lady of the Well-Spring' is a special case it is because it has a stronger smell of greenery: the poem depicts an erotic awakening. The English child Joan, sitting apart in a French drawing-room 'to be freed from the difficulty of conversation', hears gossip about one who is

> 'Quite captive to the lady of the Well-Spring
> Who will rescue him?'
> Now I have an excuse to go
> Said Joan, and walked out of the window
> Down the iron staircase and along the path
> And then she began to run through the tall wet grass . . .

At length she comes upon the lady:

> Now with her feet in deep moss Joan stands looking
> Where on a bank a great white lady is lying
> A fair smooth lady whose stomach swelling
> Full breasts fine waist and long legs tapering
> Are shadowed with grass-green streaks. The lady smiles
> Lying naked. The sun stealing
> Through the branches, her canopies, glorifies
> The beautiful rich fat lady where she lies.
> Never before in history
> In a place so green and watery

Has lady's flesh and so divine a lady's as this is
With just such an admiring look as Joan's met with.
'Quite captive to the Lady of the Well-Spring?'
What nonsense, it is a thing
French ladies would say
In sophisticated conversation on a warm day.
I do not wish to rescue him, blurts Joan,
The lady lolls, Do you wish to go home?
No says Joan, I should like to live
Here. Right, says the lady, you are my captive.
The child Joan fully sees the beauty her eye embraces.
Do not think of her as one who loses.

So this world, too, is magical and freeing—though at the same time *not* freeing: Joan will remain the grateful captive of this lolling lady in the timelessness of transport as if in the endlessness of a great painting. Another rapturous stasis, only now on that plane where the sensual cools and is sublimated into the aesthetic, being perhaps all the more insidiously enchanting for that. And that it should be a Victorian or Edwardian child who thus succumbs (the poem is subtitled 'Renoir's "La Source"') throws an awesome and disturbing light on its power. But then had not the child Joan, in her reluctance to converse, shown her ripeness for this fortunate fall? The lady herself is more natural and then more aesthetic than human, a creature of form, divine white flesh, and grass-green streaks, as alien to the drawing-room as the towering cornflowers or the pike that prettily stalks his prey. Like Watchful, she is the desired, the freeing, the strange and inescapable occasion for ecstasy.

'The Lady of the Well-Spring' is not only more startling and convincing than 'Watchful'; like 'The Blue from Heaven' and 'The Ass' it has more of the formal life of art. As is true of several of Smith's other long narrative poems, 'Watchful' weighs towards prose. Once past the opening stanzas it relinquishes the secret of the poetic line—the elastically cadenced, wholly *experienced* duration that is the measure in which a poem breathes.

> Often we gave parties
> In London
> For Senior Civil Servants
> And barristers
> and Junior Members
> Of the Government . . .

Lacking poise in themselves as well as balance in each other, these
lines have an arbitrary air of the disposed. By contrast, those
of 'The Ass' show volition, seem unified from within:

> In the wood of Wallow
> Mash, walked Eugenia, a callow
> Girl, they said she was,
> An ass.

The alliteration and off-rhymes pull back playfully while the
syntax winds forward irresistibly, as unstoppable as Eugenia
herself. And the last line is the weight that brings the roaming
scales into balance. In 'The Lady of the Well-Spring', too,
mimesis and formal measure give the lines simultaneous drama
and poise. The poem fairly blurts with Joan's eager, wide-eyed
disposition:

> . . . Into a little wood
> She runs, the branches catching at her feet draw blood
> And there is a sound of piping screaming croaking clacking
> As the birds of the wood rise chattering.
> And now as she runs there is the bicker
> Of a stream growing narrower in a trickle
> And a splash and a flinging, it is water springing . . .

Headlong and panting, the lines are so at one with the subject
that the latter seems to dash into them unconsciously, as blindly
and inevitably as Joan finds the lady. The same happy agreement
governs the rhymes. These come thick and fast as the branches and
noises, and through their insistent stumble-down endings seem
to portend Joan's captivation. On the other hand the couplets
are reassuring. They hint that Joan's behaviour is not really
without rhyme or reason and that she will not be one who loses.
The rhyme reflects her unison with her destiny.

In two other superior poems, 'The Frog Prince' and 'I had a
dream . . .', the magical globe of fantasy rolls round into the
darkness. Here enchantment is an oppression, a spell of *non*-
transcendence. Dialectic these poems have, but between comedy
and despair, not comedy and bliss; and the comedy not only
relieves but sharpens the despair, as in the other poems it both
mocks and graces the bliss. In 'The Frog Prince', one who is
already enchanted, however dubiously, wishes to become still
more enchanted—for, such is the funny-sad irony of the poem,

the frog prince thinks it would be '*heavenly* / To be set free', heavenly to be human. He has misgivings:

> I have been a frog now
> For a hundred years
> And in all this time
> I have not shed many tears,
>
> I am happy, I like the life,
> Can swim for many a mile
> (When I have hopped to the river)
> And am for ever agile.
>
> And the quietness,
> Yes, I like to be quiet
> I am habituated
> To a quiet life . . .

The delightfully stolid tone, the naïve, obliging exactitude of 'When I have hopped to the river', the stretched vowel in the last syllable of 'And am for ever agile', the charming nursery metre, endear this frog at the same time that they confirm his sense of limitation, the absence of 'Eternal Delight'. But when the short lines and balanced quatrains give way to distraught irregularity, we can only pity the human remnant in him, his unsatisfied and unsatisfiable consciousness:

> But always when I think these thoughts
> As I sit in my well
> Another thought comes to me and says:
> It is part of the spell
>
> To be happy
> To work up contentment
> To make much of being a frog
> To fear disenchantment
>
> Says, It will be *heavenly*
> To be set free,
> Cries, *Heavenly* the girl who disenchants
> And the royal times, *heavenly*,
> And I think it will be . . .

The three emphases on 'heavenly' make it ring like an alarm bell: the word is a swoony adolescent's cry. '*Heavenly* the girl who disenchants', thinks the frog, unaware of the treacherous *double entendre* in 'disenchants'. The conclusion is, alas, reversible: 'Only disenchanted people / Can be heavenly'. So the original fairy tale withers in ambivalence, irony, scepticism. The tale has been wittily turned against the assumption that it is finer to be human than a frog. And yet, of course, the poem does not exalt the frog's life either. It is itself an expression of restless human consciousness.

If enchantment only begins to prove stultifying in 'The Frog Prince', in 'I had a dream . . .' it is all but intolerable. Fabling waking life, the dream ('I had a dream I was Helen of Troy / In looks, age and circumstance, / But otherwise I was myself') poisonously concentrates time's strangely heavy, strangely ethereal atmosphere. Stasis, so desirable a release in 'Watchful' and 'The Ass', is here just an appalling standstill:

> . . . Oh, I thought,
> It is an ominous eternal moment I am captive in, it is always
> This heavy weather, these colours, and the smell of the dead men.
> It is curious to be caught in a moment of pause like this,
> As a river pauses before it plunges in a great waterfall.
> I was at home with these people at least in this, that we wished
> It was over and done with. But oh, Cassandra, I said, catching hold
> of her,
> For she was running away, I shall never make
> That mischievous laughing Helen, who goes home with Menelaus
> And over her needlework, in the quiet palace, laughs,
> Telling her story, and cries: Oh shameful me. I am only at home
> In this moment of pause, where feelings, colours and spirits are
> substantial,
> But people are ghosts. When the pause finishes
> I shall wake.

It is too much knowledge of time, for she is ages down in her own past, indeed partly a woman of the twentieth century ('But otherwise I was myself'), that weighs on this Helen, crushing her spirit to the moment; this that accounts for the dull tonelessness, the dragging add-on syntax, the long lines woefully underpowered in accents and growing even longer as the poem progresses. In their approach to unleavened discourse (yet how quick with mood they remain), the lines enact the humdrum, crawlingly linear pace of life. To know so much of what will happen is to know almost everything and find it nothing, and this dreamed

Helen inhabits a dream. How can she leave the moment, go home to Menelaus, laugh, when her spirit has lost belief in the future? She has already been there and it too was only a series of moments stuck like snails to an unscaleable wall, though not quite this ominous eternal moment, which is the sum of all moments in one, time drawn back on itself, comprehended in an endless point. So she merely waits for the dream to end, too sunk within it or too afraid to wonder what lies beyond—waits in the smallest line of the poem, its three words giving on to silence.

Meanwhile she is innocently obnoxious—well, perhaps only half innocently. After all, one gets bored, one must act, if only to speak; and, being not simply Helen but a well-read Stevie Smith, can she be blamed if she speaks the truth and it hurts? Besides, helplessness is the paralysing sting that makes one want to sting back. So Helen strikes out at others rather freely if also heartily, as if expecting accord with the truth she speaks and not the horrified reactions in fact provoked—reactions that pain her and make her cross. When she sings the song of the First World War, 'We're here because, we're here', she notes

> . . . This was the only time
> I heard Cassandra laugh. I said:
> There you are, you laugh . . . that shows you are not nearly so
> Religious as you think. That's blasphemous, that laugh,
> Sets you free. But then she got frightened. All right, I said,
> Don't be free, go along and finish up on Clytemnestra's sword-point,
> Pinked like a good girl. I used to get so cross.
> Paris was stupid, it was impossible to talk to him.
> Hector might have been different, at least he understood enough
> To be offended—fear of the gods again, I suppose—because
> When I said: Well, you know what the Trojan Women
> Are going to say about the sack of Troy and being led away
> Into captivity, they are going to say: If these things
> Had not happened to us we should not be remembered. I hope that
> Will be a comfort to you. He was angry and said
> I should bring ill luck to Troy by my impiety, so I laughed
> But I felt more like crying . . .

One rather likes this Helen, who is hard enough for the truth—though it leaves her outside of everything. She enjoys and suffers her dreamer's own capacities for pique and honesty—suffers also her essential loneliness, including the peculiar loneliness of the artist for whom 'feelings, colours and spirits are substantial, / But people are ghosts'.

Combining a single moment with centuries, pungent naturalism with dry profundity, humour and cruelty with pathos, prose rhythms with poetic measure, 'I had a dream . . .' is as brilliant a synthesis of diverse elements as 'The Ass' or 'The Lady of the Well-Spring'. It has the imaginative surprise and bareness, the subtle depth, the delicate adjustment of manner to attitude, the piquant humour and oddness, the captivating voice, that distinguish this poet at her best.

None of Stevie Smith's poems summarize her view of life, for finally she had no view, only views. She knew perhaps everything the emotions can know with a knowledge as heavy as the earth and a brilliance as light as the air. She could touch any subject and give it truth. Bold and queer mixture of vivacity and honesty that she was, author of numerous poems of wit, force, and unexpectedness, we may find ourselves saying of her: it was improbable that such a poet should ever happen along, but now that she is with us she is indispensable.

W. S. Graham

W. S. GRAHAM is the most piquantly original poet now writing in English. Stevie Smith had rivalled him but at present no one else works so elfin a touch upon the language—is so capable of an unremitting, delightful, and authoritative surprise. Like Smith he is a tart mixture of the apparently naïve and the formidably knowing. At first it was the naïveté that dominated, and Graham wrote with a wonderful freshness, as if just breaking out of the shell. For instance, he could describe a sunrise at sea in a style so brusquely self-tutored, so imperiously unexpected, that his words themselves seemed new risen:

> . . . The old defender
> Towers. His head soars.
> He stands like downfall over
> The high gables of morning
> In kindling light. Under
> His eye that blinds us now
> We go down dazzled into
> The crowded scroll of the wake.
> As silence takes me back
> Changed to my last word,
>
> Reply. Present your world.
> Gannet of God, strike.

This gives a rich astonishment, convincing us simultaneously of the momentousness of the physical world and of the power of language to prove equal to it. It has motion, life, luminosity, grandeur. The sunrise is enacted by clauses that are themselves events. 'He stands like downfall', for instance, dazzles in its own right: the brilliant tension of the clause scatters us in opposite directions. The style of the passage is at once unique and effortless, fully, commandingly itself. And this is the utmost piquancy of style, this daring that seems innocent of what it is.

This was the Graham of eighteen years ago. Now he is even odder, with a taunting, sinisterly comic, often harsh piquancy that is as surprising as the resplendent tonality of former years. Graham (it is part of his elfin quality) has done what might have seemed impossible, made himself over from one originality to another. Now there is slyness in his work, a menace caught from the age:

> I found her listed under Flora
> Smudged on a coloured, shining plate
> Dogeared and dirty. As for Fauna
> We all are that, pelted with anarchy.

The poem has the prickly crispness of a pinecone—is as uncomfortable, as closed, as achieved. Its import—that to track down the Ideal is to find it already sullied by man, by history—becomes the more upsetting, the more unspeakable, through its disturbing laconicism. At once quaintly and magisterially metaphoric, almost all vehicle, the poem banishes the human to alien terms.

So Graham has gone from strangeness to strangeness, in fact has become even stranger, like a troll dragging us farther into the forest. Yet this wizard of idiosyncrasy began—it is one of the strangest things about him—as a dazed disciple of Dylan Thomas, in the Forties copying not only his sheer heart-in-the-throat tone but his loftily mannered phraseology ('Day through my prison walked', 'God as the day is good can tell no fraud'): it was as if he had simply been taken over by the Welsh poet, had no resistant fibre of his own. Graham's early poetry drains away as you read it, partly because it flows back into Dylan Thomas and partly because, detail by detail, it undoes itself. For Graham follows Dylan Thomas at his worst, where his images crowd pell-mell. Of all greatly gifted poets the youthful Dylan Thomas was the messiest, mixing and smearing entities like a child in the mud. 'Breaking / Through the rotating shell, strong / As motor muscle on the drill, driving / Through vision and the girdered nerve', for instance, hurls flesh and metal together like a collision. And Graham is often just as manic, as witness 'The swords / Of ancient eyes bloodbell above' or 'ptarmigan rocked in a rod of battles'. Writing of this sort evokes the visual only to black it out; it is world-blind. Turning imagery against its own substance, reducing it to an abstract code, it displays a kind of creative bad faith.

Graham's earliest volumes—*Cage Without Grievance* (1942), *The Seven Journeys* (1944), and *2nd Poems* (1945)—widen to absurdity, indeed to wide-eyed absurdity, the characteristic element of modern poetry: the enlarged space between words, lines, stanzas, poet and reader, poet and poem. At the theoretical level the same exaggeration occurs in Roland Barthes's *Writing Degree Zero*, with its hermetic depiction of modern poetry as a rejection of syntactical relationships, 'an explosion of words'. In this poetry of autonomous and 'terrible' words, says Barthes, the Word 'can never be untrue, because it is a whole': '. . . it is the Word which gratifies and fulfills like the sudden revelation of a truth'. But in fact words by and to themselves are not even fragments, let alone wholes; they are merely latencies. Poetry begins in the resurrection of words from the tombs of their denotations, and only a new context, a delicate and directed association, can trumpet life back into them. Poetry enters words as the subtlest intelligence of their relationships. Consequently, poems in which connections are, in Barthes's words, 'merely reserved areas, parodies of themselves', are merely parodies of poems. Here are two extracts from Graham:

> Then holier than innocence, like ten commandments
> Any workman in these seas
> The man and his labour no man can say . . .
>
> Yet look where my saint's value pads in snow turrets
> Like down a polar spiral in a berg of bone
> And scrawls on keels of glaciers governed in glass
> The sign of a nervous leglong crucifixion . . .

If 'the density of the word' is to 'rise out of a magic vacuum', Barthes says, relationships must be voided. But from these prime examples of cancelled syntax what rises is only a skittering of verbal noise. The concepts have been decapitated from their syllables; the sounds are familiar but mean nothing. Failing to join up the words disappear, one by one, into silence. They pass us along like a man above the shoulders of a crowd—but a crowd of which we had wanted to be a part.

'SHEER I break AGAINST those EVERMORE GLITTERING SEASONS', writes the young poet as he sets out, like every other romantic writer, to meet life and language anew. 'We fall down darkness in a line of words', he announces; 'This drop no man descends / To death or depth of meaning if there's day'. Day, then, not meaning: the Word as Being, animal innocence. But in fact the consuming light in his phrases is self-reflective, a lyric egotism. It is this that overwhelms the only other light perceivable, the glimmer of vestigal connections. For, in truth, often the poet neglects to draw the blinds of syntax all the way. Sit long enough before most of his lines and you begin to discern, dim as starlight, an intended meaning. But he has backed so far from common discourse that he makes us conscious less of what he sees than of his effort to esacpe convention:

> Let me measure my prayer with sleep as an
> Infant of story in the stronghold eyelid
> Left by a hedge with a badge of campions
> Beats thunder for moles in the cheek of Spring . . .

So prayer will consist of a dream inspired by a glimpse of nature (the hedge) and joyfully participate in its fertility (beating thunder for moles). Still, the lines do not so much offer this 'story' as betray it; they rise less directly from their own logic than from the poet's intention to be sheer. Writing like this chiefly says, 'I want to feel my consciousness tossing in a freedom from ordinary language, which is everyone's language, the language of death'. This is the poetry of the whirligig, the words spinning so fast that the imperial order of the world, its arrangement of time and death, is lost in the blur.

If Graham gradually accepted syntax as a wall against which his singular shadow could be cast, perhaps it was because, having moved out into the 'beyond' of a dumbly ecstatic language, he found himself without either individuality or the world. 'My heart is headhung on a peartree girl / Whirled from the season's pollen flume', for instance, achieves liberation, affects passion, at the expense both of inflected expression and of actual perception. It is, as it were, mere words. In trying to save himself Graham was losing W. S. Graham. Not only did he recall Dylan Thomas, someone *else*; he failed to sound like a human being whom the world had touched, formed, limited. He could just be anyone; he could be no one at all. Though it was precisely limitation that he was trying to escape, it was yet himself that

he wished to make into dialogues with 'those fairer flocks . . .
Over the pitheads', the 'bright keys' of space—dialogues that
would 'spring / Past tempest'. He had now to create himself in
order not only to recognize himself, *exist* as himself, but even to
have company in his own mind. He had gone straight and blankly
into idiosyncratic impersonality; he was now to cultivate the
natural idiosyncrasy of personality, so as to hold both time and
the evermore glittering seasons, both individuality and univer-
sality, in the same words, the same glass jar.

Graham's first undoubted syntactical successes, however,
proved, in the modesty and timidity of his new commencement,
almost as without living voice as before. 'Shian Bay' and 'Gigah'
in his fourth volume, *The White Threshold* (1949), are so conventional, so toneless, as to share the anonymity of the common
tongue. 'Shian Bay' concludes:

> Last gale washed five into the bay's stretched arms,
> Four drowned men and a boy drowned into shelter.
> The stones roll out to shelter in the sea.

Chastely impersonal, the last line is majestic in its unhesitating
swing to an inhuman perspective; in its ironic simplicity it both
pains and frees. The other lines, by contrast, as if compensating
for their expository role, are slightly touched up. None, however,
has either style or voice, and the strengths of the passage are
traditional: the paradox of 'drowned into shelter' and the poignant poised heartlessness of the final line.

Here is 'Gigah' entire:

> That firewood pale with salt and burning green
> Outfloats its men who waved with a sound of drowning
> Their saltcut hands over mazes of this rough bay.
>
> Quietly this morning beside the subsided herds
> Of water I walk. The children wade the shallows.
> The sun with long legs wades into the sea.

Another surprising reversal (though now tiered and warm in
feeling); and another strong last line. Like 'Shian Bay' the poem
is composed in the Spartan sense prescribed by Valéry: '. . . the
poem's only aim is to prepare its climax'. Yet it, too, is almost
characterless. Except for the end, it scarcely attempts the felicitously simple. Nor does it speak with an imagined voice. It is

in other, less nearly perfect poems in the volume that this momentous self-creation is under way.

Here in 'Since All My Steps Taken', fittingly the first poem in the volume, Graham takes, as it were, his first steps on his own, and how lonely he sounds:

> Since all my steps taken
> Are audience of my last
> With hobnail on Ben Narnain
> Or mind on the word's crest
> I'll walk the kyleside shingle
> With scarcely a hark back
> To the step dying from my heel
> Or the creak of the rucksack . . .

Hard and spare, the lines have an isolated ring of validity. They echo like frozen ground to their own steps; they listen to themselves. Lilting and withering simultaneously, they cannot quite get into the swing of a happy walk, for the step heard dying from the heel makes the speaker half his own ghost. The movement falters, is almost squeakily dry, because, even as this venturer resolves not to hark back, he yet does, perhaps must, the present being simply an imminence, almost too sheer for breath. Fixed as he is on the 'word's crest' of self-consciousness, Ben Narnain and the shingle engage him but feebly compared to the sounds of the hobnail and the rucksack—sounds he originates; and even from these he seems estranged. Ben Narnain, with its capitalized name, broad with resonance, simply stands and is; the speaker, by contrast, is a movement without rest. Indeed, he steps past his own thought so quickly that he allows 'since' where the logic needs 'though'—he is determined, no matter what, to go buoyantly on.

In the later Graham, syntax will grow soberer, the glowing tonality even here endangered will flicker out, the edgings of the style become more cutting, seem the threatening edge of night. But much of what will come is already here, roughly knocked out. The starkness, the echoing loneliness, the homely hobnailed diction, the knocking succession of short syllables, the metre that lacks the heart to crystallize—these will persist even as they vary.

The Nightfishing (1955), Graham's next and first major volume, develops from 'Since All My Steps Taken' on the lyrical side, wonderfully transmitting the circumambient solar radiance that would help explain the lilt (struggling as it is and unexplained) of the earlier poem. Yet, in keeping with the eremitic spareness of that poem, the lyricism is curiously ethereal. Heady with sea air, suggestive of luminist painting, it seems at the same time subdued to the considering and self-gravitating mind. With the partial exception of the title poem, the volume is more blindly abstracted than visual—at once dazzled and dazzling, as in the description of the 'old defender'. As a result, the mind is thrown back on itself; it both is and is not in the world:

> Let the signs start and peer
> Us into light. We drift
> Above fathoms that move
> Their friendly thunders through
> This breathless thoroughfare . . .

The principle here is a worldly abstractness, at once salty and phantasmal, like spindrift. So 'signs', if less sensuous than 'stars', or even 'constellations', is yet quickened by 'start', which makes the signs both begin and startle, pricking them into life. Conversely, the animating 'peers', being divided between the stars and ourselves, is by that much etherealized and removed from each. Then 'friendly' settles, perhaps wisely, for a simple emotional impression, humble before its great object, taking hold by not struggling to take hold. 'Thoroughfare' is kinetic but visually indistinct, its usual connotation of the narrow and linear tugging against the openness of the sea. And 'breathless' renders the description even more a part of the poet as against the world. All in all, this is a lyricism more certain of its delight than of its objects, and Graham carried it through the volume like a flame through the wind. When he was ready to produce another volume, fifteen years later, it had gone out.

The muse, Graham says towards the end of *The Nightfishing*, 'Appreciates the starkest man / Her length and breadth to be', and his next volume, *Malcolm Mooney's Land* (1970), is to the starkness of 'Since All My Steps Taken' what *The Nightfishing* is to its lilt—a heightening, a further creation. Here Graham follows the clue of a period so jaded, overtaxed, and suspicious that the minimal, the severe, the stripped, the ironic, the broken, most readily seem new to it. And yet Graham is as easily unique in his new spareness as he was in his lyricism, combining as he does a pungently oblique conceptual power with a bony sound, a bare effect—riches with poverty. Indeed, he is stark as much in defiance of as in obedience to the times, stark in order to be audible, recognizable as W. S. Graham. His ostensibly awkward spareness represents a rejection of social volubility—in particular, of glib authority. The opposite of a poet like Donald Davie, who wants to wear the common language like a consecrated robe, Graham wants to cut his own cloth, show by his style that he is *not* the public. His cultivated eccentricity argues the right to stand alone.

Not that he necessarily thinks well of himself, but he scorns collectively, its code of repression and corruption. If no poet has been more openly fond of his readers, few have been more slyly aggressive—for we, alas, number among the *others* and, if not the victimizers, are very likely their victims. In 'Ten Shots of Mister Simpson', a long recent poem, the poet menaces his protagonist, who is all of us, by insinuating that to international history he is just a number or, worse, fuel:

> Mister Simpson, kneedeep in the drowned
> Thistles of not your own country,
> What is your category? What number
> Did you curl into alone to sleep
> The cold away in Hut K
> Fifty-five nearest God the Chimney? . . .

On the mantelpiece 'A photograph of five young gassed / Nephews and nieces fading brown'. The poem scrutinizes those who would scrutinize its oddness, its infractions of the rules. As in all the recent Graham the thistled style (of not our own country) reclaims a little of the linguistic ground trodden bare by history, bristling against its massive authority.

So in *Malcolm Mooney's Land* Graham speaks 'a lipless language / Necessarily squashed from the side / To make its point against the rules. / It is our poetry such as it is'. 'Clearly they try to frighten me / To almost death', he says of the Keepers of Communication —showing his resistance by placing 'almost' awkwardly. His rhythms and phrases are those of a man squeezing around the bulging shape of custom:

> Today, Friday, holds the white
> Paper up too close to see
> Me here in a white-out in this tent of a place . . .

This does not even breathe. The rhythm is almost totally lacking in *relief*. And as if grimly or numbly holding themselves back, the images are scarcely depicted, bare bones. (If nonetheless they prove powerfully present it is partly because they are clever and partly because they simultaneously imply and stand out from absence.) Typically, Graham's lines are now all elbows, angularly breaking:

> Tonight in sadly need
> Of you I move inhuman
> Across this space of dread
> And silence in my mind . . .

As for his frequent monosyllables, Graham favoured their spareness even in *The Nightfishing*, letting them rap drily, sound lonely.

All together, with his nipped lines, his prepositions like frozen thumbs out at the ends of sentences, his teeth-chattering monosyllables, and his anxious avoidance of caesuras, Graham gets himself out in a 'clumping taliped disguise'. And in part it functions precisely *as* a disguise. Let his lines hobble as they will, clearly a master of language lurks behind them:

> Or am I always only
> Thinking is this the time
> To look elsewhere to turn
> Towards what was it
> I put myself out
> Away from home to meet? . . .

Indeed, their refused power and glory, their mock clumsiness, endears them to us. Graham's lines have become a kind of act, but a necessary one—right for him and a creative response to the times.

Graham, of course, not only shapes himself as he reshapes the language; he shapes a new pleasure for his readers. His homely, awkward style is, as it were, unapparent beauty—an ugly duckling. Its clumsiness is calculated less to affront than to delight provocatively. With its roughly cut angles and raw surfaces, it is like a handcarved wooden bowl that is *meant* to look handmade. It conveys a renewing fondness for the texture of its materials and at the same time a kind of greeting to the reader such as the more precision tooled could not imply. 'I made them all by hand for you', Graham's ballad maker, Baldy Bane, says of his words, 'To use as your own'. This is the sunlight on the frost of Graham's style, the compensation for its guardedness and aggression.

Syntax proved necessary and useful to Graham not only in creating his individuality but, for a time, in approaching animal innocence—that sea lit by the sun of youth. The spontaneity, the democratic gathering of words in the early poems is really too blustering to be ingenuous. Retreating from the great objects that *invite* forgetfulness, however nostalgic for them, Graham's poetry was confined to its own delirium. The only approach to natural innocence through words is sensory enchantment, and in poetry this is somehow dependent on syntax, on a framed description or an idea, on more than the senses themselves. Compared to words, mere words, syntax is a broadly reflecting river that leads the mind in exaltation from itself.

It was in 'The Nightfishing' that Graham finally broke as 'sheer' against sensuous reality as his extraordinary talent would allow. Here, at the prow of syntax, he fronted Appearance—'Appearing' being, in Heidegger's words, both 'that which . . . brings-itself-to-stand in its togetherness' and 'that which, already standing there, presents a front . . . an appearance to be looked at'. Through images and the focal, cinematic quality of syntax, Graham found himself facing the sheerest of objects, the sea. This was the right subject for him, the compelling Appearance; for, born in a tenement in Greenock, Scotland, he had grown up with a 'seaboard outlined heart'. In *The White Threshold* he breasted its vastness:

> Very end then of land. What vast is here?
> The drowning saving while, the threshold sea
> Always is here. You may not move away . . .

'I rise up loving', he said, 'and you may not move away.' He apprehended the sea as a great accumulated Appearance: 'Your while in all your mighty times is here'. Still, it was not until 'The Nightfishing' that he was able to bring the waves themselves down on the page.

The poem is a profound experience; its nineteen pages put us amid Being. Few poems in the language resonate with so full and immediate a response to life. We are with Graham, fishing

for herring, and somehow the sea, the voyage, fishes in us. We
start before dawn. 'Landvoices and the lights ebb away / Raising
the night round us'. The boat rides in the oily fires of the sea;
'our bow heaves hung on a likely / Bearing for fish'. Soon the
swells lengthen 'Easy on us, outride us in a slow follow / from
stern to stem'. The keel is 'in its amorous furrow'. 'The early
grey / Air is blowing'. And there at length 'is the water gone /
Lit black and wrought like iron into the look / That's right for
herring'. Dense moment gives way to dense moment, until we
have never been anywhere except on the herring boat, the roused
gulls slanting with 'Swelled throats screeching', everything deeply
and as if forever abandoned to 'Time's grace, the grace of change'.

The boat is 'lapped / At far last still', the nets are out, the fish
caught. We return:

> The long rollers,
> Quick on the crests and shirred with fine foam,
> Surge down then sledge their green tons weighing dead
> Down on the shuddered deck-boards. And shook off
> All that white arrival upon us back to falter
> Into the waking spoil and to be lost in
> The mingling world . . .
> . . . .
>
> For it sailed sore against us. It grew up
> To black banks that crossed us. It stooped, beaked.
> Its brine burnt us. I was chosen and given . . .
> . . . .
>
> It rose so white, soaring slowly, up
> On us, then broke, down on us. It became a mull
> Against our going and unfastened under us and
> Curdled from the stern. It shipped us at each blow.
> The brute weight
>
> Of the living sea wrought us, yet the boat sleeked lean
> Into it, upheld by the whole sea-brunt heaved,
> And hung on the swivelling tops . . .

'And we went keeled over / The streaming sea'. At length, 'A
sailing pillar of gulls', we come in, 'riding steady in the bay water'.
The quay opens its arms. Moored, 'we cut the motor quiet'. We
lie down. Somewhere men shout. We are our 'fruitful share'.

The writing throughout has a sensitive flexibility. From the
delicate opening, 'Very gently struck / The quay night bell',

through the booming kinetic tension of the voyage itself, with its verbal and accentual crowding, its washing assonance and alliteration, to the lovely refrain of section IV, 'O my love, keep the day / Leaned at rest, leaned at rest', the style is upon the moment, a style like the tautened skin of a rolling wave. It makes us a gift of its own fruitful share.

Yet even in this poem the sentiment of Being (if rarely more magnificently served) is attenuated by self-consciousness. In small part this is owing to syntax itself, which, however impelling, however mimetic of arrival, is like a river that turns to rapids before it reaches the sea: temporal where innocence is sempiternal, establishing relationships where innocence is Oceanic. But in truth Graham suffers anyway from an extraordinary liability to *reflection*; like the waves, his mind bends round on itself. Even in the drench of the sensual wonders of 'The Nightfishing', and even as his words receive it, his time-bound mind protects him like an oilskin. A swelling chorus of self-consciousness distances the physical immediacy—until finally Appearance is like thunder heard from a muffling cave.

Graham's self-consciousness speeds syntax before it as if one of the puff-cheeked winds on an old nautical map. By dint of *listening* for the fading rush of words, he hastens their passage. 'It is this instant written dead', he will say, as if confirmed in his expectations. More, as a man looking into a shaded window sees himself, so Graham finds his own linguistic consciousness reflected back by experience, which he thereupon interprets as an utterance ('I uttered that place / And left each word I was'). He inhabits a world of time that is also a world of words, and the words pour away down the horizon, and the actual words used to hold them snap and fly after. Indeed, the wonder is that Graham's poem is as full of sheen and tumult, of the miracle of morning, the hues and lifts of the sea, as it is. In 'The Nightfishing' the ancient instinct of Being and involuted modern consciousness exist side by side.

Then this exquisite, novel balance is lost. If 'The Nightfishing' hangs poised between the acceptance of life as something we subserve and the fear that it runs off us too quickly to be absorbed, the seven 'Letters' that fill out the volume seem to blanch with this fear, prove luminously ethereal. Substance they have, precise and subtle thought, great elusive beauties of language; but it all comes to us with the light fingering touch of mist. Sensuous as some of the details are ('Orion / Is brightly barbed'; 'What blinded tons / Of water the world contains'), they seem to flare up in a twilight discourse, burning just long enough to betray, rather than establish, an objective world. And the poet's words fall against a silence awesomely at large. The last letter ends,

> My love my love anywhere
> Drifted away, listen.
> From the dark rush under
> Us comes our end. Endure
> Each word as it breaks at last
> To become our home here.
> Who hears us now? Suddenly
> In a stark flash the nerves
> Of language broke. The sea
> Cried out loud under the keel.
> Listen. Now as I fall.
>
> Listen. And silence even
> Has turned away. Listen.

But it is precisely silence we hear. The last word gives on to nothing—on to an active, blinded nothing that swallows the words, keeping them from becoming 'our home'.

From the 'Letters' onward Graham assumes the vocation of self-consciousness with the unrelieved thoroughness, the unsparingness, with which he once pursued a numinous Nonmeaning. Hereafter he will listen more than look—indeed, relying almost entirely on distant memories, his eyes will furnish his now symbolic or fantasizing imagination merely generically: with 'the curving / World's edge' or 'the line of the sea' as against the tracking observation formerly our 'fruitful share'. Appearance receding, Silence will rush into the vacancy. Teasing, almost malicious, undermining his confidence in Being as steadily as Appearance had supported it, it will set him scrambling to hold on to himself. Now when the world appears to him (but this it will do infrequently), it will burst into consciousness as through the resistance of preoccupations. Identified chiefly with the sky—which, however vast, is remote and still, not present 'in all its mighty times'—it will come to epitomize all the unproblematical beauty, the simple certainty of Being, that his poetry (so he now feels) can never be:

> This is no other place
> Than where I am, between
> This word and the next.
> Maybe I should expect
> To find myself only
> Saying that again
> Here now at the end.
> Yet over the great
> Gantries and cantilevers
> Of love, a sky, real and
> Particular is slowly
> Startled into light.

This itself unfolds exquisitely. Yet the sense of being left forlorn between one word and the next, the absence of companionable particularity, even the brevity of the lines, tell of the essential loneliness that thus, in its low station, is startled from on high.

In *The Nightfishing* and *Malcolm Mooney's Land* loneliness stems—as premonitorily in 'Since All My Steps Taken'—from the exclusive, estranging nature of the present: that coming-into-time which seems to be a coming-out-of-the-world. It is a loneliness inseparable in experience from the eternal withdrawal of time from itself—from its recessive silence. Suddenly emergent, alone, at a loss, the present moment is a beached shell nostalgic for the thunders of the past ('Sometimes like loneliness / Memory's crowds increase'). If the past befriends and dilates the present, it is in a kind of death that aches to be life. Or what *was* may overwhelm what *is*, question its separation, call it in like a hypnotic field of snow:

> The centuries turn their locks
> And open under the hill
> Their inherited books and doors
> All gathered to distil
> Like happy berry pickers
> One voice to talk to us.
> Yes listen. It carries away
> The second and the years
> Till the heart's in a jacket of snow
> And the head's in a helmet white . . .

Yet to come into the present is simultaneously to miss, expect, and grope for the future; and even if this intimate absence is faced lovingly—

> Listen. Put on morning.
> Waken into falling light.

—still it is an absence, a separation, a delay. The present looks
on the eternally receding future as on perpetually unattainable
potential. 'Somewhere', Graham says in 'Implements in Their
Places', a recent long poem, 'our belonging particles / Believe in
us. If we could only find them'. And so the poet peels time from
himself, even as it peels from him, in the hope of uncovering
his essence. Hence it is that, at once elegiac and excited, the
miraculous scene of simultaneous death and birth ('Now he
who takes my place continually anew / Speaks me thoroughly
perished into another'), divided between self-abandonment and
self-anticipation, the present is always the plus sign between
zero and a number yet to be determined—a perpetual distraction
that somehow forms the only continuity of Being.

By now Graham's poetry has become the open and relentless
expression of this predicament—his style having gained the surprised ring of one who had never expected to hear himself speak,
not here in this tenantless place where the echo leaps. Just as his
'lifetime treads a rolling ball', so his lines, as earlier noted, jerk
and remain anxiously in movement. His deliberate awkwardness
has finally declared itself as the sign not merely of an unassimil-
ability to social propriety but of an incessantly renewed self-
ignorance.

The same ignorance explains his use of the poem as primarily
a vehicle for voice. Except in the recent, stunning 'Imagine a
Forest', a poem on the certainty of death, and the epigrams of
'Implements in Their Places', Graham writes as if too dislocated
and blinkered by the instant to tell just where he will come out:
an effect perhaps part truth, probably in great part cunning
pose. His poems are all baits for the moment. Their aim: to
provoke it, to counter its machinations with aggressive alertness.
And so they talk, talk as no poems before have talked,
surprising silence with living accents, questions, insinuations, a
certain eccentric charm of phrase, distinct as a brogue. . . . Intent
on keeping pace with the present, fleeing 'perfection's / Deadly
still anatomies', they avoid the symmetries of rhyme, expectable
beat, counted syllables. Indeed, they cultivate the *forward* stumble
in the irregular and dissonant. At the same time, afraid of proving
impotent before Silence, 'tripped and caught into the whole /

Formal scheme which Art is', they employ selectivity and climax as David employed the sling. They will not merely be heard; they will be heard with admiration. And so they emerge as a compromise between the unfinished character of the present and the formal pride of art. (Yet it may take several readings before one perceives that the voice knows its before and after, and is bringing the poem around.)

Conscious as he is of loneliness and silence, conscious indeed of his own consciousness of these things, Graham now writes a poetry uniquely at bay, a poetry that frequently takes its own embarrassment, its harassment by silence, as its subject. Worst of all, Graham has lost confidence in his words—his very tools, his only aides. The more his self-awareness increases, the smaller his words appear—until now he sometimes holds them up before him with conscious absurdity, like a tiny mask.

Originally he conceived the poet as a hunter, a bagger of Appearances:

> Then lean out, Love, and yearn from the window
> That ever you saw from, that far hero,
> Someone wandered into imagination
> And weed of the way, and word won . . .

Language was magical, Being was in it—the weed and the word were one. 'The nettling brine / Stings through the word'. Poems endowed their readers with the exalted essence of Appearance:

> . . . Huge
> Over the dark verge sauntered
> Half the moon. Then all
> Its shoal attending stared
> Down on the calm and mewing
> Firth and in a bright
> Breath that night became
> You in these words fondly
> Through me . . .

Hence the poet gave Being to those confined to the window, satisfied a metaphysical yearning. Moreover, at the same time that Being invested his language, his language invested Being. He worded 'the world awake and all its suns'; told 'half the country . . . / Into life by severe imagination'. Things could be found by how he called them. The poet brought the world and human beings to a fuller, articulate life in each other.

At the very least, so 'Letter V' seems to urge, language *reinvests* Being. The object exists but, as Max Picard says, 'through the word it exists all over again', the gift of language lying in a 'blessed overflow'. Words are the extended life of Appearance, carrying it into inner space, freeing it from itself:

> The tiller takes my hand
> In a telling grip. We drive
> On in the white soaring
> Meantime of fair morning . . .
> . . . .
> Under the wanderlusting
> Sky of morning waked
> And worded beyond itself
> By me to you, who leans
> Down through the fanfared lists
> To listen? A day to gladden.
> A sight to unperish us from
> The flashing wake unwinding
> Us to our end . . .

The phrase 'waked / And worded beyond itself' is the tiller of this beautiful passage: it is this that steadies the poet in his perishing. A lifeline thrown to a disappearing moment, his string of words will, with the help of those who lean down to listen, preserve the morning, preserve his meeting with it, indefinitely. Even as his words observe and subserve it (an intimacy emulated by the lovingly repeated sounds), they give it a serenity beyond itself, the permanence of memorable language. 'This present place', the poet writes at the end of 'The Nightfishing',

> . . . is
> Become made into
> A breathless still place
> Unrolled on a scroll
> And turned to face this light . . .

Thus braced, Graham was once emboldened to delight in 'the grace of change'. He was 'Trusted on the language'.

But after fading from the incarnational to the reproductive, a function hardly less miraculous, words further diminished for him into the *sounds of a voice*. And this was a fall indeed, though not to the bottom. At least words retained significance—not only their own individually but, taken together, as a proof of his existence. Where once they formed his identity with the world ('words / Bird-printed, sharing the lad I am'), they became the stark sign of his difference from it—a difference like the distinction between life and death. This remnant, being all there was, the world itself having frozen silent in the interim, was seized almost gratefully. No longer able to view experience itself as a naming, places and events as speaking him 'to the bone' —his words merely completing the utterance in an audible range —at least he could use words to position himself in the great hollow remaining: 'And why is it there has to be / Some place to find, however momentarily / To speak from, some distance to listen to?' Poetry became an 'aside from the monstrous', a space to 'think in'.

Yet when a poet has only words for company, there in the tent pitched in Silence, they get on his nerves, and Graham began to question their good faith. Were they out to preserve or destroy him? Declare or hide him? Drag him forward or keep him decently out of the way? More and more he wrote around and despite them, took up a position 'between' them, as a trainer keeps a wary distance from his beasts.

The trouble, as was noted, began in *The Nightfishing* when Graham first leaned to words and heard the tick of a clock. 'Each word', he complained, 'speaks its own speaker to his death'. As if signing his own death certificate, a poet speaks into the ear of a present that is passing him, going the other way. His constant cry: 'And I burn my words behind me. Silence is shouted out'. His identity moving at a faster rate than his consciousness, he is forever cast 'through' who he thought he was. 'When you hear from me / Again', Graham says in the brilliant 'Clusters Travelling Out', '. . . Whoever / Speaks to you will not be me. / I wonder what I will say'.

Yet, once he has buried himself at the 'grave's table', won't his ghost be after him to 'shout farewell'? Yes, but this revenant is our good company, not his. He is even less strange to us than to Graham, who naturally expects him to be the same as himself, what he *is* in the present moment. So in *Malcolm Mooney's Land*, rereading 'Letter VII' of *The Nightfishing*, Graham feels affronted by the 'new expression' on the face of his 'Dear Pen / Pal in the distance'. And, alas, he has seen this pal (as he none too kindly observes) 'standing / Older' losing himself in 'The changed

Mooney's mirrors'—the mirrors of the poet's own imaginative self-knowledge.

Graham came to see his words not merely as agents of time but, just as disquietingly, as social agents, panderingly ready to betray the truth he knew and was. A new fear seized him: that his words were less his than ours. After seeing them down the road, waving farewell, how could he tell what 'lonely meanings' might be read into them? Yet if not *his* meanings he would die twice over in his poems: first through composing them, then through failing to rise again in the reader.

If Graham now begins to address the reader as 'dear' and 'love', uttering 'you' in fond though quizzical tones, it is because he has grasped that this unknown being—this threat, this stranger, this companion—is his saviour. 'Unperish me', he entreats him in 'Letter VII', 'burning in these words . . .'; 'Be for me still', he asks in 'Letter V', 'steering / Here at my keeling trade. . . .' But in truth he doubts us, suspects us of being an alien immortality. 'Dear you who walk', he says,

> Your solitude on these
> Words, walk their silences
> Hearing a morning say
> A welcome I have not heard
> In words I have not made . . .

Though in so recent a poem as 'Implements in Their Places' Graham no longer burns in his words—on the contrary, they freeze him—still they are his message, and 'Why do you persist', he asks in his new goading way, 'In holding my message upside-down?' He tries not to mind: 'What you do with them', he elsewhere says of his words, 'is nobody's business'. All the same, his ignorance of their fate exacerbates his loneliness. 'And yet / I would like to see where they go / And how without me they behave'.

And if Graham should blunder as he writes? The poet's act of creation is at one and the same time a 'formal death' and a struggle not to die at his own hands. Above all he must keep the poem itself alive, for only through *its* strength can he continue to live, like the aborted Dionysus in the thigh of Zeus. Whence his need, however pungent or eccentric his personality, to make of the poem his own sublimation in truth, in imaginative space:

> Terrible the indignities of one's self flying
> Away from the sleight of one's true hand
> Then it becomes me writing big
> On the mirror and putting a moustache on myself.

So Graham levels a strict eye on his words, those 'dear upstarts' whom he has so often to refuse ('Tomorrow / Same place same time give me a ring'). And what troubles he has with the muse! Notoriously so faithless a mistress:

> Under my pinning arm
> I suddenly saw between
> The acting flutters, a look
> Catch on some image not me . . .

So vulnerable, besides, to the poet's egotism, and ambiguous:

> I love you paralysed by me.
> I love you made to lie. If you
> Love me blink your right eye once.
> If you don't love me blink your left.
> Why do you flutter your just before
> Dying dear two eyes at once?

So terrible when not herself:

> Who's there I shouted. And the face
> Whitely flattened itself against
> The black night-glass like a white pig
> And entered and breathed beside me
> Her rank breath of poet's bones . . .

More, as in section IV of 'Five Visitors to Madron', terrible when she *is* herself, pressing truths. . . . And finally, now that the dews of Appearance no longer sweeten or saturate his poems, now that he has ceased to *be* in his words, Graham has begun to fear the poeticide of the explicit:

> Out into across
> The morning loch burnished
> Between us goes the flat
> Thrown poem and lands
> Takes off and skips One
> 2, 3, 4, 5, 6, 7, 8, 9,
> And ends and sinks under.

Yet, even as Graham expresses his doubts, he proves them unnecessary. Like Wallace Stevens, he makes witty, original, astonishing poetry out of the subject of poetry itself—makes poetry out of his doubts that he can make it. Let him voice misgivings:

> But when they're not about in the morning I shout
> HOY HOY HOY and the whole corridor rings
> And I listen while my last HOY turns the elbow
> With a fading surprised difference of tone and loses
> Heart and in dwindling echoes vanishes away . . .

Still, the very skill, the happy surprise, with which he exhibits his qualms, as here (for instance) the sudden faltering enacted between 'loses' and 'Heart' and the gripping, stark conception itself—these ensure that, for all its inversion, his poetry remains an intense experience. In the passages on the blinking paralysed muse, the flat thrown poem, Mister Simpson, and the white-out, indeed in all his recent poems, Graham somehow writes as startlingly as if his subjects, familiar as they are, had never before been conceived. Almost frighteningly novel, his imagination is now a strange power all its own. Far from being debilitated by its repeated collisions with self-consciousness, it has only grown more resourceful. His recent poems are full of verbal life, witty stratagems.

Though Graham seldom surprises us any longer into healing relationships with Appearance, he enlivens us, all the same, by manœuvring us into disturbing and delightful relationships with his subjects, indeed with him, frequently exhorting us to 'See' or 'Listen', to join him in collusion over silence. Full of edged dialogue, addressing friends or imaginary characters or the muse or the reader or words themselves in a manner now humorous, now fond, now hard, now faintly plaintive, his poems transform self-consciousness into drama, into a tartly realized, wittily challenged *Angst*. The isolation almost all modern poets feel, having lost their sense of an audience, Graham has had the inspiration to theatricalize; and in so doing he has revealed more about loneliness, about the give and take of words, and about the moment, than poetry had laid bare before.

No age but ours—so self-conscious, so ready to be extreme yet rigorous, so philosophically honest—could have produced

Graham and yet, like all triumphant and original artists, he is more than his age deserves. In a period so humanly appalling as ours, and excepting a few of the morally brave, only the greatness of art can make one proud to be human, and Graham is one of those, like Tomlinson and Stevie Smith and Davie and Larkin, like Kinsella and Hughes and R. S. Thomas, who have given stature to the day.

Bibliography

Donald Davie (*born* 1922)

Purity of Diction in English Verse, Chatto & Windus, London, 1952; Oxford University Press, New York, 1953.

Poems (The Fantasy Poets, 8 pp.), Oxford, 1954.

Brides of Reason, Fantasy Press, Swinford, 1955

A Winter Talent and Other Poems, Routledge & Kegan Paul, London, 1957.

Articulate Energy: An Enquiry into the Syntax of English Poetry, Routledge & Kegan Paul, London, 1955; Harcourt Brace, New York, 1958.

The Late Augustans: Longer Poems of the Later Eighteenth Century (edited, with an introduction and notes by Davie), Heinemann, London, 1958; Macmillan, New York, 1958.

The Forest of Lithuania (a poem), Marvell Press, Hessle, Yorkshire, 1959.

Six Epistles to Eva Hesse, London Magazine Editions, 1960.

The Heyday of Sir Walter Scott, Routledge & Kegan Paul, 1961; Barnes & Noble, New York, 1961.

A Sequence for Francis Parkman, Marvell Press, Hull, 1961.

New and Selected Poems, Wesleyan University Press, Middleton, Connecticut, 1961.

Language of Science and Language of Literature, 1700–40, Sheed & Ward, London, 1963.

Events and Wisdoms: Poems 1957–1963, Routledge & Kegan Paul, London, 1964; Wesleyan University Press, Middleton, 1964.

Ezra Pound: Poet as Sculptor, Oxford University Press, New York, 1964; Routledge & Kegan Paul, London, 1965.

The Poems of Dr Zhivago (translated with a commentary by Davie), Manchester University Press, 1965.

Russian Literature and Modern English Fiction (A collection of critical essays; edited, with an introduction by Davie), University of Chicago Press, Chicago and London, 1965.

Essex Poems 1963–1967 (drawings by Michael Foreman), Routledge & Kegan Paul, London, 1969.

Pasternak (edited by Donald Davie and Angela Livingstone), Macmillan, London, 1969.

The Survival of Poetry: A Contemporary Survey (edited by Martin Dodsworth; with a contribution by Davie), Faber & Faber, London, 1970.

Collected Poems 1950–1970, Routledge & Kegan Paul, London, 1972; Oxford University Press, New York, 1972.

Thomas Hardy and British Poetry, Oxford University Press, New York, 1972; Routledge & Kegan Paul, London, 1973.

W. S. Graham (*born* 1918)

Cage Without Grievance (with drawings by Benjamin Creme and Robert Frame), Parton Press, Glasgow, 1942.

The Seven Journeys, W. MacLellan, Glasgow, 1944.

Second Poems, Nicholson & Watson, London, 1945.

The Voyages of Alfred Wallis (a poem, 2 pp.), Anthony Froshung, Cornwall, 1948.

The White Threshold, Faber & Faber, London, 1949; Grove Press, New York, 1952.

The Nightfishing, Faber & Faber, London, 1955; Grove Press, New York, 1955.

Malcolm Mooney's Land, Faber & Faber, London, 1970.

Ted Hughes (*born* 1930)

The Hawk in the Rain, Faber & Faber, London, 1957; Harper & Row, New York, 1957.

Lupercal, Faber & Faber, London, 1960; Harper & Row, New York, 1960.

Meet My Folks (illustrated by George Adamson), Faber & Faber, London, 1961.

Selected Poems (Thom Gunn and Ted Hughes), Faber & Faber, London, 1962.

The Earth Owl and Other Moon People (illustrated by R. A. Brandt), Faber & Faber, London, 1963.

How the Whale Became, Faber & Faber, London, 1963 (illustrated by George Adamson); Atheneum, New York, 1964 (illustrated by Rick Schreiter); Penguin, Harmondsworth, 1971.

Five American Poets (edited by Thom Gunn and Ted Hughes), Faber & Faber, London, 1963.

Here today (introduced by Ted Hughes), Hutchinson Educational, London, 1963.

Nessie the Mannerless Monster (pictures by Gerald Rose), Faber & Faber, London, 1964.

Recklings, Turret Books, London, 1966.

The Burning of the Brothel, Turret Books, London, 1966.

Scapegoats and Rabies: A Poem in Five Parts, Poet and Printer, London, 1967.

Wodwo, Faber & Faber, London, 1967; Harper & Row, New York, 1967.

Animal Poems, Richard Gilbertson, Crediton, 1967.

A Choice of Emily Dickinson's Verse (selected, with an introduction by Ted Hughes), Faber & Faber, London, 1968.

Poetry in the Making: An Anthology of Poems and Programmes from Listening and Writing, Faber & Faber, London, 1967; under the title *Poetry Is*, Double-day, New York, 1970.

The Iron Man: A Story in Five Nights, Faber & Faber, London, 1968 (illustrated by George Adamson); under the title *The Iron Giant*, Harper & Row, New York, 1968 (illustrated by Robert Nadler).

Five Autumn Songs for Children's Voices, Richard Gilbertson, Crediton, 1968.

Seneca's Oedipus (adapted by Ted Hughes), Faber & Faber, London, 1969; Doubleday, New York, 1972 (introduced by Peter Brook; illustrated by Reginald Pollack).

A Crow Hymn, Sceptre Press, Farnham, 1970.

The Martyrdom of Bishop Farrar, Richard Gilbertson, Crediton, 1970.

The Coming of the Kings, and Other Plays, Faber & Faber, London, 1970.

Crow: from the Life and Songs of the Crow, Faber & Faber, London, 1970; Harper & Row, New York, 1971.

Shakespeare's Poem, Lexham Press, London, 1971.

Eat Crow (illustrated by Leonard Baskin), Rainbow Press, London, 1971.

Crow Wakes, Poet and Printer, London, 1971.

A Choice of Shakespeare's Verse (edited by Ted Hughes), Faber & Faber, London, 1971; under the title *With Fairest Flowers While Summer Lasts: Poems 1564–1616*, Doubleday, New York, 1971.

Allsorts 4 (edited by Ann Thwaite; with a contribution by Ted Hughes), Macmillan, London, 1971.

Orghast at Persepolis (by Anthony Smith), Eyre Methuen, London, 1972. (An account of the experiment in theatre directed by Peter Brook and written by Ted Hughes.)

Selected Poems 1957–1967, Faber & Faber, London, 1972 (illustrated by Leonard Baskin); Harper & Row, New York, 1973.

In the Little Girl's Angel Gaze (illustrated by Ralph Steadman), Steam Press, London, 1972.

The Tiger's Bones and Other Plays for Children, Viking Press, New York, 1973.

Thomas Kinsella (born 1928)

Three Legendary Sonnets, Dolmen Press, Dublin, 1952.

The Death of a Queen (illustrated by Bridget Swinton), Dolmen Press, Dublin, 1956.

Poems, Dolmen Press, Dublin, 1956.

Thirty Three Triads (translated by Kinsella from the Irish), Dolmen Press, Dublin, 1957.

Faeth Fiadha (The Breastplate of Saint Patrick), Dolmen Press, Dublin, 1957.

Another September, Dolmen Press, Dublin, 1958; Dufour Editions, Philadelphia, 1958.

Moralities, Dolmen Press, Dublin, 1960.

Poems and Translations, Atheneum, New York, 1961.

Downstream, Dolmen Press, Dublin, 1962.

Longes mac n-Usnig: being the exile and death of the sons of Usnech (translated by Kinsella), Dolmen Press, Dublin, 1964.

Wormwood, Dolmen Press, Dublin, 1966; distributed by Dufour Editions, Philadelphia, 1966.

Nightwalker, Dolmen Press, Dublin, 1967; distributed by Dufour Editions, Philadelphia, 1967.

Nightwalker and Other Poems, Dolmen Press, Dublin 1968; Oxford University Press, London, 1968; Knopf, New York, 1968.

Poems (Kinsella, Douglas Livingstone, and Anne Sexton), Oxford University Press, London, 1968.

Tear (a poem), Pym-Randall Press, Cambridge, Mass., 1969.

The Táin (translated by Kinsella; brush drawings by Louis le Brocquy), Dolmen Press, Dublin, 1969; distributed in USA by Irish University Press, New York. New edition published by Oxford University Press, London and New York, 1970.

Tradition and the Irish Writer, Dolmen Press, Dublin, 1970.

Butcher's Dozen, Peppercanister, Dublin (distributed by Dolmen Press), 1972.

Notes from the Land of the Dead, Cuala Press, Dublin, 1972.

Finistere, Dolmen Press, Dublin, 1972.

A Selected Life, Peppercanister, Dublin, 1972.

Notes from the Land of the Dead (limited edition), Cuala Press, Dublin, 1973; Knopf, New York, 1973.

New Poems, Dolmen Press, Dublin, 1973.

Philip Larkin (born 1922)

The North Ship, The Fortune Press, London, 1945.

A Girl in Winter (a novel), Faber & Faber, London, 1947; St Martin's Press, New York, 1963.

The Less Deceived, Marvell Press, Hessle, Yorks., 1955; St Martin's Press, New York, 1960.

Jill (a novel), Faber & Faber, London, 1964; St Martin's Press, New York, 1964.

The Whitsun Weddings, Faber & Faber, London, 1964; Random House, New York, 1964.

The North Ship (new edition), Faber & Faber, London, 1966.

All What Jazz: A Record Diary 1961–1968, Faber & Faber, London, 1970; St Martin's Press, New York, 1970.

The Oxford Book of Twentieth-Century English Verse (compiled by Philip Larkin), Clarendon Press, Oxford, 1973.

Stevie Smith (1902–1971)

Mother, What Is Man? (illustrated by Stevie Smith), Cape, London, 1942.

Not Waving But Drowning, Deutsch, London, 1957.

Over the Frontier, Cape, London, 1958.

Some are more Human than Others (sketch book), Gaberbocchus, London, 1958.

Cats in colour, Batsford, London, 1959; Viking Press, New York, 1960.

Selected Poems, Longmans, London, 1962; J. Laughlin, Norfolk, Conn., 1964; also New Directions, Norfolk, Conn., 1964.

The Frog Prince and Other Poems (with drawings by the author), Longmans, London, 1966.

Selections (edited by Edwin Brock; with contributions by Stevie Smith), 1966.

The Best Beast (illustrated by the author), Knopf, New York, 1969.

The Poet's Garden (edited by Stevie Smith), Viking Press, New York, 1970.

The Batsford Book of Children's Verse (edited by Stevie Smith), Batsford, London, 1970.

Novel on Yellow Paper, Cape, London, 1969; Penguin, Harmondsworth, 1972,

Two in One: Selected Poems and The Frog Prince and Other Poems, Longman, Harlow, 1971.

Scorpion and Other Poems (with drawings by the author; introduced by Patric Dickinson), Longman, London, 1972.

R. S. Thomas (*born* 1913)

The Stones of the Field, Druid Press, Carmarthen, 1946.

Song at the Year's Turning: Poems, 1952–1954 (introduced by John Betjeman), Hart-Davis, London, 1955.

Poetry for Supper, Hart-Davis, London, 1958; Dufour Editions, Philadelphia, 1961.

Judgement, Poetry Book Society, London, 1960.

Judgement Day, Westerham Press, London, 1960.

Tares, Hart-Davis, London, 1961; Dufour Editions, Philadelphia, 1961.

The Batsford Book of Country Verse (edited by Thomas), Batsford, London, 1961.

The Penguin Book of Religious Verse (edited by Thomas), Penguin Books, Baltimore, 1963.

The Bread of Truth, Hart-Davis, London, 1963; Dufour Editions, Philadelphia, 1963.

Words and the Poet, University of Wales Press, Cardiff, 1964.

Pietà, Hart-Davis, London, 1966.

A Choice of George Herbert's Verse (edited by Thomas), Faber & Faber, London, 1966.

Pergamon Poets No. 1 (edited by Fuller & Thomas), Pergamon Press, Oxford and New York, 1968.

The Mountains (illustrated with ten drawings by John Piper, engraved on the wood by Reynolds Stone, with a descriptive note by John Piper), Chilmark Press, New York, 1968.

Not that He Brought Flowers, Hart-Davis, London, 1968.

Selections, Longmans, Harlow, 1969.

An Exercise in Redeployment (edited by Thomas), Pergamon Press, Oxford and New York, 1969.

A Choice of Wordsworth's Verse (selected with an introduction by Thomas), Faber & Faber, London, 1971.

H'm, Macmillan, London, 1972.

Young and Old, Chatto & Windus, London, 1972.

Charles Tomlinson (*born* 1927)

Solo for a Glass Harmonica, Westerham Press, San Francisco, 1957.

Seeing is Believing, McDowell, Obolensky, New York, 1958; Oxford University Press, London, 1960.

Versions from Fyodor Tyutchev 1803–1873 (with an introduction by Henry Gifford), Oxford University Press, London and New York, 1960.

A Peopled Landscape, Oxford University Press, London and New York, 1963.

Machado: Castilian Ilexes (translated by Tomlinson with Henry Gifford), Oxford University Press, London and New York, 1963.

Poems (with Austin Clarke and Tony Connor), Oxford University Press, London and New York, 1964.

The Necklace, Oxford University Press, London and New York, 1966.

American Scenes and Other Poems, Oxford University Press, London and New York, 1966.

The Poem as Initiation, Colgate University Press, Hamilton, New York, 1968.

The Matachines, San Marcos Press, New Mexico, 1968.

Engraved on the Skull of a Cormorant, The Unaccompanied Serpent, London, 1968.

Selected Poems (in Penguin Modern Poets), Penguin Books, Harmondsworth, 1969.

The Way of a World, Oxford University Press, London and New York, 1969.

America West Southwest, San Marcos Press, New Mexico, 1970.

Marianne Moore: A Collection of Critical Essays (compiled by Tomlinson), Prentice-Hall, Englewood Cliffs, New Jersey, 1970.

Ten Versions from Trilce (by Cesar Abraham Vallejo, translated by Tomlinson), San Marcos Press, New Mexico, 1970.

An Octave for Octavio Paz (by Tomlinson and others, edited by Richard Burns and Anthony Rudolf), Sceptre Press; Menaid Press, Farnham, 1972.

William Carlos Williams: A Critical Anthology (edited by Tomlinson), Penguin Books, Harmondsworth, 1972.

A New Kind of Tie, Tarasque Press, Nottingham, 1972.

Written on Water, Oxford University Press, London and New York, 1973.

Notes

These notes annotate the poems cited in the book. The numerals at the left refer to page numbers in this volume; those concluding entries for extracts from poems list the pages on which those words occur.

Charles Tomlinson

2 'The Gossamers', *A Peopled Landscape*, p. 43
4 'Four Kantian Lyrics', *A Peopled Landscape*, p. 20
4 the steady roar / 'Through Binoculars', *The Necklace*, p. 8
5 Out of the shut cell / 'Something: A Direction', *Seeing is Believing*, p. 66
6 'Return to Hinton', *A Peopled Landscape*, p. 1
6 'The Farmer's Wife', *A Peopled Landscape*, p. 13
6 'The Hand at Callow Hill Farm', *A Peopled Landscape*, p. 16
6 'Oxen: Ploughing at Fiesole', *Seeing is Believing*, p. 5
6 'Geneva Restored', *Seeing is Believing*, p. 32
6 'Maillol', *A Peopled Landscape*, p. 34
6 'The Castle', *Seeing is Believing*, p. 45
6 'Antecedents', *Seeing is Believing*, p. 57
6 'Black Nude', *A Peopled Landscape*, p. 38
6 'Up at La Serra', *A Peopled Landscape*, p. 23
6 'Mr. Brodsky', *American Scenes*, p. 29
6 No hawk at wrist / 'Portrait of Mrs. Spraxton', *A Peopled Landscape*, p. 12
7 'Clouds', *The Way of a World*, p. 18
7 'In the Fullness of Time', *The Way of a World*, p. 12
8 'Something: A Direction', *Seeing is Believing*, p. 66
8 A trailed and lagging grass / 'Logic', *The Way of a World*, p. 13
10 Two stand / 'The Meeting', *American Scenes*, p. 15
10 'Canal', *A Peopled Landscape*, p. 6
11 It happened / 'How it happened', *A Peopled Landscape*, p. 22
11 Cloudshapes are destinies / 'Clouds', *The Way of a World*, p. 18
13 'Distinctions', *Seeing is Believing*, p. 8
13 'Farewell to Van Gogh', *Seeing is Believing*, p. 33
13 'Maillol', *A Peopled Landscape*, p. 34

Donald Davie

(*CP* indicates *Collected Poems*)

40 'Ezra Pound in Pisa', *Essex Poems*, p. 19 (*CP*, p. 188)
41 Solicitations / 'The Evangelist', *Brides of Reason*, p. 27 (*CP*, p. 22)
41 Not just in Russian / 'Hearing Russian Spoken', *A Winter Talent*, p. 45 (*CP*, p. 61)
42 'Heigh-ho on a Winter Afternoon', *A Winter Talent*, p. 53 (*CP*, p. 66)
43 'Low Lands', *Events and Wisdoms*, p. 7 (*CP*, p. 137)
43 'Treviso, the Pescheria', *Events and Wisdoms*, p. 9 (*CP*, p. 139)
43 'Housekeeping', *Events and Wisdoms*, p. 6 (*CP*, p. 136)
44 'Across the Bay', *Events and Widsoms*, p. 19 (*CP*, p. 145)
44 'New York in August', *Events and Wisdoms*, p. 26 (*CP*, p. 149)
44 'In California', *Events and Wisdoms*, p. 25 (*CP*, p. 147)
44 'Time Passing, Beloved', *A Winter Talent*, p. 2 (*CP*, p. 35)
44 'Poreč', *Events and Wisdoms*, p. 29 (*CP*, p. 151)
44 'The Prolific Spell', *Events and Wisdoms*, p. 10 (*CP*, p. 139)
44 'The Feeders', *Events and Wisdoms*, p. 16 (*CP*, p. 143)
44 'A Meeting of Cultures', *Events and Wisdoms*, p. 38 (*CP*, p. 156)
45 'In California', *Events and Wisdoms*, p. 25 (*CP*, p. 147)
46 'The Mushroom Gatherers', *A Winter Talent*, p. 11 (*CP*, p. 40)
47 'After an Accident', *Events and Wisdoms*, p. 47 (*CP*, p. 160)
47 'Viper-Man', *Events and Wisdoms*, p. 27 (*CP*, p. 150)
48 'Woodpigeons at Raheny', *Brides of Reason*, p. 39 (*CP*, p. 30)

R. S. Thomas

51 'Ninetieth Birthday', *Tares*, p. 23
52 It was like a church / 'The Moor', *Pietà*, p. 24
52 'Green Categories', *Poetry for Supper*, p. 19
53 'The Dance', *Pietà*, p. 38
55 This man swaying / 'The Muck Farmer', *Poetry for Supper*, p. 23
55 Consider this man / 'Affinity', *Song at the Year's Turning*, p. 25
55 Farmer, you were young / 'Age', *Poetry for Supper*, p. 21
55 My name is Lowri / 'Lowri Dafydd', *Poetry for Supper*, p. 20
55 The men took / 'The Minister', *Song at the Year's Turning*, p. 87
56 'The View from the Window', *Poetry for Supper*, p. 27
57 There were larks / 'A Line from St. David's', *The Bread of Truth*, p. 7
57 O, hers is all / 'Farm Wife', *Poetry for Supper*, p. 47
57 You who never / 'The Minister', *Song at the Year's Turning*, p. 87
57 I blame the earth / 'The Slave', *Song at the Year's Turning*, p. 104
57 I remember also / 'Death of a Peasant', *Song at the Year's Turning*, p. 59
57 Prytherch, man / 'Absolution', *Poetry for Supper*, p. 44
57 Mother, he said / 'Mother and Son', *Tares*, p. 37
57 No, no / 'The Airy Tomb', *Song at the Year's Turning*, p. 41
58 sin was the honey / 'The Minister', *Song at the Year's Turning*, p. 83

Philip Larkin

69 'Wild Oats', *The Whitsun Weddings*, p. 41

70 'Dockery and Son', *The Whitsun Weddings*, p. 37

70 'I Remember, I Remember', *The Less Deceived*, p. 38

71 This was Mr. Bleaney's room / 'Mr. Bleaney', *The Whitsun Weddings*, p. 10

73 I was sleeping / 'XXI', *The North Ship*, p. 34

74 And in their blazing solitude / 'Night-Music', *The North Ship*, p. 23

75 'As Bad as a Mile', *The Whitsun Weddings*, p. 32

75 black flowers / 'XXI', *The North Ship*, p. 34

75 birds crazed / 'I', *The North Ship*, p. 11

75 wintry drums / 'I', *The North Ship*, p. 11

75 Home is so sad / 'Home is so Sad', *The Whitsun Weddings*, p. 17

76 'Dockery and Son', *The Whitsun Weddings*, p. 37

77 She was slapped up / 'Sunny Prestatyn', *The Whitsun Weddings*, p. 35

78 When getting my nose / 'A Study of Reading Habits', *The Whitsun Weddings*, p. 31

78 'Toads', *The Less Deceived*, p. 32

78 'Wild Oats', *The Whitsun Weddings*, p. 41

78 'Send No Money', *The Whitsun Weddings*, p. 43

78 'Self's the Man', *The Whitsun Weddings*, p. 24

78 Talking in bed / 'Talking in Bed', *The Whitsun Weddings*, p. 29

78 'MCMXIV', *The Whitsun Weddings*, p. 28

78 'Ambulances', *The Whitsun Weddings*, p. 33

79 'As Bad as a Mile', *The Whitsun Weddings*, p. 32

79 'Toads Revisited', *The Whitsun Weddings*, p. 18

79 'An Arundel Tomb', *The Whitsun Weddings*, p. 45

79 Life is slow dying / 'Nothing to be Said', *The Whitsun Weddings*, p. 11

81 'Days', *The Whitsun Weddings*, p. 27

81 'Next, Please', *The Less Deceived*, p. 20

81 'No Road', *The Less Deceived*, p. 26

82 'Whatever Happened?', *The Less Deceived*, p. 25

82 'Age', *The Less Deceived*, p. 30

82 'Triple Time', *The Less Deceived*, p. 35

82 'Latest Face', *The Less Deceived*, p. 41

82 'If, My Darling', *The Less Deceived*, p. 42

82 'Arrivals, Departures', *The Less Deceived*, p. 44

82 'Church Going', *The Less Deceived*, p. 28

84 'Lines on a Young Lady's Photograph Album', *The Less Deceived*, p. 13

84 'Dockery and Son', *The Whitsun Weddings*, p. 38

85 'Deceptions', *The Less Deceived*, p. 37

86 'Coming', *The Less Deceived*, p. 17

86 'Dublinesque', *Encounter* (October 1970), p. 41

Ted Hughes

102 'November', *Lupercal*, p. 49

102 the wolf is small / 'The Howling of Wolves', *Wodwo*, p. 179

103 Squealing and gibbering / 'Skylarks', *Wodwo*, p. 171

103 A dance / 'Gnat-Psalm', *Wodwo*, p. 181

103 I seem separate / 'Wodwo', *Wodwo*, p. 184

103 the one sun / 'Gnat-Psalm', *Wodwo*, p. 180

103 In a nightmare / 'Skylarks', *Wodwo*, p. 170

103 I'll go on looking / 'Wodwo', *Wodwo*, p. 184

104 stronger than death / 'Examination at the Womb-door', *Crow*, p. 11

104 In the beginning / 'Lineage', *Crow*, p. 10

104 His wings / 'Crowego', *Crow*, p. 50

104 battered itself featureless / 'Crow and Stone', *Crow*, p. 70

104 word / 'The Battle of Osfrontalis', *Crow*, p. 29

104 The sun / 'Hawk Roosting', *Lupercal*, p. 26

104 the fossil / 'Crow's Nerve Fails', *Crow*, p. 38

105 Lonely Crow created / 'Crow's Playmates', *Crow*, p. 49

105 'Robin Song', *Crow*, p. 43

105 His utmost gaping / 'Crow on the Beach', *Crow*, p, 34

105 Yet the prophecy / 'Crow Hears Fate Knock on the Door', *Crow* (Harper and Row), p. 11

105 Crow saw the herded mountains / 'Crow Alights', *Crow*, p. 17

105 Crow thought of a fast car / 'Magical Dangers', *Crow*, p. 42

106 Otherwise, he would / 'Crow's Theology', *Crow*, p. 30

107 sob contentment / 'A Modest Proposal', *The Hawk in the Rain*, p. 25

107 would shriek / 'Secretary', *The Hawk in the Rain*, p. 21

107 hedge-scratched pig-splitting arm / 'Complaint', *The Hawk in the Rain*, p. 33

107 like flies / 'The Casualty', *The Hawk in the Rain*, p. 49

107 and I, / Bloodily grabbed / 'The Hawk in the Rain', *The Hawk in the Rain*, p. 11

107 'Fair Choice', *The Hawk in the Rain*, p. 31

107 'Egg-Head', *The Hawk in the Rain*, p. 35

107 Stamp was not / 'The Martyrdom of Bishop Farrar', *The Hawk in the Rain*, p. 59

107 Where admiration's giddy mannequin / 'Fallgrief's Girl-Friends', *The Hawk in the Rain*, p. 28

107 blackouts of impassables / 'Incompatibilities', *The Hawk in the Rain*, p. 26

108 after the drills / 'The Jaguar', *The Hawk in the Rain*, p. 12

108 Here's no heart's more / 'The Casualty', *The Hawk in the Rain*, p. 49

108 Love you I do not say / 'Billet-doux', *The Hawk in the Rain*, p. 24

108 falsifying dream / 'Hawk Roosting', *Lupercal*, p. 26

108 Pike, three inches long / 'Pike', *Lupercal*, p. 56

Stevie Smith

W. S. Graham

160 ptarmigan rocked / 'Endure no conflict. Crosses are keepsakes', *Cage Without Grievance*, p. 22

161 Then holier / 'The Bright Building', *2nd Poems*, p. 18

161 Yet look / 'The Fourth Journey', *The Seven Journeys*, unpaged

161 SHEER I break / 'The First Journey', *The Seven Journeys*, unpaged

162 We fall down darkness / 'No, listen, for this I tell', *Cage Without Grievance*, p. 27

162 Let me measure / 'Let me measure my prayer with sleep', *Cage Without Grievance*, p. 21

162 My heart is headhung / 'This fond event my origin knows well', *Cage Without Grievance*, p. 20

163 those fairer flocks / 'A Letter More Likely to Myself', *2nd Poems*, p. 19

163 'Shian Bay', *The White Threshold*, p. 39

163 'Gigah', *The White Threshold*, p. 40

164 'Since All My Steps Taken', *The White Threshold*, p. 9

165 Let the signs start / 'Letter III', *The Nightfishing*, p. 44

165 Appreciates the starkest man / 'The Broad Close', *The Nightfishing*, p. 65

166 'Ten Shots of Mister Simpson', *London Magazine* (February/March 1972), p. 8

166 a lipless language / 'Clusters Travelling Out', *Malcolm Mooney's Land*, p. 61

166 Today, Friday / 'Malcolm Mooney's Land', *Malcolm Mooney's Land*, p. 13

167 Tonight in sadly need / 'Letter II', *The Nightfishing*, p. 40

167 Or am I always / 'The Dark Dialogues', *Malcolm Mooney's Land*, p. 34

167 I made them all / 'Baldy Bane', *The Nightfishing*, p. 71

168 'The Nightfishing', *The Nightfishing*, p. 15

168 Very end then / 'The White Threshold', *The White Threshold*, p. 55

171 Orion / Is brightly barbed / 'Letter VII', *The Nightfishing*, p. 58

171 My love my love / 'Letter VII', *The Nightfishing*, p. 62

172 This is no other / 'The Dark Dialogues', *Malcolm Mooney's Land*, p. 36

172 Sometimes like loneliness / 'To My Mother', *The White Threshold*, p. 69

172 The centuries turn / 'Listen. Put on Morning', *The White Threshold*, p. 11

173 'Implements in Their Places', *The Malahat Review* (April 1972), p. 9

173 Now he who takes / 'The Nightfishing', *The Nightfishing*, p. 28

173 lifetime treads / 'The Children of Lanarkshire', *The White Threshold*, p. 23

173 'Imagine a Forest', *The Malahat Review* (January 1971), p. 14

173 perfection's / Deadly still anatomies / 'To My Mother', *The White Threshold*, p. 69

173 tripped and caught / 'Approaches to How They Behave', *Malcolm Mooney's Land*, p. 47

174 Then lean out / 'The Lost Other', *The White Threshold*, p. 30

174 The nettling brine / 'The White Threshold', *The White Threshold*, p. 55

174 Huge / Over the dark verge / 'Letter IV', *The Nightfishing*, p. 46

174 the world awake / 'Explanation of a Map', *2nd Poems*, p. 7